AMONG THE
LIVEWIRES

100 YEARS OF PUGET POWER

By Arthur Kramer

Dedication

This book is dedicated to young people with budding curiosity to know what lies behind a light switch; and to Old Timers who with devotion and zeal carved new careers for themselves and for others in the use of electricity.

Published by:

CC

Creative Communications
PUBLISHING AND PRINTING SERVICES
529 Dayton Street
Edmonds, Washington 98020
(206) 775-5877

Cover: Glenn Jansen

LIBRARY OF CONGRESS
CATALOG CARD NUMBER: 86-91152

ISBN 0-939116-14-6

ACKNOWLEDGMENTS

The writer is indebted to a variety of research sources. These are noted in a bibliography. In addition he could not have written the book without the help of "old timers," their families and friends. He values the bundle of personal papers sent by Frank McLaughlin with encouraging letters, and the incisive conversations held with Jack Clawson, who had the rare experience of working closely with two electric company presidents — Alton W. Leonard and Frank McLaughlin — then himself became president. Frank Peters, an attorney, helped in an unusual way. He had been a law clerk to Homer T. Bone and admired him. Without Peters' help the author could not have written a fair personality sketch of the testy, provocative adversary of the private electric industry, Homer T. Bone. Above all, the author is deeply indebted to the people of Puget Power, who cheerfully provided photographs, records and factual statistics.

Preface

When March winds blow and kids fly kites, just as surely boys and girls will study social sciences in their schools. They will be coaxed by their teachers to write letters to the Electric Company, asking, "How is electricity made and how does it come over wires to our homes? Please also tell us about your company." Adults ask questions too. Electricity never lost its wonder and glamour since it first was brought to the Northwest one hundred years ago.

This book searches the thoughts of bold pioneers who started the infant electric industry in the dim past. They were strong leaders who grappled with great problems of survival in alternating booms, panics, and depressions, in changing times and changing political moods. They made prodigious efforts to change our way of life. We respect and honor them. But to a youngster who writes a letter, it is only the present that has luster; he wants to know what things are like today.

We received and welcomed such letters. One struck us as different. It was singularly thoughtful and direct, written by a young miss, a Virginia McCammon.

We sensed that she trusted us implicitly to explain the age-old mystery of electricity. Another Virginia had asked a newspaper editor the timeless question, "Is there a Santa Claus?" With awe and humility we answered our Virginia's letter, now forty years ago, before the era of television, air-conditioning and computers. Couched in present day terms we said in effect:

Yes, Virginia, we have learned how to produce electricity and how to bring it over wires to homes, to give light, heat, power, run radios, spin food mixers, cook, or do a hundred other things. But right down deep, we are baffled, and the best of us cannot explain electricity any more than we can explain how the earth, the moon or the stars were made.

Electricity, when traveling safely inside wires, alternating over and over, never wears them out. But if you touch the bright wires it will bite you, for it wants to go right through your body. So don't touch.

By flipping switches, turning knobs or pressing buttons, electricity will do your bidding. To be sure, we know how electricity is generated in power plants and we can explain how it reaches your home.

The key to this kind of magic is that when a moving magnet passes near a wire it induces an electric current in the wire. In huge electric generators, some producing 800,000 horsepower, coils of wires are placed in slots set in circular stators, and the magnets are on rotors, like spokes of a wheel, that spin around and around past the coils. The awesome field of the many magnets continually spinning past the wires produces electrical energy in huge amounts, enough for the needs of cities, towns, homes and farms.

It is the power of falling water, or the energy in oil or lumps of coal, that turns the rotors. In hydroelectric plants, the rotor of a generator is turned by a water wheel of some type which is driven by falling water. In steam plants oil or coal is burned to heat water for high-pressure steam which likewise is injected into turbines that turn the rotors.

The electricity in the wires of your home is also unique. All in a split second it is produced, delivered and used. So, simply stated, your home is wired right to the generator.

Of course it is not that simple; the transmission system is quite special. The voltage, which is the pressure that makes the current flow, must be maintained from the generator all along every part of the system. So, for a very good reason there are many power plants, many miles apart, that feed electricity into a common "pool" over high voltage power lines to large substations. From these more power lines extend to smaller distribution substations at cities and towns. From the local substations more lines emanate, extending down roads and streets. At all substations are large transformers to step down the voltage. Near your home will be a small transformer, either pole-mounted or in an underground vault. Here the voltage is finally stepped down to 230 and 115 volts for wires to your home.

When you flick a switch, all in a split second electricity is produced, delivered and used in your home, made possible through highways of power. The electric lines of Puget Power add up to over 10,000 miles of pole lines. If extended end to end from the North Pole they would stretch to the middle of South America.

If you will look, you will see electric lines extending even to remote beaches and mountain tops to light lodges, energize microwave transmitters, or run ski lifts as at Snoqualmie and Crystal Mountain.

In our modern day of microwave communications for line-of-sight projection, power lines extend to such transmitters right to tops of peaks, many in number. Here power cables are not on poles but are buried, for the weather is often blustery, winds incessant, snowfall may be twenty feet deep and roads obscure. To bury cables right on mountain tops may seem incredible. It is done with a heavy diesel tractor fitted with an indestructible prong that breaks a groove right among rocks into which the power cables are threaded. Also submarine cables laid below sea level provide crossings of Puget Sound to Whidbey Island, Bainbridge Island and to the Olympic Peninsula.

There are many glamorous and unusual aspects in the electric business. Because lines extend across mountains and under the sea the Company must be responsive to the elements and be prepared to operate in heavy snows, silver thaws, floods and earth slides. Often it faces real emergencies so it uses special machines and devices.

With radar it can locate line trouble, miles away, probably on a mountain pass. To get to such rugged terrain it may use a snow "weasel" or a helicopter. Jeeps and four-wheel-drive trucks bring workmen to places at bays, inlets and backroads. Other special equipment includes earth-boring machines, tree trimming rigs and chippers, bull-dozers, machines for burying power cables and a cable-laying ship.

For communications it has the regular telephone service, its own private microwave system, carrier-current telephone (speaking over power line wires), and two-way radios in cars and trucks.

The electric company uses many electronic devices. Why shouldn't it? It is in the electric business. Whole power plants are operated remotely, unattended, with electronic supervisory controls. With telemetering it gets readings of power flows at remote interconnections. Such readings show at the load dispatcher's desk, separately and also at a totalizing meter, so he can make decisions readily about distributing loads between power plants. Such technology helps to give electric service of a high order.

Electric facilities are heavy, intricate and expensive. For the large investment in a modern power company there are relatively few employees. These men and women are highly skilled and professionally trained. Job classifications tally nearly 500. The range is rather amazing. The basic jobs are engineers, electricians, linemen, wiremen, machinists, hydro and steam operators, certified public accountants, analysts, home service advisors, industrial consultants, and many related positions.

Its management setup is flexible, ranging from executive offices, to division centers, service headquarters and local offices which are on "main street" in small towns. People of the electric company are well known as neighbors and members of the community.

The most vital part of the electric business is its power plants. In its early history it built its own power projects; in recent years new energy sources have been developed in partnership with other utilities. Now generally shared with others are the massive resources of the Northwest Power Pool. Today, new multiple plants, hydro and coal-fired, have been built or are under construction, that cost millions of dollars. In building them in partnership risks are shared.

Managed as a private business the electric company is subject to the laws of the state, many federal laws and licenses, and to all ordinances of each city and town where its customers live.

Though its history goes back to the horse and buggy days, when there were no automobiles, airplanes or radios, the electric company has many dynamic plans for the future.

Virginia, we thank you for writing.

The foregoing is a profile of a present-day electric company. The following chapters are of fledgling beginnings facing startling uncertainties, which in unpredictable ways were shaped and melded into this one enterprise.

It is a story of men, alive with personal anecdote, surprising successes and disheartening disappointments, who reflect the spirit of American free enterprise. They staked their fortunes on a magnificent dream.

This history is written in two sections. Section One covers 45 years, 1885 to 1930, devoted to the growth and emergence of a unified electric system, as gleaned from early records. Book Section Two is dedicated to the fifty-five following years, 1930 to 1985, of ever-changing times marked variously by shocks, successes and serenity. This part is written in the first person, because the author's experience parallels these years.

Arthur Kramer

Seattle, Washington
January, 1986

ABOUT THE AUTHOR

The author's understanding of the electric utility industry comes from spending a lifetime with the utility at a number of imaginative jobs. Hired in 1930 by Puget Power, Arthur Kramer recalls that because of the Depression and battles with public power advocates, "I was recycled constantly." He worked in operations, in executive offices, power plants, substations, the load office, research, sales, right of ways, advertising and even wrote a monthly employees' publication.

Arthur Kramer was born in 1908, at Ritzville, Washington, and grew up on a wheat ranch that his father had homesteaded in 1895, where he learned to be self-reliant and use good work ethics. In 1930 he graduated from the University of Washington in electrical engineering; within two years he also earned a master's degree and a professional engineer's license.

He has a keen interest in people and community services, including his church, PTAs, service clubs and scouting. In scouting he held various leadership roles and received the Woodbadge Award, the Silver Beaver Award, was on the staff of two National Jamborees and president of the Tumwater Area Council of Boy Scouts.

Why a writer? In one of his "recycled" jobs he had been assistant to the advertising director. Years later, while assistant superintendent of the Baker River Hydro Plant, he received a call. "Your file shows advertising experience — we'll raise your salary, come down and be director of advertising and editor of *Puget Power News.*" He took the challenge. Through the years, he has honed and sharpened his writing skills as bulletin editor of various organizations and has published historical items, personality sketches and family genealogies.

Contents

Illustrations

BOOK SECTION ONE

*The growth and emergence of a unified electric utility
company, from 1885 to 1930.*

PART ONE

WHEN DYNAMOS BEGAN SPINNING

This is the story of the Puget Sound Power & Light Company from its beginning. Its roots go back to more than 150 separate beginnings of the electric systems started in young and buoyant towns in the Northwest. In this story we savor the spirit, the wit and moments of truth of its pioneers. Most of these beginnings of the electric industry sprang up in the 1880s. Dynamos then started spinning, not to power factories or heat homes, but in these early days for lighting only.

It is the purpose of this history of an industry, past and present, to name events and tell of bold personalities who gave prodigious amounts of energy towards changing our way of life. The events echo the past of one hundred years. The electric industry in the Pacific Northwest did not spring up in full-bloom, but began haltingly in the days of wagon trails, split-rail fences, coal oil lamps and tallow candles. Talent, courage, and flexibility were demanded of its leaders to cope with the industry's survival. Their lives were marked with alternating booms and depressions, even wars, and changing political moods.

A Look at the Times

There were only fifty million Americans in 1880, most of them east of the Mississippi. Deer, bear and cougar were in the woods nearby and buffalo roamed the prairie. There were animals alive that are now extinct. There were social systems, too, of that time that no longer exist. Europe was dominated by kings, queens, emperors and czars who were not just figureheads. In America Rutherford B. Hayes was president of the United States, and the Northwest was known as the Washington Territory but was claiming attention as a developing country.

The trans-continental railroads were still a national excitement. In the Territory of Washington, in 1873 the Northern Pacific Railway had pushed its line to a terminus at Commencement Bay in Tacoma. Here the railroad meant to spark a city. Tacoma's population was a scant 200. Seattle and Olympia were the established metropolises of Puget Sound, each claiming over 2,000. They had been by-passed and were deeply pained.

The Panic of 1873 was ushered in by the clanging shut of the doors of the New York bank which had financed Jay Cooke's railroad. The Northern Pacific was broke. Other empires came crashing down. Still heard were the words, "Now, just watch the West grow!"

The eyes of the nation were turning West. Ours was a country of rugged people, and the names of Seattle, Tacoma, Olympia and Bellingham caught the attention of adventurers back East. Heading West were men whose names were to stand out in Northwest history: John Leary, Robert Moran, Edmond Meany, Thomas Burke, Sam Shuffleton, James Colman, Hazard Stevens and Ezra Meeker.

Another newcomer was Colonel Dan Gilman, who claimed he became a Seattle resident because of a pair of buckskin pants which he unwisely wore on his arrival in town in the midst of an autumn rain. "Those buckskins stretched so when they got wet that the seat dropped down and snagged on a nail in the sidewalk," he explained. "Then the sun came out and dried 'em up so tight I couldn't move. By that time I'd decided I might as well stay permanently."

A Glamour Industry

The glamour of electricity would soon be introduced to

FIRST KITCHEN LIGHTING IN THE WORLD, 1879, in the home of Mrs. Sarah Jordon, New York City. The light was from Edison's new invention, the incandescent electric lamp. (Photo by General Electric Company)

frontier towns like Seattle. In the 1880s Thomas A. Edison was electrifying the minds of the world with his discoveries. The electric age was dawning. Electric lighting had just become a commercial achievement holding out great possibilities, a few electrically operated cars were in service and the transmission of electric power over long distances was being discussed as a likely development in the near future.

Electricity came into use first for arc lights in mines, in signal lights for ships, for stage effects, and especially for street lighting. In 1879 Thomas Edison introduced the incandescent lamp and the age of electricity began.

Then the Chicago World's Fair of 1893 with its bewildering variety of electrical exhibits emphasized that the electrical age had arrived. Edison's showmanship was superb. He and his men had brought 250,000 handmade electric light bulbs to the fair in clothes baskets and installed them on the grounds. At the end of the first day at twilight as people still lingered, to their amazement the buildings and grounds were instantly gleaming with electric light.

Young men on seeing the fair were hooked — henceforth their lives would be tied to the world of electricity. One such yearning young man was Magnus Crawford, an 8-year-old from Louisville, Kentucky. The fair had fired his ambition. In his adult life he came to the Pacific Northwest and became a top man in the industry.

At 14 young Magnus was a machinist's helper and moved on to switchboard builder, draftsman, designer of electrical machinery, estimator and installer of power plant equipment. Mixing jobs with schooling, he attended Polytechnic School in Louisville and later, upon arriving in Seattle, he obtained a master's degree in electrical engineering from the University of Washington — all this before 1910.

In 1906 he was employed by the Seattle-Tacoma Power Company (one of five electric systems consolidated in 1912 as the Puget Sound Traction, Light & Power Company). In time he became chief engineer of the modern-day highly integrated power system, the present Puget Sound Power & Light Company. Magnus Crawford died in 1971. He had witnessed in his lifetime of 86 years the unfolding of a very rich American heritage.

Part Two

BEGINNINGS IN TERRITORY OF WASHINGTON

The power systems of the Northwest are now interconnected and today electric businesses are meaningful to everyone, so let us look at their beginnings.

Before Washington attained statehood (1889), forerunners of its present electric systems were already established within its boundaries. The earliest electric plants were located in Tacoma, Seattle and in the village of Spokane Falls. An original electric plant whose output was measured in "lamps" was small. Such plants were the pioneers that marshalled forces of nature which now, through mighty hydro and steam plants, release a powerful array of kilowatts to serve homes, industries, highways, and byways, over a great network of energy carrying copper and aluminum.

Tacoma Had First Steam Plant

The very first electric light plant in the territory of Washington was built in 1882 by the Tacoma Mill Company, a dockside mill. It was installed so that the mill could operate day and night and load lumber in ships at night too. The system consisted of a number of arc lights arranged in a one-series circuit. Being steam driven, it was the first "steam" electric plant in Washington.

First Hydro Plant Built in Spokane

The first hydroelectric plant was installed at Spokane Falls in 1885. It is told that the steamship *Columbia* engaged in the coast traffic was equipped with an electric dynamo and wired to power 15 arc lamps of 1,200 candlepower each. This plant was replaced, dismantled and sold. The buyer was George A. Fitch, who shipped the plant to the village of Spokane Falls. The dynamo was installed in the basement of the C. & C. Flouring Mill and driven by a hurdy-gurdy wheel, an impulsive wheel similar to a Pelton wheel. On September 2, 1885, Mr. Fitch secured a franchise for en electric lighting system. Early in 1886 some of the leading businessmen of the village organized the Spokane Electric Light & Power Company, bought out Mr. Fitch and replaced the first generator with a small bi-polar dynamo of about 30 kilowatts. Difficulty with high water and an increased demand caused the company to build a new plant in 1887 of about 120 kilowatts. This installation was made

OTHER PLANTS very similar were quickly built, as the one shown above, of the Seattle Gas & Electric Company. They became predecessors of Puget Sound Power & Light Company. John Quinn, right, served over 50 years with Puget Power.

by John B. Fiskin, who remained with the firm and its successor, The Washington Water Power Company, for more than fifty years.

John B. Fiskin had previously helped install a hydro plant in Tacoma. The records show, "on December 26, 1886, incandescent electric street lights were turned on for the first time in Tacoma." Dissatisfied with their water service, in 1893 the voters purchased this private company, and so began municipal operation, of water and electric service in Tacoma. The plant was hydroelectric and located at Gallagher's Gulch in Tacoma.

Seattle First With Central Station Lighting

In Seattle electric service had its inception with the organization of The Seattle Electric Light Company, October 19, 1885, by J.M. Frink, George D. Hill, S.Z. Mitchell and F.H. Sparling. The present Puget Sound Power & Light Company stems from this beginning. The plant had two steam generators, each with a capacity of 600 lamps.

Lights were turned on March 22, 1886, at an exhibit given at the company's headquarters. Eleven 16-candlepower lamps were placed around the room and one 30-candlepower lamp over the street.

The Post Intelligencer of March 23, 1886, in reporting the matter, stated, "When the dynamo was started, instantly the room was made brilliant with a clear white light."

The company obtained a twenty-five year franchise, Ordinance No. 693, approved November 28, 1885, "to erect poles and stretch wires for electrical purposes." George D. Hill was its president, James M. Frink its vice president and superintendent, and S.Z. Mitchell and F.M. Sparling were the electricians.

The first customer of this electric company was a store, Toklas & Singerman's San Francisco Store, later known as MacDougal & Southwick Department Store. The big event occurred on the evening of April 24, 1886. Crowds came to witness the transition from greasy candles, smokey kerosene lamps and flickering gas lights. C.T. Conover, writing for *The Seattle Times* in 1955, under the caption "JUST COGITATING," tells it this way:

Some thought it was an advertising stunt, others were uncertain it would work, but all were curious. The questions asked would be thought amusing in this day and age, but in that period new discoveries and momentous developments were rare. Even the advent of gas lights still was something of a novelty and the first horse cars had made their appearance only two years previously.

As the hour hand on the clock in the San Francisco Store reached 9 o'clock on the memorable evening the store was jammed to the doors with spectators. Crowds were milling outside.

Over on lower Jackson Street in a little frame shack, James A. McWilliams, engineer for the Seattle Electric Light Company, pulled a switch. In the San Francisco Store, two blocks away, Paul Singerman pulled another switch. The gas lights had been turned off. There was a barely noticeable interval of darkness and then, as if by magic, the store was flooded with brilliant new light of five 2,000 candlepower lamps.

Those who witnessed the change hardly could believe their eyes. For hours crowds thronged in and out, some still almost unbelieving.

Seattle's little electric plant was the first west of the Mississippi to install incandescent lighting with central station service, although there had been small electric light installations in San Francisco and Portland and the larger sawmills on Puget Sound.

The new electric lights were successful beyond expectation, and it was not long before the original little plant gave way to a larger plant at Post Street. This was destroyed by the Seattle Fire of 1889. The company rebuilt at Eighth Avenue South and it was in operation within five weeks after the fire.

First Horse-Drawn Railway Car

The men who came to Seattle felt they were destined for success, and Seattle certainly challenged them with multiple and knotty problems. By the year 1885 Seattle's population had grown to 10,000. Its greatest asset was a deep harbor that was magnificent as a seaport. But its terrain was a massive problem. From the beginning there was mud. In coping with its terrain, rain and mud, transportation problems played a large role in the growth of Seattle and the electric industry.

The town had started on an eight-acre spot of land, at its highest point only sixteen feet above sea level. On one side was the sea and on the other a wall of cliffs which had seven ravines, so streets were on trestles and also had a habit of sliding into the bay. The waste from Henry Yesler's Mill and ballast from ships were used to make land fills. Streets tended to run only north and south as the steep cliffs were too forbidding.

So with the town stretching north from its original eight acres, a new form of transportation was added in 1884. Horse-drawn cars pulled on steel tracks were installed.

Frank Osgood, an outsider from Boston, upon arriving in Seattle had thought the time right, so with the urging of Judge Burke, David Denny and George Kinnear, he became the determined leader in building the first horse-drawn railway in Seattle. When service on the railway was begun on September 23, 1884, it was a prestigious thing for the city and the first street railway in Washington Territory.

Start of an Electric Railway

Osgood, ever a promoter, then got the gleam in his eyes to replace the horse-drawn cars with an electric railway and to parley his capital into a fortune. He began looking for a franchise to build his electric railway.

As in any frontier town, townspeople were drawn into the discussion. It was solemnly argued at the Council meetings that Osgood's scheme would be a menace to life and limb. Electricity had been seen as crooked lighting. Everybody knew it traveled in a zigzag fashion.

A Colonel Haines addressed the Honorable Body with this dire prediction:

"Steadiness of movement in the running of cars is essential, electricity is eccentric and shocking. Its shocks will make the cars jump off the track and endanger the lives of passengers. Water is a con-

FRANK OSGOOD, *builder of Seattle's first railway*

OCCASION OF THE FIRST RAILWAY IN SEATTLE, *September 23, 1884.* (**Seattle Times** *photo*)

ductor and rain will divert the electric current from the wires, leaving the cars dead on the tracks, collisions and appalling accidents will occur. The rails will be electrified and horses stepping on them will be shocked and fall.

Osgood was further told: Besides, Seattle already had streetcars pulled by sober, sedate and unemotional horses who could make all the speed necessary, and the City could not see why it wanted to monkey with any new-fangled mysterious toy as electricity.

Osgood did not laugh. He believed it was time to replace the horses. The citizens, too, decided it was worth the risk. Going along with the popular opinion, the city fathers granted a franchise to the Seattle Electric Railway & Power Company, which was incorporated on October 8, 1888. There were eight prominent men on the board of directors, Frank Osgood became president and manager.

On the morning of March 31, 1889, Seattle's first electric railway commenced regular service. The running cars were a sight for rubber-necking and eye-swiveling. All Seattle, it seemed, lined 2nd Avenue to watch the cars go by. Curious men and boys caused difficulties at most stops. They ducked under the cars trying to fathom what made them go.

George Lee, a Chinese man, stood for a long time and watched the streetcars go by. Finally he summed up his bewilderment by exclaiming, *"No pushee, no pullee, all same go like hellee!"*

By April 5, the last horse-drawn car was seen. Horses went to pasture. And so began another use for electricity in the lives of Seattle citizens. Furthermore, it might be said that streetcar service started a business boom.

After that everybody seemed to want to build a streetcar line. David Denny soon had three of them in operation, one running clear to the town of Fremont and beyond to tap the distant wilderness around Green Lake. Judge Burke and William Ballard built a line to Ballard's booming town. Osgood started laying tracks along the Rainier Valley towards Renton.

In 1890 Frank Osgood was also busy building an electric railway in Portland, and during the following years carried to completion similar undertakings in Tacoma, Bellingham, Port Townsend, Spokane, Fildelgo Island, as well as in the British Columbia towns of Victoria and Vancouver. He was an enthusiastic builder.

The streetcars made Seattle boom as it had never boomed before — until the inevitable bust, which came in the Panic of 1893. Most of the lines went into receivership then.

The Ballard line escaped the fate of the others. It kept solvent and kept running, after a fashion, until Stone & Webster bought the other bankrupt lines and consolidated them into a single system. Then Judge Burke, following the break-down of his generator, let the big company have his line, too.

The records show that the Ballard Line survived only because Judge Burke had made heroic efforts to economize, including shutting down the railroad's power-house. The engine and generator were moved to the basement of the Burke Building to replace an already inadequate generator. So the railroad's generator now furnished light for the offices and power for the elevators of the Burke Building and also was expected to energize the trolley system.

He did get by, with the cars barely crawling along at the end of the line. Everyone in the Burke Building suffered with them, for the car's demand dimmed the lights and elevators paused between floors until the trolley made it.

Burke's overloaded generator flew apart in the early months of 1900. It let go with a bang that shook the solid brick building. Blue sparks buzzed across the basement while the premises lit up like a Fourth of July fireworks display. Flywheels ran wild, snapping belts.

Sam Shuffleton, the electrician, had made it perform miracles, and when he put in his appearance at a running walk, he went straight into the roomful of fireballs and pulled the right switches. Those who had seen the drama were not surprised in later years when Sam Shuffleton emerged as a top man in the electrical business and had

One of Seattle's early streetcars.

named after him a large powerhouse, the Shuffleton Steam Plant at the foot of Lake Washington in the City of Renton.

Tumwater Falls First to Power a Mill

The oldest American settlement in the Puget Sound area is at the falls of the Des Chutes River at Tumwater, Washington, established in 1845. The story of Tumwater is an admirable example of struggles by pioneers to harness a natural resource, and in it is a capsule history of the piecemeal emergence of water power and the electric industry in the Northwest, which reveals its continuing restructuring. Here settlers built the first mill on Puget Sound.

In the history of Tumwater Falls we get an insight of changing times, from water wheels spinning for one hundred years, to their complete removal because in recent years they were too small, and to the restoration of the Falls, once unfettered, to a recreation area for tourists.

Sam Shuffleton

The Tumwater Falls site is picturesque and beautiful with exquisite waterfalls, pools, rockwork, shrubs and native trees. Today one can view much of it from a dining table at the Falls Terrace Restaurant, see ducks dive and swim in pools, or take a walk along shaded pathways on either side of the Des Chutes River for a closer view of the Falls. This scenic park of fifteen acres is maintained by the Olympia–Tumwater Foundation and is visited by over 250,000 people a year.

In contrast, the settlers of 1845 found the Falls wild and awesome. From accounts of early members of the community, they found three monstrous waterfalls — the upper, the middle and the lower falls — where the water went bounding, billowing and roaring along and over the rocks with a noise resembling the roar of ocean surf at high tide beating against rocky shores.

The Falls, now set aside as a recreation area and a park, once powered grist mills, sawmills and electric generators. When viewed by the early settlers in 1845 the Falls held enough attraction for them to start this oldest Puget Sound community. (Settlers arrived in Seattle at Alki Point six years later in 1851). Upon arriving they named their little community New Market but later changed it to Tumwater, adopting the name given it by Chinook Indians, who likened the sound of falling water to the repeated throb of a human heart, expressed in the jargon as "thum-thum."

The hardy group to first set foot on the site were Michael T. Simmons, George Washington Bush, David Kindred, Jesse Ferguson, Gabriel Jones, Samuel B. Crocket and James McAllister. To reach it the men and their families had to cut a road a distance of 58 miles and to clear a space for a camp.

Simmons took a claim near the Falls which held promise

8

MIDDLE FALLS, at Tumwater

of some kind of mill; the others staked out land on the adjacent prairie for farming. These were honored frontiersmen.

Bush, a mulatto and a man of true merit and sterling manhood, at the age of 54 had left a prosperous farm in Missouri when that state passed a law banning free Negroes,

MICHAEL T. SIMMONS
(State Capitol Museum photo)

GEORGE W. BUSH
*(Copyright, **Los Angeles Times** reprinted with permission).*

bringing his wife and six sons West. Upon arriving in Oregon he found a similar ban. It was hard for him to stomach for he had been born free in Pennsylvania, had fought in the War of 1812 under Andrew Jackson, roamed the West as a fur trader with the Hudson Bay Company and was accustomed to answer to no man. They decided to settle north of the Columbia in what was considered British territory. At Tumwater Bush again became a successful farmer who, on many occasions, helped his neighbors and travelers with both food and finances. Despite his good deeds Bush was able to remain only through special permission of the legislature, and his 640-acre claim became his only by special act of Congress.

Two years after arriving at the Falls, in the summer of 1847, Bush and Simmons built a combination grist and sawmill at the lower falls, where timber rafts and small vessels could come in at high tide. Bush financed the mill and Simmons provided the know-how in setting up the first sawmill in the Puget Sound area.

They built the sawmill from discarded machinery of the Hudson Bay Company's sawmill which had been established at Fort Vancouver in 1827 — the first in the West and the grandfather of all the thousands of sawmills, big and little, which subsequently were built. It was a "muley" with an up and down, or upright saw. Floods washed out this mill at Tumwater, and within three years the men had a workable plant named the Puget Sound Milling Company.

Soon others were diverting water from the Falls to turn waterwheels for various uses. In time there were three grist mills. Ira Ward owned one on the upper falls which he also converted into a sawmill that remained in operation for many years. George Gelbach owned a grist mill at the middle falls, and the Simmons mill, the first to be built, was located at the lower falls.

The lower falls became a veritable water power center. Around it was a sizeable industrial community. A blueprint prepared by A. J. Gillis, an engineer, dated 1892 and titled "Contour Map of Des Chutes Canyon at Tumwater," reveals a network of water flumes to serve an ice factory, a shingle mill, a flour mill and a box factory. Here also was a waterwheel for an electric generator.

Clanrick Crosby bought the Simmons' flouring mill in 1849 which he replaced with a six-story mill in 1864. A very significant home was built in 1857 just west of the mill. The mill is gone now, but this home is still standing as the oldest house in Tumwater. It was the home of Nathaniel Crosby, grandfather of Bing Crosby, the famed Hollywood singer, and it is maintained as a historic dwelling by the Daughters of the Pioneers.

The water-powered businesses prospered for many years; however, other competition developed. Olympia, dedicated as a townsite in 1850 and situated at the head of Bud Inlet, the most southerly tip of Puget Sound with a harbor for ocean-going ships, became a rival of Tumwater. Moreover, by the 1880s, with a railroad terminal at Tacoma and the presence of larger mills there, in Seattle and in Portland, the Tumwater mills went into a decline.

Furthermore, by now the news of the glamour industry, electricity, was splashed in headlines in local and distant newspapers. No longer was it necessary to locate mills at waterfalls to be driven by water wheels. They could be located dock-side and powered by electricity transmitted by wires.

Beginnings of the Electric Business in Olympia

The first electric light plant was built in Olympia — not at Tumwater Falls — by Allen C. Mason for street lighting; still, just as the Falls had caught the fancy of frontiersmen who built grist and sawmills using water power, again when electricity grew with sizable demands the Tumwater Falls became the pride of electric power men. Street lighting was a beginning.

Allen C. Mason had obtained a city franchise on April 16, 1887, with the plan of supplanting gas lights which had been installed in 1885. The Olympia Gas Company had secured a franchise on April 6, 1884, "to build works for generating hydrogen gas for illumination purposes." Mason felt that electric lighting was the coming thing.

With astute persuasion, on September 17, 1887, the gas company purchased Mason's system, which had an inventory of an electric light plant with a 30 horsepower engine and boiler, 15 arc lamps and 50 incandescent lamps, poles and wires. Now a Roman horseman, handling both gas and electricity, the company changed its name to the Olympia Gas & Electric Company.

This was the time of excitement in Olympia over becoming the capitol of the new State of Washington (1889). In rapid succession other franchises were obtained by various interests for telephone, street railways, a private water system and for electric service. There was a scramble to get into the act. For example, a franchise had been granted to the Olympia and Tumwater Railway, Light & Power Company on March 7, 1889. The same privilege was granted to George M Savage and Associates, who was the first man to make use of his franchise when he laid a track along Main Street from 4th to 13th and in the winter put on two horse cars.

The company with the greatest foresight, the Olympia Light & Power Company, was incorporated on May 9, 1890. E. T. Young was president and George D. Shannon secretary. Young had obtained a franchise on December 27, 1889, "to erect poles, wires and works for the production and supplying the city of Olympia and its inhabitants with light, heat and power by means of electricity." Young had also purchased a site for a hydro plant at Tumwater Falls, where the company built a modest electric hydro plant at the middle falls. There still remained ample water in the Des Chutes River to operate the existing flour mills, shingle mill, the ice factory and a box factory.

The Olympia Light & Power Company had its sights set for a much bigger operation. It proceeded to acquire, consolidate and enlarge all electric services — power, light, street lighting and street railways. Incorporated in May of 1890, it also secured a franchise on June 6 to operate a street railway; then on August 13 it purchased its competitor, the Olympia Gas & Electric Light Company, to secure the street lighting business. This company was willing to sell, for its electric generator was steam driven and wheezy; besides, gas street lighting was now considered old-fashioned.

Then, with the Panic of 1893, plans went awry. The company went into bankruptcy. Other businesses at the Falls were also shutting down.

On March 10, 1897, a decree of foreclosure and order of sale was made by the U.S. State Circuit Court in favor of the American Loan & Trust Company against the Olympia

TUMWATER HYDRO PLANT, (1900), built of stone from the Tenino quarry, as was the Old State Capitol Building. The hydro plant used the full capacity of the Des Chutes River. Today only the foundations of the powerhouse remain, decked over as a 40 by 80 foot viewing platform of lower falls.

Light & Power Company. Then on July 8, at noon at the front door of the Courthouse in Olympia, said property was struck off and sold to Lester B. Falkner for the sum of $100,000. Falkner purchased the electric utility as agent for a committee of bond holders consisting of Hazard Stevens, Frank W. Wilder, John F. Souther and N. W. Jordon, all of Boston. Hazard and Wilder left Boston and followed their money to Olympia to pursue further investments.

Shortly after the foreclosure sale took place the depression ended miraculously with the arrival of the ship *Portland* in Seattle on July 17, 1897, from the Yukon with a ton of gold.

The new owners again saw a bright future in the electric utility business, and the Olympia Light & Power Company secured all water rights at Tumwater Falls. Thereupon it planned for the full development of the Falls and built a new hydroelectric plant at the lower falls for which water of the Des Chutes River was brought from the upper falls through a 10-foot steel pipe to utilize the 74-foot fall of the river. Two generators were installed in the powerhouse with a combined rating of 1,667 kilowatts.

Within ten years the use of electricity had outraced the supply at Tumwater. In fact, a consulting engineer, Henry L. Gray, in a report made in 1916, rated the Tumwater Plant at 1,000 kilowatts, pointing out that it was severely handicapped by lack of water, even though the company had expended a considerable sum of money in acquiring storage at Lake Lawrence.

Now with the demand of electricity multiplying greatly, especially with needs of World War I, the company set about to buy power. To the east of Olympia were the plants of Electron, White River and Snoqualmie operated by the Puget Sound Traction, Light & Power Company. In 1919 this larger company came to the help of the Olympia utility. It extended its 55,000 volt transmission line from Dupont to Olympia. Olympians were relieved.

Then in 1924, when Puget Power consolidated many separate systems into one integrated area-wide system, the Olympia Light & Power Company was also purchased and consolidated into the Puget Sound Power & Light Company. The use of electricity expanded greatly; however, the street railway patronage declined and the trolley line was discontinued for bus service with its sale on December 1, 1933, to the Olympia Transit Company.

Puget Power continued to operate the Tumwater Falls Plant until the 10-foot pipe line wore thin and rivets began to squirt water, and when this quarter-mile-long supply line could be seen to bulge and throb with water surges flowing inside, the Company considered the plant unsafe.

So the small 1,000 kilowatt power plant was dismantled in 1950. In the span of 100 years the use of water power at Tumwater Falls had gone full circle. In 1950 the Olympia-Tumwater Foundation was established which in 1962 restored the scenic beauty of the Falls by building the Tumwater Falls Park, with landscaping, reception area, restrooms and picnic facilities. There are walking trails on the east and west banks of the river connected by foot bridges. One of the bridges is a replica of the wooden truss foot bridge spanning the picturesque Tumwater Falls that served the people of Tumwater before the turn of the century.

Strangely, as one industry gave way to another, each owing its life to power from Tumwater Falls, one industry still remains which never directly depended upon energy from the Falls, the Olympia Brewing Company.

In 1895 Leopold F. Schmidt discovered the brewing qualities of artesian water in the Des Chutes Valley, and the Olympia Brewing Company, brewers and bottlers of Olympia Beer, was born, and the trademark "It's The Water" of Tumwater was originated. This $100,000,000 a year business is still managed by the descendants of Leopold Schmidt. It was his son, Peter G. Schmidt that led in the organization of the Olympia-Tumwater Foundation.

In contrast to Tumwater, where development and growth took place with natural changes, elsewhere on Puget Sound, the City of Seattle, in 1889 a shabby lumber town, suffered a ruinous fire and abruptly rebuilt as a city of intrinsic beauty. The Great Seattle Fire was a vital turning point in the future of that city.

The Great Seattle Fire

Nowadays a wrecker's ball is used to quickly demolish old unwanted structures in a city. In 1889 it was a devastating fire that hardy men in one instance believed as good for the city. After downtown Seattle burned to the ground, the city was rebuilt with brick and stone, business boomed and the population doubled in one year.

The Great Seattle Fire on June 6, 1889, wiped out sixty square blocks in its fierce sweep through the heart of downtown Seattle. The fire was devastating primarily because the whole downtown area was on stilts to raise the buildings above sea level. Wooden sidewalks and street trestles were great fire carriers. At University Street the fire was stopped from going north by tearing up the streets and sidewalks and throwing them over the cliff into the Bay.

The fire had started in a cabinet shop from an overturned burning glue pot, which hit shavings.

Though no one had worried before the fire about Seattle being a shabby lumber town, three weeks after the fire an ordinance was passed raising the streets, and men of vision rebuilt the town with brick, stone and mortar, erecting buildings and business structures for permanence, some with inherent beauty.

Seattle, though burned and shocked, reacted in a lusty way. Badly scorched, it was healing fast. Within a year the six-story Pioneer Building was topping the skyline. Moreover, in less than a year after its destruction, the city had more than doubled its population. The 1890 census gave a population count of 42,837, eleven times the figure of 1880. A dozen electric streetcar lines were now doing a booming business.

Panic of 1893

Although the nationwide Panic of 1893 struck Seattle a little late, its effects went deeper. All but one of the independent streetcar lines went into receivership. Jim Hill had brought a transcontinental railway, the Great Northern, to Seattle in 1893. It was not a spectacular event with financial panic all around. The worsening depression saw some of the new brick schools closed because there was no money to pay teachers. A person with money could buy a seven-course dinner with wine for fifty cents. A wool suit cost $3.90.

Gold from Alaska

The four years of frustration and poverty were ended with a whoop and holler on July 17, 1897. The occasion was the arrival of the ship *Portland* from the Yukon River, with a ton, more or less, of raw Alaska gold aboard. True, another ship had also gone to San Francisco, with gold aboard worth millions of dollars, but Seattle grabbed off national publicity. As in all periods of distress there was a man of the hour.

Erastus Brainerd, a journalist, was alert as no one else. He fast-talked himself as press agent for the Seattle Chamber of Commerce, and immediately he and his associates coined the phrase that became a banner headline in newspapers across the nation: "A Ton of Gold in Seattle."

People read, heeded and headed for Seattle. The city soon swelled and roared with teeming life as every steamer and train poured out miners who came to Seattle headed for Alaska to get rich. Seattle was busy making up for those four long, lean years of the depression.

A hundred thousand miners passed through Seattle, dropping $50,000,000 on the way north. In the ten years following the gold strike they brought back with them over $200,000,000, of which about half remained in Seattle. The gold ran out in 1908.

There were many men attracted to Seattle for the excitement and adventure to be found in a booming city on the crest of the gold rush. One such person was Frank Seibert, who in time became assistant treasurer of the Puget Sound Power & Light Company. Frank was a violinist who subsequently played in the Seattle Symphony. As a member of a string ensemble playing dinner music at the Globe Hotel, he related that tips were fabulous in the gold rush fever. Instead of applause, approval was by way of sliding silver half dollars and dollars across the floor to the music makers.

Moments of Truth

The small pioneering electric railway and lighting companies, hard hit by economic depressions and even fire, seemingly were not benefited by gold rush money. For them the decade 1890–1900 was a struggle for survival.

Most of them did not make it. They had problems in common, whether in Seattle, Olympia, Bellingham, Tacoma, Port Angeles, Port Townsend, or elsewhere across the nation. The struggles for survival of these predecessor companies is a poignant story.

Nearly thirty competing units sprang up in Seattle in the decade 1885–1895. Many were little power plants in basements of buildings. All were privately owned. In these first plants power was steam generated under conditions of high costs. Added to inefficient machinery there was lack of experience and little regard to economy. The men who built the systems and wired the buildings had never run an electric light setup before. With the first flush of success in seeing lights burn, others went pell-mell into building another electric plant.

Minor mergers absorbed half of these companies in Seattle, for operating separately survival was a vain hope. Elsewhere the story was the same. Hundreds of electric systems had been rushed into existence all over the nation in the hasty anticipation of a new golden era. Then came the 1893 panic. Many of these ventures, unwisely conceived, poorly managed and badly financed, failed.

Stone & Webster

During the soul searching and shake-down of the electric business across the nation, when insolvency was so common, the firm of Stone & Webster was organized as a group of experts whose specialty was the appraisal, financing and management of electric properties. They expanded their activities in response to calls for assistance and advice. This firm which began as a partnership in 1889 of two young consulting electrical engineers, grew until its activities covered every phase of the business. So, during the moments of truth as witnessed by Seattle firms, Stone & Webster was persuaded to look over the local electric systems.

In 1899 Stone & Webster came to aid the troubled electric companies and purchased the Union Electric Company, and in 1900 began to merge with it the remainder of the small and mostly insolvent street railway and electric firms under the name of The Seattle Electric Company. It consolidated the following electric properties, with date of

CHARLES A. STONE, EDWIN S. WEBSTER

acquisition shown:

Seattle Traction Company	(1900)
Third Street & Suburban Railway Company	(1900)
Grant Street Electric Railway Company	(1900)
Madison Street Cable Company	(1900)
First Avenue Cable Railway Company	(1900)
Union Trunk Line	(1900)
Consumers Electric Company	(1900)
Burke Block Light Plant	(1900)
Union Electric Company	(1900)
Seattle Steam Heat & Power Company	(1900)
Seattle Railway Company	(1901)
West Seattle & North End Railway Company	(1901)
Arcade Electric Company	(1903)
Seattle Gas & Electric Company	(1903)
West Seattle Municipal Street Railway	(1907)

There were other predecessor companies not shown; for example, the first plant in Seattle, the Seattle Electric Light Company, was reorganized as the Seattle General Electric Company in 1890, and consolidated with the Union Electric Company in 1892. There were about fifteen such short-lived companies.

The year 1900 therefore marks the first step toward unified electric service in Seattle with astute management, qualified engineers and sound funding. In 1900 the new company set the following rate for electric lighting:

20¢ per KWH for first 30 hours use of maximum demand

8¢ per KWH for next 120 hours use of maximum demand

4¢ per KWH for all in excess of 150 KWH use
Minimum $1.10. 10% discount for prompt payment.

12

Rates had been reduced several times since the first plant was started fifteen years previously. The area served by the newly formed Seattle Electric Company (1900), predecessor of the present firm, Puget Sound Power & Light Company, served Seattle only. Similar consolidations in other seaports, together with the advent of interurban electric railways running between cities, set the pattern for area–wide merging of electric utilities later (1912).

Engineer With an Elegant Dream

The City of Seattle which emerged at the close of the 19th century had the makings of a Queen City in a setting of Charmed Lands. The scenic beauty of Mount Rainier, the Cascades and the Olympics, and Seattle's location on a remarkable inland harbor on Puget Sound, became a constant source of interest and wonderment. Seattle soon had a champion for projecting an elegant dream, that of its city engineer, Reginald H. Thomson. Thomson had come West in 1881 to survey the roadbed for Judge Burke's Lakeshore and Eastern Railroad. Thomson was sort of a Paul Bunyan.

With resolve and audacity Thomson accomplished for Seattle most of his plans, a water system and a sewer system built for needs far into the future, and an ambitious plan to cut down the City's seven hills and fill its tidelands.

The seven hills were an impediment to the City's growth. Thomson planned to sluice them into Elliott Bay, using the same sort of huge hoses the Alaskans used in hydraulic mining. Denny Hill was attacked first. Five million yards of dirt were sluiced down to fill the tideflats and provide level ground for industrial expansion. Another five million yards came off Dearborn and Jackson Hills.

At Thomson's request in 1903 the City Council hired a nationally known firm of landscape architects, the Olmsted Brothers, to make a park and recreational survey of the City. Now Seattle was destined to be beautiful. Created were the Lake Washington Boulevard, Seward Park, Volunteer Park, other smaller parks and green belts, and Green Lake as a jewel inside the city.

In ten years Seattle had more than tripled its population, paved its streets, acquired 2,000 acres of parks and playgrounds, reduced the grade of its once almost perpendicular streets to a maximum of five percent and achieved a skyline of handsome new buildings. In this environment the Seattle Electric Company extended streetcar lines, built substations and gave electric service of a high order.

PART THREE

THE ELECTRIC NORTHWEST IN 1900

Electricity in 1900 was considered the youngest science, and significantly the youngest states of the nation, those of the Northwest, were in the forefront in finding new ways of generating and distributing electricity.

The New Northwest

At the time it was often repeated that "electricity is still in its infancy." Some contended this was simply a platitude, explaining that when a boy reaches the age of twenty-one and is able to do as much work as a man he is no longer called an infant, although admittedly his development does not cease when he reaches his majority. The use of electricity was constantly discussed and there was real pride in seeing what more could be done with it. Its promoters insisted that electricity was a way of life.

To all it was a mystery. Whether by instinctive wisdom, or by sheer good fortune, the first use of electricity was that of supplanting older modes of work, applying its use to the commonplace, and gaining instant acceptance. Electricity replaced horse-drawn cars, steam engines, coal and gas. It was clean and by a flick of a switch it would do its work. It was liked.

The pioneers by nature were receptive to new ideas for they were innovators. In building the Northwest, first settlers came in wagons over torturous trails, then came the Pony Express, the Overland Stage, and finally by emphatic demand came railroads. Railroads were a gigantic undertaking, yet eventually steam engines were climbing mountains and drawing millions of tons of freight across the country. Electrical men drew on this parallel.

They replaced the horse cars with trolley cars, rolling them along on steel rails, an idea borrowed from the railroads. They soon would also invade the country and run electric trolleys between towns and cities many miles apart.

Next coal burning steam power plants were supplemented and then replaced by hydroelectric plants. The use of "white coal" in place of "black diamonds" opened up a new realm of engineering and established the Northwest as the unchallenged area of low-cost electric power. The new Northwest was learning fast.

Residence Lighting

At the turn of the century, 1900, electricity in the home was just a novelty. The house without a chimney was a pipe dream. A few wealthy home owners had wired their houses for lights. A chandelier was hung in the parlor and in the dining room; single drop lights were hung in the kitchen, bath, bedrooms, pantry and porch. Wires were No. 14 copper placed in walls with knob and tube insulators. Switches were high on the walls out of reach of children or as part of the lamp socket. Within a few years, however, electric appliances such as hand irons, toasters and space heaters, came into vogue. Immediately the wiring became obsolete, wires were too small, and new wiring had to be added.

Speaking of the novelty of lights in a home, in the town of Port Townsend at about 1888 the Port Townsend Electric Company had been founded and kilowatts were like diamonds then. Three street railroads were clanking up and down streets with capacity loads and the electric company had been organized by W. J. Grambs, S. Z. Mitchell and E. B. Downing, with slab wood providing the fuel for making steam. It ran only nights. For many years the townsfolks talked about one of the society women who "put on the ritz" by throwing an afternoon social affair at her home with the electric lights on. Her swankiness caused a daytime run of the light plant and cost her husband slightly in excess of $75.

At that time the cost of electricity was based on lamps used. For one 16-candlepower lamp the cost was $3 per month, and for one 32-candlepower lamp it was $5.50 per month. The lamps themselves cost $1 and $1.50 apiece.

By 1912 with the introduction of an improved Mazda lamp and miscellaneous appliances, most new houses were being wired for electricity. Hardly a home was without an electric hand iron or some kind of heating device. There was a continued downward trend in the cost of electricity. A rate for electric heating and cooking was being discussed. A study of residential lighting for Seattle in 1912 revealed that the average home used about $21 annually (also the national average).

The home owner watched his pennies and his electric consumption closely, with 32% using only the minimum charge. The average use per year was 25 kilowatt-hours. It was predicted that there was a wonderful future in residential lighting.

Central Heating

Two of the pioneer electric systems should be recognized for their ingenuity in developing by-products. The Seattle Heat and Power Company sold exhaust steam from its boilers for heating downtown buildings. The Diamond Ice Company, principally engaged in ice making, also organized a subsidiary, the Mutual Light and Heat Company, which likewise sold electricity and exhaust steam. In time, ice making and electric power were separated from these ventures, and central heating evolved on its own, which today is an independent service supplied by a successful company, the Seattle Steam Corporation.

It is doubtful that the small group of men who initiated the sale of steam for heating downtown buildings realized that from their side ventures a network of high pressure and low pressure steam mains would total miles of lines, and that they were early-day ecologists who were first to eliminate smoke from chimneys of many downtown buildings.

The distribution of steam had its inception in 1893 when the Seattle Heat and Power Company obtained a franchise in the south half of the city to install mains for supplying steam for heating and for water to operate hydraulic elevators. Their operations extended within a radius of two blocks of their plant.

In 1900 this company was merged with the Seattle Electric Company. By 1902 it completed a steam electric generating plant at Post Street (see Part Four), with eight boilers and a total boiler capacity of 4,000 horsepower. Now the steam heating distribution was enlarged to serve the greater part of the buildings located south of Madison Street.

The district north of Madison Street was served similarly by the Mutual Light and Heat Company. It began as a small heating business in 1897.

About 1904, the Seattle-Tacoma Power Company purchased the properties of the Mutual Light and Heat Company (along with its parent company, the Diamond Ice Company), and with this merger the Western Avenue plant was enlarged to eleven boilers for a total boiler capacity of 5,100 horsepower. The new owners also enlarged the heat distribution system to serve the growing business north of Madison Street.

In 1912 there was a merger of five major electric systems to form the Puget Sound Traction, Light and Power Company. The heating systems of the Seattle Electric Company and of the Seattle-Tacoma Power Company were then joined.

In 1917 considerable experimental work was done at Western Avenue Station in the burning of pulverized coal. The source of fuel was the Renton Coal Mines. The pulverized coal was ground to the fineness of talcum powder or flour, mixed with the proper amount of air, and blown into the furnaces. The pulverized coal burned in suspension without grates like oil. This had never been done before, so credit should be given to these pioneers for originating the idea which is now used in steam plants throughout the world.

When in 1951 the Puget Sound Power & Light Company was forced to sell its electric facilities to the City of Seattle, the City did not want the steam heat business. So on October 24, 1951, Puget Power sold the steam heat properties to a group of steam users, owners of downtown buildings. They named their company the Seattle Steam Corporation, and under good leadership this firm has grown into a fine enterprise. Within two years this new company modernized and doubled its plant capacity and extended its mains. The system is modern and clean.

The heating mains vary in size from six to eighteen inches and are buried at a minimum depth of six feet, although in one instance, due to the contour of the ground, the main is laid a depth of 43 feet below the street level. Pipes are heavily insulated. Those who take the historic Underground Tour of Seattle can see some of the steam mains located under sidewalks.

There Was Competition

In 1898 the Snoqualmie Falls Plant was built by parties backed by Chicago capital.

Prior to 1903 the Snoqualmie Falls Power Company sold electricity to wholesale customers only in Tacoma, Everett and Seattle, including the newly organized Seattle Electric Company. After 1903 it was in competition with the Seattle Electric Company. The Gas Company also entered the field with the Welsbach lamp which had just appeared.

In November, 1904, the Seattle Electric Company adopted the following lighting rate:

12¢ per KWH for first 60 hours use of maximum demand as shown in November, December and January

3¢ per KWH for all excess. Maximum taken at 50% of connected load

The City of Seattle had been engaged in constructing a municipal power plant at Cedar Falls, where the City obtains its water supply, and in January, 1905, the street lighting system of the private company was taken over and served by the City. The municipal lighting plant also began to serve private consumers in 1905.

The municipal lighting plant was hardly a factor in the competition for business prior to 1910. The Snoqualmie company was the real competitor, and the fight waxed stronger and stronger until lighting was often taken as low as $40 per horsepower-year regardless of hours of use. Rate schedules were not strictly adhered to.

Though the "12 and 3" rate was still retained as an alternative, in 1908 business meter rates were adopted as follows:

6¢ per KWH on Min. monthly guarantee of $35 per HP per year

5½¢ per KWH on Min. monthly guarantee of $40 per HP per year

5¢ per KWH on Min. monthly guarantee of $45 per HP per year

4½¢ per KWH on Min. monthly guarantee of $50 per HP per year

4¢ per KWH on Min. monthly guarantee of $55 per HP per year

3½¢ per KWH on Min. monthly guarantee of $60 per HP per year

3¢ per KWH on Min. monthly guarantee of $70 per HP per year

2½¢ per KWH on Min. monthly guarantee of $80 per HP per year

2¢ per KWH on Min. monthly guarantee of $90 per HP per year

Free lamps with rates of 3½¢ and above, net.

On June 7, 1911, a legislative act creating a Public Service Commission in the State of Washington became law. On the following day a new schedule of rates was filed by the Seattle Electric Company covering residential lighting, business lighting and power service. The residence rate filed was:

9½¢ for first 20 KWH use per month
8½¢ for next 20 KWH
7½¢ for next 20 KWH
5¢ all over 60 KWH
Minimum $1.10 per month, 10% discount for prompt payment. Free renewal standard carbon lamps.

PART FOUR

A GROWING COUNTRY: 1900-1910

At the turn of the century times were not tranquil nationally. Our nation was growing lustily. Its stature loomed large as it entered into international disputes, righted its boundaries, dug the Panama Canal, sent its Navy around the world, experimented with a flying machine, built wireless telegraph units, grew enormous industrially, was deeply beset by labor strikes, and on the local scene, Seattle sponsored a World's Exposition.

War with Spain began in 1898 and concluded with a treaty of peace in 1899, which created international tensions; it brought America into possession of the colonies of Cuba, Puerto Rico, Guam and the Philippines which in time were given home rule. In China the Boxer uprising with its purpose to murder all foreigners in China was quelled by American troops capturing Peking.

The presidential campaign of 1900 gave President McKinley a second term with Theodore Roosevelt as his vice president. Within three months McKinley was assassinated and Theodore Roosevelt became president.

By this time industrial America had grown broadly, and many large companies were organized which were joined further as large trusts. As their counterpart, workers were organized into large labor unions. Strikes by railroad workers and mine workers became a national concern. Coal strikes of 1900 and 1902 more than doubled the price of coal.

The discovery of gold in the Klondike and the Yukon regions made it necessary to definitely locate the line between Alaska and Canada. In 1903 a commission of the two nations set fixed boundaries.

The Panama Canal was begun in 1904 and completed in 1913. The American Navy made its first sailing around the world in 1908-1909, receiving warm reception at every city where the fleet stopped. An explorer, Commander Robert E. Peary, discovered the North Pole in 1909.

Wireless telegraph units were installed in one hundred shore stations and in nearly two hundred stations on naval vessels in 1909. The Wright brothers of Ohio made successful flights with their flying machine and received the government's prize of $30,000.

The City of Seattle sponsored the Alaska-Yukon-Pacific Exposition. What began as a zany, impossible idea proposed at a civic banquet by Godfrey Chealander, "that the city hold a little exposition to celebrate the 10th anniversary of the arrival of the first Klondike gold ship," before long the little exposition idea embraced Alaska, the Yukon and all of the Pacific. The opening day was June 1, 1909, of an audacious ten million dollar undertaking. When it closed on October 16 it had been a financial success and the townspeople were radiant. Visiting the exposition were 3,740,551 people. They found Seattle an exciting city, a natural port of entry for the Orient and a "second" home for Alaskans visiting outside their territory.

The Exposition Monument, eighty feet high, was covered with gold from Alaska and from the Yukon. Another monument, the Electric Tower, stood at the other end of the Fair's Court of Honor. It was slender, 250 feet high, and inside its open construction was a central winding stairway. At night the monument had a festive shimmer of countless filaments. Its latticed architecture gave it a radiant beauty planned to be symbolic of the properties of electricity, the youngest science. The civic-minded sponsor of the Electric Tower was Jacob Furth, a banker, and also president of the two firms that erected the tower, the Vulcan Iron Works and the Seattle Electric Company.

Emergence of a Profile

With vigor, imagination and subtlety, the leaders of the Seattle Electric Company were unerringly shaping the profile of the present Puget Sound Power & Light Company. During the decade of 1900-1910 stable utility operations had emerged within cities all along the Puget Sound, large electric steam plants and hydro plants had been built for low cost power, electric interurban railway lines now linked cities and towns hauling passengers and freight, and the hinterlands were being exposed to power lines which tied cities together. There was an orderly growth of the electric utility business.

To emphasize the strong points of each, the history of five electric utility companies and two interurban railway systems follow: The Seattle Electric Company, The Seattle-Tacoma Power Company, The Puget Sound Power Company, The Pacific Coast Power Company, The Whatcom County Railway & Light Company, The Puget Sound Electric Railway and The Pacific Northwest Traction Company. The five firms were consolidated in 1912 as the Puget Sound Traction, Light & Power Company.

Each had its day in the sun and special expertise, and time brought them traumatic and rare experiences. But all faced moments of decision that came swiftly upon them either from competition or changes in life styles. As pioneers of an industry men labored mightily and we value their story.

The Seattle Electric Company

In the fall of 1898 with encouragement from local businessmen, Charles A. Stone, a lone figure of the Boston firm of Stone & Webster, came to Seattle for the purpose of acquiring the street railway and lighting properties and to consolidate them into one system.

He enlisted the help of the local leaders. William J. Grambs, a manufacturer's representative of dynamos, bought the first electric property, the Union Electric Company, of which Dr. E.C. Kilbourne was president. Then they encountered difficulties. At Grambs' suggestion the

JACOB FURTH

There was no stumbling. Within a few years they also set the stage for a merger of electric utilities area–wide, serving Seattle, Everett, Bellingham, Puyallup and Tacoma. Officers of the newly incorporated Seattle Electric Company were:

Jacob Furth	President
F. S. Pratt	Vice President
R. T. Laffin	Vice President
Geo. W. Dickinson	Manager
Dwight P. Robinson	Assistant Manager
Henry B. Sawyer	Treasurer
Frank Dabney	Asst. Treasurer
A. S. Michener	Controller
C. A. Homond	Claim Agent
H. E. Wilmot	Chief Clerk
W. J. Grambs	Purchasing Agent
A. L. Kempster	Supt. of Transportation
J. G. Roseman	Supt. of Light & Power
H. Day Hanford	Chief Engineer
D. J. Blackwell	Asst. Engineer
E. C. Kilbourne	Sales Manager
R. J. Santmyer	Chief Steam Engineer
S. C. Lindsey	Station Electrician
F. A. Hill	Supt. of Coal Mines

help of Jacob Furth was sought.

Furth was a banker and industrialist and one of the most respected men of Seattle. He was persuaded to join them and became the president of the newly organized Seattle Electric Company, and the dynamic force in the consolidation of the electric properties in Seattle. (For a list see Part Two).

The company was set up in 1900 under the guidance of Stone & Webster to unify the multiple little companies and to engage in building both steam and hydro plants. They had ample funds.

People of the present day can have no adequate idea of the enormous difficulties which confronted the Seattle Electric Company, which began operating these properties under the management of Stone & Webster in 1900. All the railway and lighting properties were inadequate and badly rundown, and the demands for service were so great that it was almost impossible to meet them. Seattle's population was 80,000 in 1900; by 1910 it had zoomed to 237,000

It was necessary to practically rebuild all of the existing street railway lines and increase the generating capacity in the various railway stations by whatever means were found most readily available. Spare generating equipment

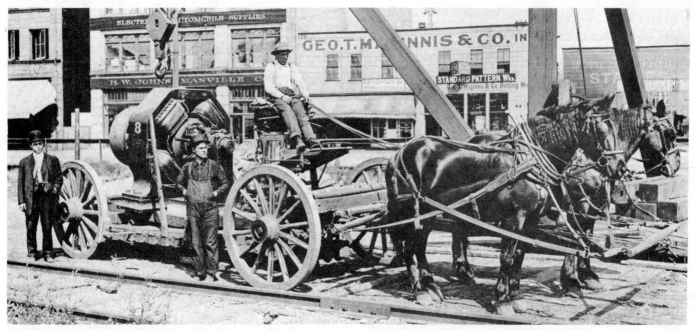

A DYNAMO, hauled on a lowbed wagon of THE LLOYD'S HEAVY HAULERS. Spare generators and other parts were obtained from across the nation. Emil W. Peters, a driver, was a distant ancestor of Vincent Ferrero, presently employed by Puget Power. (Photo courtesy of Bessy Hudack of Wilkeson.)

18

NEW STREETCAR, 1903, on the Fremont line. The motorman was Jens Nissen, grandfather of Carl Nissen a present-day Presbyterian pastor.

was assembled from various parts of the United States.

Almost every make of engine and generator had been in use by the predecessor companies, and the physical condition of their plants was poor. Until such time as a new steam plant was built (Post Street, 1902), other secondhand engines and generators were purchased and added to keep abreast of rapidly growing electrical demands.

The Snoqualmie Falls Power Company had built a hydro project at the Snoqualmie Falls in 1898, and a contract was made with them by the Seattle Electric Company for 3,000 horsepower or half of its output. The Seattle Electric Company also immediately started on the construction of the new Post Street Steam Station.

By 1903 a large amount of the old railway lines had been rebuilt, seven miles of old lines abandoned and twenty-four miles of new line built making a total of ninety-five miles of street railway at the end of 1903.

Stone & Webster engineers were also engaged in building a hydro-electric plant on the Puyallup River at Electron. This was completed in the fall of 1904 and operated as a sub-

sidiary named Puget Sound Power Company. More power was available by the completion of the new Georgetown Steam Plant in 1906. The public was never aware of a power shortage.

By 1914 the Company had approximately 198 miles of single track covering 111 miles of city streets with 417 cars in use and one of the best street railway systems in existence.

The Electric Building

In 1910 the Company moved into the Electric Building at 7th and Olive, their new headquarters. It was a substantial six-story steel reinforced concrete structure, specially designed for a utility company.

The first floor of the Electric Building was then entirely given over to the Sales Department with a showroom of one of the most unique displays of electrical devices in the United States. It consisted of a complete five-room flat, known as "The Home Without a Chimney." Each separate

SNOQUALMIE
(1898)

POST ST
(1902)

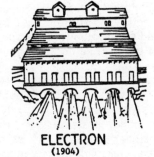

ELECTRON
(1904)

GEORGETOWN
(1906)

THE ELECTRIC BUILDING, DECORATED FOR A FOURTH OF JULY CELEBRATION. The sign on the roof was placed there in 1911. It was an animated sunburst lighted in sequence with the Company's name, visible for miles.

room was of practical size, and in each were found installed articles appropriate to the use of that room. Floors were of polished hardwood. There were imported rugs. The dining room was paneled with Philippine mahogany, its furniture was of Mexican mahogany, and electric adjuncts vied with a handsome showing of silver, cut glass and porcelain.

This elegant showroom was in high style, and salesmen subtly called attention to the electrical installations in their "house without a chimney."

The idea of a lighted sign on the roof of the Electric Building was borrowed from the top of a cake created by Mathew Beginn, a pastry chef of the Butler Hotel, who baked a special cake for a dinner party at the opening of the new headquarters building.

He used a lamp bulb design centered in a burst of light rays upon the Company's name. The president, Jacob Furth, liked the cake decoration so well he asked permission to use the idea for a lighted sign on the roof of the building.

Running A Trolley System

When the Seattle Electric Company was first organized its principal electrical business was its trolley system. Electric trolleys held a fascination. A streetcar ride meant the clanging of steel wheels on rails, the click-clop as wheels sped over rail joints, the commanding voice of the

motorman calling out street names as he sped along, a grinding and squealing of wheels on rails around sharp street corners, and the clanging of the motorman's bell. Even smells such as the air-brake exhaust and ozone from trolley arcing and motor brushes were identifiable with streetcars. The trolley system was the mark of a busy city.

The streetcars ran along on tracks out in mid-street, powered by poles with electrical wires overhead. The cars commanded attention. They were center stage. With a clanging of his bell the motorman could claim the right of way. People when aboard felt a companionship with the motorman, they rode regularly and knew their conductor and motorman, the urgency of the bell spoke for them. They had paid their fare of 5 cents and once aboard felt the motorman was doing his best to get them home fast.

Strangers often commented on the motormen and conductors for their bright intelligent appearance and their courtesy. Over 1,200 in number, they were the largest single body of men employed by the Seattle Electric Company.

Morale was excellent. Every month an honorary list was published, and most of the men appeared on this list. They were valued and appreciated.

Rules governing the employment of trainmen were very strict. Applicants were required to be of good moral character, physically sound, well informed and of robust constitution. They were expected to be able to read understandingly and to write legibly, neatly and rapidly.

In their examination the list of conditions for rejection was long and detailed. The physical examination by a doctor was rigorous. Sight, color perception and hearing had to be normal. Minimum height was 5 feet eight inches. Management considered them an elite group and selected them carefully. Until World War I the Company had no trouble getting all the men it needed.

Trolleys Hauled Freight

Hauling freight began in a small way in 1890. The crew consisted of a man and a boy running a supply car to serve the Green Lake District. It handled a considerable wood tonnage on the inbound trains which originated from the extensive clearing of land then going on in that district.

Then other lines too began hauling freight. Freight was hauled to and from the Ballard District, the University section set up a tri-weekly freight run, and eventually runs were put on to Madrona, Fort Lawton, West Seattle, and in time to the Meridian and Phinney lines. There was no agent or freight office; the conductor handled all the bills, cash and records. This was at the turn of the century.

By 1910 the freight business of the street railway system had been divided into two separate classes or divisions, package freight and carload service. Package freight was operated by light cars, each making twice daily trips over a scheduled route during the day, while the carload service was performed at night by heavy railroad cars, including box cars and flat cars.

Until 1911 the freight business amounted to a very satisfactory tonnage totalling well over $100,000 annually; however, after April, 1911, the packaged freight service had fallen off to an alarming extent. Why?

There were various reasons, such as discontinuing the Madison Street run and loss of some spurs and sidings, but chief above all was the improvement by the City of street grades and paving. This made outlying districts easily accessible to teams and autos—so much so, in fact, that almost simultaneously there sprang into existence regularly organized auto freight companies. To all this, when asked why he had not opposed sluicing down Seattle's hills, changing road grades and the expensive relocation of trolley tracks, Jacob Furth, president of the Seattle Electric Company, replied, "I couldn't oppose such improvements to the City for I believed Seattle was better off for making the changes."

Historically, packages and freight were hauled by streetcars, then with improved streets and roads they lost this business; in the meantime electric trolleys also were the pioneers in extending their runs between cities as interurban traction companies. The interurbans too became carriers of packages and freight. When interurban traction companies were displaced by motor vehicles traveling on paved highways, busses such as Greyhound and Trailways took on the hauling of packages; and now many systems of auto freight lines travel the vast interstate and national highways. These in turn are challenged by air-freight carriers, such as the Flying Tigers, with national and international routes.

This miracle of modern transportation never ceases to amaze one who can remember horses and wagons, early 1920 autos, and five-day train rides across the nation, when today passengers and freight are zipped across the nation in a matter of hours by jetliners.

The movement of goods and produce by rapid transportation has bridged the gap of space and time. Fryers, berries, pineapple or carrots grown in Florida, California, Hawaii, Texas or Washington, can be purchased anywhere in the United States at practically the same price. When the demand is there the product can be delivered promptly. Exotic fruits brought halfway around the world too are competitive with local produce. To men like streetcar conductors who pioneered fast freight should go some of the credit.

Model-T Ford a Competitor

With changing times came new competition. No two decades in the present American century were even remotely alike. During the first decade of the 1900s the electric trolleys reached an outstanding success. By the end of the next decade they went into a sharp decline. The challenge came from the gasoline automobile. Model-T Fords were catching on.

The challenge was dramatically made clear at the Alaska-Yukon-Pacific Exposition of 1909 in Seattle, when a transcontinental auto race was begun from New York to Seattle at the same instant President Taft pressed a telegraph key which officially opened the Fair. The race demonstrated the durability of the automobile.

A Ford came in first, a Shawmut second, and another Ford third. The winner covered 4,106 miles in 20 days and 52 minutes, driving clear across the United States. The Fords were Model-T, 4 cylinder, 20 horsepower and each weighed 1,200 pounds. At no time did the winning cars need outside help to get them out of quicksand, mud or snow. The Fords were light enough for the driver and his mechanic to lift up a wheel or the end to ease them out of the mud. Roads were hazardous enough to frighten a buffalo.

The trip was almost unbelievable. A diary of one of the drivers preserved by the Ford Motor Company reveals that some trails traveled were no better than when crossed by pioneer covered wagons drawn by oxen. Streams were crossed by driving through them or haltingly crossed upon railroad trestles. Some mountain roads had six inches of road outside the wheel with 1,000 feet of sheer drop below. Hired guides at times themselves were lost and off course.

The Seattle Post Intelligencer, on June 24, 1909, carried the following comments:

The Snoqualmie Pass was the worse piece of going that we encountered on the road, said Scott in telling of the trip. We crossed Lake Keechelus at 5 o'clock last night, and as we toiled up to the summit we were soon floundering in snow, which, in places, was five feet deep. We reached the summit at 8 o'clock and continued on our course until 9:30, when we stopped for the night at a railroad camp, and slept in a siding car until 2:30 this morning, when we started off again. In many places we had to dig our way out of the snow, and practically climb over logs which lay across the road...

In spite of the rough knocks of the long, hard drive, the Ford No. 2 (the first place winner) was in perfect condition when it was put to rest at the

THE WINNER OF A TRANCONTINENTAL AUTO RACE, a Model–T Ford, upon arrival at the Alaska–Yukon–Pacific Exposition in Seattle, 1909. Bert Scott was the driver and C.J. Smith (with goggles) was the mechanic. There to greet them was Henry Ford (extreme right with long coat and derby), and Harry Guggenheim (man with beard left of Smith) sponsor of the race. Price of a Ford Roadster, f.o.b. Dearborn, October, 1909, was $900. (Photo from Ford Archives, Henry Ford Museum).

Mines Building at the Exposition grounds yesterday afternoon.

A story told hereabouts was that in coming down the Snoqualmie slope, drivers of the auto race tied small fir trees on behind to save their brakes. This is emphatically denied regarding the Fords by the Archivist of the Ford Motor Company; explaining that Fords always had good brakes.

The drivers were guests of the Good Roads Association at an impromptu meeting held at the fairgrounds, and later the winners were taken to the Kent Valley to inspect a newly paved brick roadway.

Not only did the hardy Fords and other cars in growing numbers travel ordinary country roads, but soon families driving automobiles would gaily drive to campgrounds along streams and even to mountains. As roads improved more vehicles were purchased and the trolley business declined.

Resiliency of The Electric Company

The leaders of the utility company showed resilience, vigor and creativity in meeting competition. Diversity of use kept them in business. Trolley wires and substations were handily converted to other demands.

In running the streetcars the trolley wires were energized at 600 volts direct current over many miles of roads. Direct current was used to obtain variable speed control of the streetcar motors. So central station power transmitted at 13,000 volts and 55,000 volts alternating current required step-down substations and additionally a grouping of trolley substations to convert the power to direct current. The trolley substations housed motor generators, transformers and switches.

To gain diversity in electricity sales the power lines were extended from the substations, both direct current and alternating current, to serve industrial and residential customers nearby and also along the route of the trolley lines.

So in the evolution of the electrical business there is a transition: What began as power for electric streetcars, in time would see the total disappearance of the streetcars and the removal of the motor generators, followed by enlarged substations for alternating current facilities to serve expanding commercial, industrial and residential loads. It came about as a natural diversity of usage.

The Seattle Electric Company had acquired or built the following substations for streetcar trolleys, which later became general distribution substations: Ballard, Post Street, Jefferson, James Street, Georgetown, West Seattle,

Fremont, Massachusetts Street, North Seattle and Union Street.

Other electric companies contributed much to the growing electric industry. Leaders sensed a new trend and were eagerly building large hydroelectric power plants. They also were alert to meeting competition by consolidating holdings.

The Seattle-Tacoma Power Company

The Seattle-Tacoma Power Company, with its principal power source the Snoqualmie Falls Plant, was a dominant force in the electric power business during the decade 1900-1910. In vigorous competition with the Seattle Electric Company it came out second best; even so, it produced outstanding leaders.

The Seattle-Tacoma Power Company was organized in 1904 by the consolidation of the Snoqualmie Falls Power Company, the Tacoma Cataract Company and the Seattle Cataract Company. In the same year it also purchased the Mutual Light & Heat Company and the Diamond Ice Company, both of Seattle.

In this merger the Snoqualmie Falls Company was the largest unit and the leader. It held the largest assets including a hydro generating station and a network of power lines extending to Seattle, Tacoma and Everett. Boldly and with true pioneering instincts the leaders of the Snoqualmie Power Company had built ingeniously, ventured into difficult transmission line construction and had pursued new service areas and power sites. Its history has a fascinating background.

Snoqualmie Falls Power Plant

What now appears to be the world's first underground power plant is not in Europe, as most people believe, but in the State of Washington beneath the cliffs of Snoqualmie Falls. Designed and built by Charles H. Baker, a civil engineer whose father was a prominent Chicago broker, completed in 1898, and still in use today, this little plant has been almost overlooked in the discussion of underground plants stemming from building of a number of large underground plants, such as Kitimat in Canada, and many in Scandinavian countries, during and since World War II.

Unlike many of the recent plants in Europe, the Snoqualmie Falls Plant was not put underground as a protection against bomb attack, an unknown method of warfare when it was built. It was put underground to avoid trouble from freezing spray from the falls in winter.

Precedent for putting the plant underground came from the first Adams Plant at Niagara Falls, built about 1890. In the Adams Plant the hydraulic turbines were set at the bottom of shafts 135 feet deep at Niagara and discharged into a tunnel extending 450 feet to the gorge below the falls.

The generators in the Adams Plant, however, were at the surface in a conventional powerhouse, being driven by long vertical shafts from the turbines.

At Snoqualmie Falls, both turbines and generators are in a chamber forty feet wide, thirty feet high and two hundred feet long, cut out of solid rock about 250 feet below the river level above the falls. A low dam above the falls diverts water to the penstock through a small intake structure.

The turbines are served by a steel penstock, 7½ feet in diameter, down a 10 by 27 foot shaft, in which also is the elevator serving the plant and conductors to carry power to the surface.

In the underground station, four horizontal turbines of 2,000 horsepower capacity each drive four 1,500 electric generators. There also is a turbine-driven exciter dynamo. Water from the turbines is discharged below the falls through a tailrace tunnel twelve feet wide, twenty-seven feet high and four hundred fifty feet long.

An account of the plant, published in *Engineering News* of August 31, 1899, says that the water wheels are of a design invented by Thomas T. Johnston, a pump representative, "and resemble in form the double impellers used in rotary blowers and pumps." They were reported to have an efficiency of 90 percent.

In operation, though, these water wheels proved unsatisfactory. Said S. C. Lindsey, who later became chief electrician of the Seattle Electric Company, "I spent the evening shift during the first winter in the cavity by a barrel of oil and a dipper to ladle oil on the bearings, they ran rough, and the water wheels whined and howled, in fact people could hear them five miles away at Preston." They were replaced with tangential water wheels which were satisfactory.

Power Line Design Problems

The penalty of being first is to submit to innovative and experimental ideas heretofore untested. This was the case of the gear-type waterwheels of the Snoqualmie Plant which whined and howled; similarly, the ideas on transmission line design used in the original Snoqualmie power lines needed drastic revisions.

In 1900 the company built two separate pole lines from Snoqualmie Falls to Renton, thence to Seattle, and from a junction, a line to Tacoma. From these lines power was supplied to Issaquah and Auburn in 1900, and to Renton in 1903. The Tacoma line was built in 1901 by the Puget Sound Electric Railway upon its interurban railway right of way to supply substations at Kent and Milton for its interurban service. In 1905 a transmission line was also built from Snoqualmie to Everett. At first the company agonized over some very evident design problems and then proceeded to rebuild its power lines.

The two original lines built from Snoqualmie Falls in 1900 had poles of 35 feet average height, two separate three-phase circuits per pole line, with white pin-type insulators (now rated at 13,000 volts), and energized at 15,000 volts. Within a year the voltage was upped to 30,000 volts.

The wires were aluminum-copper alloy, which gave trouble from crystallization and breaking. Spacing between wires was a scant thirty inches and it soon became apparent this was too narrow, as seagulls, owls and hawks, as well as boys throwing sticks, would short-circuit the wires.

These problems were corrected when a new wire of hard-drawn stranded aluminum cable No. 4 was strung, spacing extended to seven feet, and only one three-phase circuit strung on each pole line. In 1909 the lines were replaced with 65-foot poles, copper wires, and the voltage raised to 55,000 volts. Many major design changes were necessary. The Everett line too, of 1905, had defective insulators, so

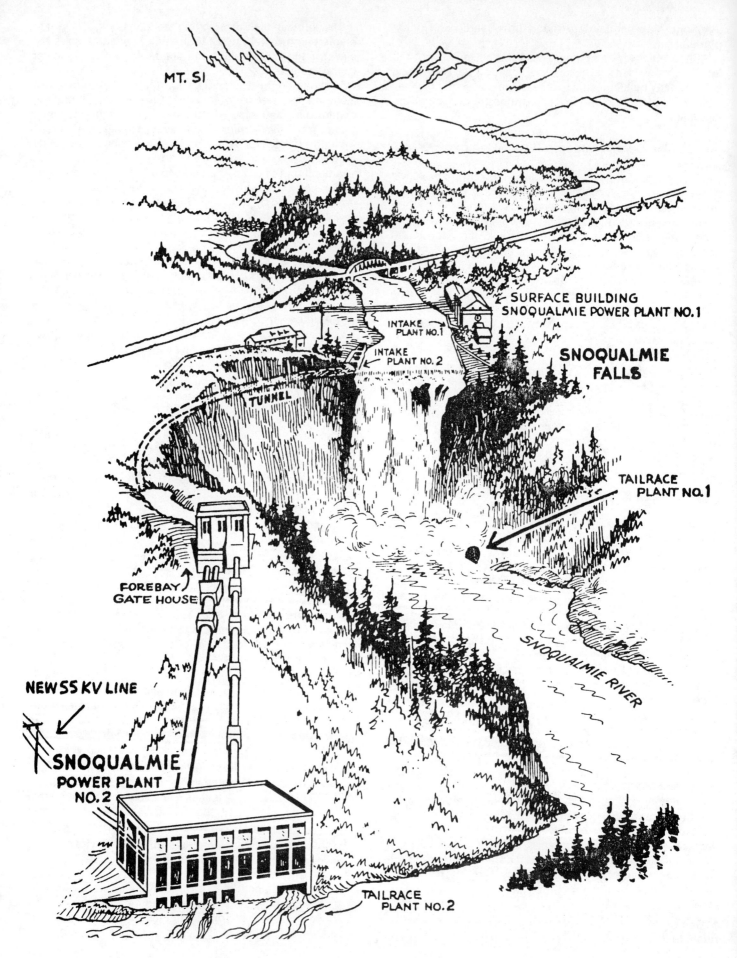

MT. SI

SURFACE BUILDING
SNOQUALMIE POWER PLANT NO. 1

INTAKE PLANT NO.1

INTAKE PLANT NO.2

SNOQUALMIE FALLS

TUNNEL

TAILRACE PLANT NO.1

FOREBAY GATE HOUSE

SNOQUALMIE RIVER

NEW 55 KV LINE

SNOQUALMIE POWER PLANT NO.2

TAILRACE PLANT NO.2

within two years it too was rebuilt for 55,000 volts. So by trial and error reliability was achieved.

A Remarkable Transmission Feat

In the year 1900, the Snoqualmie Power Company performed the then remarkable feat in electric power transmission of running an electric motor 153 miles distant from the generator. For several hours during the day the various services of the company were cut off and all the power lines were connected up into one continuous circuit running from Snoqualmie to Seattle and back to the Falls, then to Tacoma and back to the Falls, a distance of 153 miles.

These tests were made to show that power could be transmitted commercially at greater distances then heretofore contemplated. This also was a step toward the reduction of rates for electric current.

Energy Crises of 1900

Nowadays the energy crisis worries the nation. In 1898 the builders of the Snoqualmie Falls Power Plant jubilantly proclaimed that their new 6,000 kilowatt plant would supply the power needs of the area for the next fifty years. However, the new plant had hardly passed its shakedown run when its operators were faced with an energy crisis. To meet energy demands they doubled the output within five years, and five years later doubled it again. Times were booming. Seattle's population had nearly tripled from 1900 to 1910.

The demand for electricity was astounding; moreover, the competition with the Seattle Electric Company too was vigorous, which step by step more than matched the growth of the Snoqualmie system. The Snoqualmie owners added 5,600 kilowatts in the cavity in 1905. This proved to be too little too late, so in 1910 they completed a new surface powerhouse below the Falls of 11,000 kilowatts. Elsewhere they had invested millions in securing a 60,000 kilowatt power site now known as Lake Tapps. It became a battle of sites with the Seattle Electric Company.

The energy crisis was abated in 1912 by an area-wide merger of competing systems. Many years later, in 1956, the full potential of the Snoqualmie River was utilized when the then existing plant capacity was again doubled by the installation of a second power unit of 20,000 kilowatts at the lower Snoqualmie powerhouse, bringing the total to 42,500 kilowatts.

Old Plant Automated

Though the oldest major hydro plant in the Northwest, the facilities of the Snoqualmie Falls Plant have been continually modernized. In keeping with the modern trend, on November 20, 1972, the Snoqualmie Falls Plant was automated. Supervisory controls were provided for unmanned operation. So, today, with electronic controls, the hydro-electric plant is operated by remote control from Puget Power's Load Center.

Men and Mergers

One of the men who had helped build the original Snoqualmie plant was John Harisberger. When it was put into operation he became its first superintendent. Through the emergence of competition and rapid development of the Northwest he held an influential position and was a respected engineer.

In October, 1903, Harisberger became the general superintendent and electric engineer of three companies, the Snoqualmie Falls Company, the Seattle Cataract Company and the Tacoma Cataract Company. In 1904 these companies were consolidated as the Seattle-Tacoma Power Company, with headquarters in Seattle.

Other men to join the Seattle-Tacoma Power Company and who loomed large in the affairs of the power business for many years were Magnus T. Crawford and Norman W. Brockett. Crawford was assistant engineer of high tension lines and Brockett was the firm's secretary. In 1912 when a merger of five major systems formed the Puget Sound Traction Light and Power Company, John Harisberger became its general superintendent of water power, transmission and substation, Magnus Crawford became superintendent of transmission and Norman Brockett public relations officer.

A Power Site Battle

As in their contest for new customers so also the Snoqualmie company and the Seattle Electric Company were competing for hydroelectric power sites. Snoqualmie was falling behind its competitor in power development until it found it could buy the option on a Lake Tapps site held since 1895 by a White River Power Company of New York.

So as a beginning the Snoqualmie Falls Power Company in October 1902, joined the White River Power Company in purchasing lands located from Buckley to Lake Tapps and continuing to the Stuck River for a sizeable power project. On March 13, 1906, the Seattle-Tacoma Power Company having absorbed the Snoqualmie Falls Power Company purchased all the rights held by the White River Power Company for $1,250,000.

In the purchase document of the Lake Tapps power site was this statement of purpose:

To divert the waters of the White River, conduct it through a six-mile ditch into the natural basin of Lake Tapps, Kirtley Lake, Crawford Lake and Lake Church, raising the level of the lakes as a storage and settling basin, thence conducting said water through a further ditch to a point on the brow of the hill overlooking the Stuck River at which point said water will be discharged through steel pipes under a head of 465 feet to waterwheels in a powerhouse located at the foot of the hill, if to do so be found expedient or best.

This deed was signed by the White River Power Company by Alquernon S. Norton, president, and Bronson P. Reynolds, secretary.

To neatly put together this development package seemingly the Seattle-Tacoma Power Company overstretched its finances. The records show that it sold the site by deed dated January 17, 1908, to the Pacific Coast Power Company, a development company managed by the Seattle Electric Company, which actually did build the White River hydroelectric project, at Lake Tapps in 1911. The price paid was $583,333 in settlement of a mortgage. So the Seattle Electric Company finally did win the battle of the power site.

The Electron Plant

The Electron Plant was built and operated under the corporate name of Puget Sound Power Company, and a colorful person in its construction was S. L. "Sam" Shuffleton.

Sam Shuffleton was the electrician who had made the long-suffering generator of Judge Burke's Ballard trolley line perform miracles when this trolley line, through heroic economies, became the lone survivor of the Panic of 1893 when other trolley lines went into bankruptcy. Then in 1900, the generator flew apart, and Sam calmly went into the roomful of fireballs to pull the right switches. After Burke's line was purchased by the Seattle Electric Company, Shuffleton was headed for a larger career.

He was hired by Stone & Webster to make initial surveys and studies for a hydroelectric plant on the Puyallup River, the Electron Plant. Its height and scope is rarely found in a single plant. In this region hills rise abruptly from the sea and rivers are fed by everlasting snows from Mount Rainier. Acting on Shuffleton's reports, construction was started in 1902, with Sam Shuffleton the construction engineer.

The diversion dam, ten and one-fourth miles of flume,

SAM SHUFFLETON

a forebay at a plateau overlooking the powerhouse 900 feet below, and a powerhouse with four generating units for a total capacity of 24,000 kilowatts, were put into operation April 14, 1904. In the meantime two transmission lines of 55,000 volts had been built for ties to Tacoma and Seattle.

The drainage area above the flume intake begins at 1,600 feet elevation and rises to 14,530 feet or to the top of Mount Rainier. So apart from its practical aspects, the headworks and the flume also give a view of scenic grandeur and at this elevation the air is exhilarating.

The most notable features that claim the attention of the visitor of the flume are its precarious perch on the hillside above the river and its many twists and turns. It was built along the canyon wall to avoid costly cuts and tunnels, so it meanders along the natural contour of the hills.

The flume right of way was heavily timbered and all material for the flume was logged from the property; a sawmill was set up just below the intake which supplied all the lumber and timbers for the flume. Other supplies were brought in over a wagon road, later a track was laid on the substructure as the trestle-work was built, and afterwards, as the flume box was finished, this track was placed on top of the flume. The light track of standard gage laid along the top of the flume facilitates inspection and repairs. Those who ride the gas-driven speeder have affectionately dubbed it as the crookedest railroad in the world.

At the outset maintenance of the flume was critical. There were boulders loosened by thawing and freezing that crashed down the hillside. There were earth slides and there was settling, and in time, deterioration. All parts have been up-graded: precast concrete mud-blocks replaced cedar mud-blocks, new lumber and timbers are pre-treated with hot preservatives, so that maintenance that originally required a summertime crew of 50 to 60 men, today requires only 10 to 20 men. Power plant facilities have also been continually improved and modernized through the years.

When it was built the Electron Plant was among the first of high head, and the drop between the forebay and the powerhouse is 871 feet. A high head plant is conservative of water. But at the nozzles which taper to seven inches in diameter the water is like a stick of hard glass and impinges on the buckets of the water wheels at a velocity nearly 500 miles an hour. One time, during World War I, an officer stationed at the plant climbed down into the wheel pit and stuck his saber into the nozzle stream. It snapped his saber and left his arm black and blue.

With glacial silt in the water in amounts to give it a milky hue, one of the persistent problems was the wear and cutting on nozzle rings and nozzle needles. (The needle travels inside the nozzle and functions as a valve actuated by the governor to control the flow of water.) The abrasive action of the silt required replacement of the nozzle rings and needles as often as every two months during the summertime. Metalurgical technology has solved this wear problem.

Using customary steel and turning the parts to shape in a machinist's lathe, and further giving the surface a mirror-like polish, the parts are then chrome plated to a depth of 0.007 inch. With the chrome plating, which is a molecular penetration of the highly polished surface, the rings and needles will then be impervious to wear for from two to three years.

Time took its toll. Lightning destroyed Unit No. 4 of the

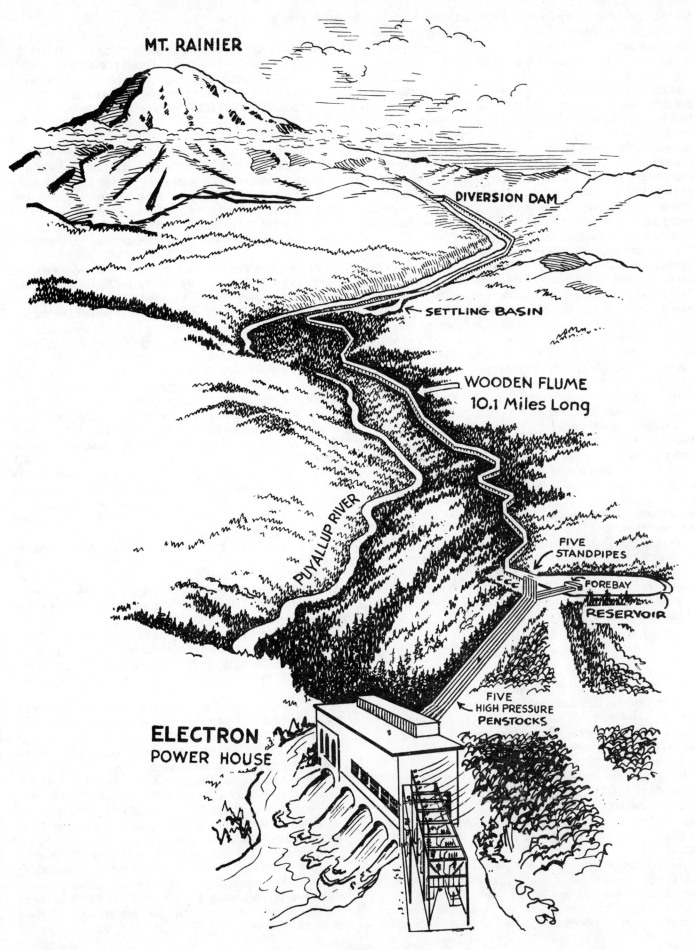

MT. RAINIER

DIVERSION DAM

SETTLING BASIN

WOODEN FLUME
10.1 Miles Long

PUYALLUP RIVER

FIVE
STANDPIPES

FOREBAY

RESERVOIR

FIVE
HIGH PRESSURE
PENSTOCKS

ELECTRON
POWER HOUSE

27

Electron powerhouse on June 20, 1928, and it was replaced by a larger machine of 7,500 kilowatts in April 1929. The plant was damaged by an earth slide on November 23, 1936, which put all of the generators out of service. Two units were back in service by July 26, 1938, and the entire station was in full operation by December 13, 1941. The cause of the slide was attributed to mountain beavers perforating the hillside above the powerhouse with their holes, and an unusually heavy rainy season softened the earth, causing the slide. There was no loss of life.

Electron challenged competitors. When the Electron Plant began delivering electric power it became a real force in the local competitive area. Whereas the Snoqualmie Power Company had extended its lines to nearby Tacoma and had a distribution system in Auburn, the Electron system now challenged this service area.

For example, in 1901 the Puyallup Electric Company was formed and built a steam generating plant in Puyallup in connection with a sawmill. In 1902 this was acquired by the Tacoma Industrial Company, and when the Electron Plant was put into service in 1904 by the Puget Sound Power Company, current was then supplied to Puyallup from its lines. Moreover, being a Stone & Webster managed company, its output strengthened the whole operation of the Seattle Electric Company also under its management, further damaging Snoqualmie competitively.

The first plant superintendent of Electron was R. V. Sprague. He had helped build the plant, and his specialty was installing generators. He served as superintendent from 1904 till 1910, when he was transferred to another plant under construction, the White River Plant. In subsequent years Sprague was placed in charge of the installation of all generators of the Boulder Dam, and in time, he became the Regional Director of the Bureau of Reclamation of the southeast area of the United States. He always maintained a personal interest in the Electron Plant.

The Electron Plant from its beginning contributed greatly to the industrial growth of the Puget Sound area. In the consolidation of electric systems in 1912 to form the Puget Sound Traction, Light and Power Company, this distinctive hydroelectric plant became another of major power plants of the new company.

The White River Plant

The White River Plant, with its water storage achieved by diking around four lakes on the Lake Tapps plateau and drawing water from the White River fed by glaciers of Mount Rainier, was built by the Stone & Webster engineering firm for the Pacific Coast Power Company. Construction began in the spring of 1909.

It was put into service in December 1911, with an initial capacity of 20,000 kilowatts, which later was enlarged to 60,000 kilowatts. A notable feature was the immense storage system impounding sufficient water to enable the original installation to operate at full load for an entire month.

Hydro sites such as that of the White River development had intrigued power men and investors even as far back as the 1890s. These men had traveled by train to the Northwest and were immensely impressed. Later, the *Electrical World* magazine of June 1912, summed up their thoughts this way:

Nature has done most of the work on the greater part of power sites . . . high heads prevail throughout the region. The region possesses numerous water–powers fed from the everlasting snows of the mountains on all sides and within easy reach of the cities.

Basic features of the White River Plant resemble somewhat those of the Electron Plant built by the same firm, in that water is diverted from a river, carried by a flume to a reservoir at a plateau and transmitted through penstocks (steel tubes) to generating units in a powerhouse below the brow of a hill. In the case of the White River development, the distance is 14 miles from the diversion dam to the powerhouse.

There are striking differences between the two plants. The flume at White River is four times larger. From the diversion dam on the White River at Buckley the ground is relatively level, and the water passes through six miles of flume and open ditch to a reservoir created by diking where necessary, raising the water level to attain one body of storage water over the area of four lakes—Lake Tapps, Kirtley Lake, Crawford Lake and Church Lake.

From the outlet of this storage reservoir another canal was cut which, at its western end, forms a forebay and the portal of a tunnel carrying the water to the generating station in the valley at Dieringer on the Stuck River. This powerhouse is located only 25 miles from Seattle. The water head is 400 feet.

The station as a whole was considered remarkably efficient. The generators, including all losses, had an efficiency of 96.8%; the waterwheels on a weir test showed an efficiency of over 90% and transformers 98.9%; giving an overall efficiency of about 86%.

With the efficient hydro plants now supplying energy to the cities and to electric interurban systems, the Seattle Electric Company used its two steam power plants, Post Street and Georgetown, only for standby or peaking needs, especially during the rush of electric trolley service at the end of the day.

While the White River Plant was being built, 55,000 volt transmission lines were also built to extend lines from other power plants to the White River Project. Lines that had been built as far back as 1903 were re-arranged for a system network.

Two transmission lines had been built in 1903 from Electron, one to Bluffs, a point about midway between Tacoma and Seattle, and on to Tacoma, the other continued on to Seattle. In 1906 the voltage of an existing line on the Interurban right of way between Seattle and Tacoma was raised to 55,000 volts and switches installed at Bluffs to serve the Interurban directly from Electron. Then in 1911 connecting lines were built to tie the lines of Electron, Snoqualmie and the Interurban directly to the White River Plant for a system network. A further improvement was made in 1912 following the consolidation of five power systems, when a tie line was built at Renton for more flexibility, allowing the Snoqualmie Plant to send all of its power to Seattle and permitting the White River Plant to carry Tacoma. The network, so comprised, totaled over 200 miles of 55,000 volt lines.

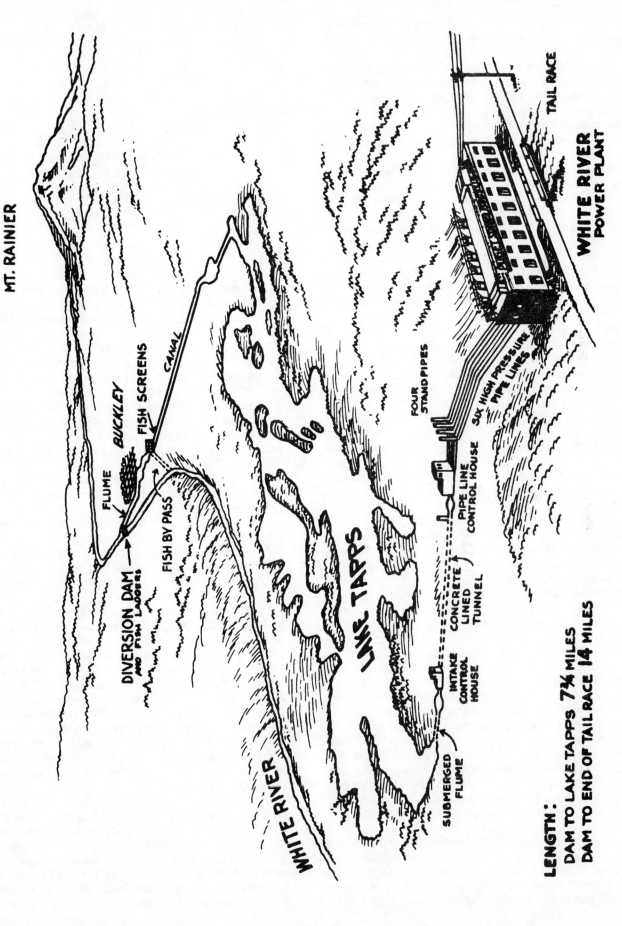

MT. RAINIER

BUCKLEY

FLUME

FISH SCREENS

CANAL

DIVERSION DAM
and FISH LADDERS

FISH BY PASS

WHITE RIVER

LAKE TAPPS

SUBMERGED
FLUME

INTAKE
CONTROL
HOUSE

CONCRETE
LINED
TUNNEL

PIPE LINE
CONTROL HOUSE

FOUR
STAND PIPES

SIX HIGH PRESSURE
PIPE LINES

WHITE RIVER
POWER PLANT

TAIL RACE

LENGTH:
DAM TO LAKE TAPPS 7¾ MILES
DAM TO END OF TAIL RACE 14 MILES

Whatcom County Railway & Light Company

For the story of electricity as it came to Bellingham, it is necessary to trace in part the early settlement of that bay area.

Located on North Puget Sound, 25 miles south of the Canadian border, is the city of Bellingham, Washington's seventh largest city. It began as a seaport of separate small settlements — Whatcom, Sehome, Fairhaven and Bellingham. Bellingham, the smallest, was conspicuous enough to send a small column of smoke above the fir trees in winter.

Fairhaven and Bellingham incorporated in 1889 under the name of Fairhaven. About the same time Sehome re-incorporated as New Whatcom, and in 1891 Whatcom merged with New Whatcom. The "New" was nixed for all cities by the State Legislature in 1901. On December 28, 1903, Whatcom and Fairhaven were formally united under the present name of Bellingham.

Mrs. Ella Higginson, the pioneer Bellingham poet, said she had the distinction of living in three cities of Washington — Sehome, New Whatcom and Bellingham — without having moved out of her house.

In 1890 the towns comprising Bellingham had a combined population of 8,135. They wanted electricity. Each settlement soon had its electric railway and power business. In time, due to financial stress, these merged, somewhat like the towns themselves, to form the Whatcom County Power & Light Company.

Power began at a sawmill. Captain Henry Roeder and Russell V. Peabody in 1853 built a little sawmill on Whatcom Creek, powered by the surging rush of waters of the stream. The mill was whining and snorting while friendly Nooksack and Lummi Indians watched with mingled awe and pleasure. The cut lumber was delivered to Bellingham Bay for the coast trade.

Later, the energy for electric railways first came not from hydro power but from steam plants fired with burning wood. The Whatcom Electric Railway Company and the Fairhaven Street Railway Company, both organized in 1891, had steam engines at Lake Whatcom.

Streetcars had their allure and excitement. For example, Michael Cosgrove was first employed in 1890 as a water boy during the construction of the Bellingham-Lake Whatcom streetcar lines, then spent a lifetime as a top-notch motorman. Freight and express would share the front platform with him, including an occasional live hog with legs corded. When progress was stopped by a broken trolley pole, Mike would cut a limb from a nearby tree, fix the line, and continue on his run. His total mileage on the Lake line would have taken him around the world twenty-five times!

In the evolution of railway lines serving the Bellingham Bay area, the Fairhaven and the Lake Whatcom lines were beset by financial troubles and in 1898 merged under the name of Fairhaven & New Whatcom Railway Company. A third company, the Fairhaven Electric Light, Power & Motor Company, was added in 1903, and again the name changed, to Northern Railway & Improvement Company.

A separate company, the Bellingham Bay Improvement Company, the first built exclusively as an electric utility company in 1888, was destroyed by fire ten years later, but replaced as the York Street Station. In 1906 this company ventured into building a hydro plant on the Nooksack River,

MIKE COSGROVE

at Nooksack Falls. It is still in operation with a capacity of 1,500 kilowatts.

Electric street railways comprised the big field for power men, next came street lighting. Historians note that the first electric light was in a little store in Whatcom in the late 1880s. The first large scale street lighting was begun on Christmas Eve, 1889, at Fairhaven with thirty-five arc lights and 250 weak incandescent light bulbs.

The gas business had preceded the electric companies and devoted its sales mostly to store lighting. The Bellingham Bay Gas Company was placed in operation in 1890, and in 1903 it merged with its competitor, the Whatcom-Fairhaven Gas Company.

In the natural growth of Bellingham the separate companies of trolleys, gas and electric service, were getting into each other's way. So in 1906 an overall merger of the various systems took place under the firm name of Whatcom County Railway & Light Company. This company became the owner of practically all the railway, gas and electric power systems in the City of Bellingham.

The Whatcom County Railway & Light Company moved from its cramped and old-fashioned quarters at Bay and Holly Streets in 1910 to what was then known as a new and sumptuous office in the Pike Building at Elk and Holly Streets.

Leslie Coffin, the manager, proved himself to be a very able and modest manager. It was said of him that he was the only manager ever to own a Ford. Coffin, when the Bellingham facilities were consolidated to become the Puget Sound Traction, Light & Power Company in 1912, became the manager of the Northern District of the company. In time he became the Eastern District manager at Wenatchee where he fathered the idea for eventual construction of the first dam to span the Columbia River, the Rock Island Dam.

It is of interest to take an intimate look at the power business of 1912. The electric company in Bellingham, in common with other early electric operations, had some rudimentary and earthy problems.

The troublemen, known as servicemen today, worked from 2:00 p.m. until 9:00 p.m. and had to walk or take a trolley to make their service calls. Street lights, ever a source of trouble, were series carbon arc lamps, and almost every

DAM

INTAKE
CONCRETE FLUME
GRAVEL BASIN

WOOD PIPE LINE

TUNNEL

NOOKSACK
FALLS

ROAD

WELLS CR.

FOREBAY AND
SURGE CHAMBER

STEEL
PIPE LINE

N. FORK
NOOKSACK RIVER

NOOKSACK
POWER PLANT

evening about 5:00 o'clock the various arcs needed carbons. By 1915 the lamp trimmer made his trips by driving a two-wheeled cart pulled by a spotted pony. During the big snow in 1915 he made all his trips to the various lights on skis.

Patrolmen of the high lines rode motorcycles which frequently got stuck. A horse and buggy had to be used to get to the Nooksack Falls Plant, and the trip was a long and tedious 50 miles.

Meter reading was done on the last four or five days of every month by members of various departments. All other operations practically ceased for the meters had to be read on time. Later three or four boys took over all meter reading.

The sales department consisted of three men, one in charge of electric sales, one who handled gas sales and one in charge of counter sales. There were no electric appliances to sell (1912), only light bulbs, wire and lamp fixtures. Gas mantles, toasters and gas ranges were popular. The home with a hundred electrical appliances was unknown, and the slogan, "Cook the Food and Not the Cook" was reserved for another generation.

The Puget Sound Electric Railway

The interurban railway fever had gripped the nation in those far-off days at the beginning of the 20th century. Interurban electric railways were fast becoming the popular links between cities. Locally, the Seattle-Tacoma interurban with its smartly designed trains became for a time one of the most prestigious lines in the nation. Then, within the

lifetime of one generation, this electric trolleyline was shoved aside by the motor busses and private automobiles. The Seattle Electric Company, and subsequently the Puget Sound Power & Light Company, anguished over its future.

Henry Bucey was the father of the interurban railway, which he incorporated on February 18, 1901, as the Seattle-Tacoma Interurban Railway, to serve two cities separated by a hilly, wooded area, of 30 miles. While Bucey was still obtaining right of way and building the railway as funds permitted, the line was taken over through major stock ownership by the Seattle Electric Company, which, on December 5, 1902, incorporated the interurban as a new company, the Puget Sound Electric Railway, often referred to as the "PSE."

On April 4, 1903, all properties of Bucey's were deeded to the PSE and funds of $5,500,000 were secured from the City Trust Company of Boston through a first mortgage and 5% gold bonds. These funds then assured full construction of the interurban line and the purchase of rolling stock and facilities. The PSE produced a saga in railroading.

The PSE became a line of distinction. In its equipment and its similarity to steam railway standards it was one of the most interesting high-speed electric three-rail systems in the United States. It had parlor cars with open observation platforms (enclosed by curved glass in wintertime) as ornately furnished as those of the transcontinental steam railroads.

In addition to operating regular trains the management kept an eye on community needs by operating special trains

A PSE TRAIN, Along the Duwamish (1906)

for community functions. With its 125-pound brass bell ringing and its third-rail arcing, residents near the tracks were attuned to hear, see, and feel those green trains roar past at forty miles an hour. The interurban had prestige.

Because it had heavy rails, an excellent roadbed, and high-grade cars, it could stretch out and travel. A frequent contest was a race with the Milwaukee's passenger trains on a parallel track not more than a hundred feet away. Passengers even laid bets on the speeding trains.

The 8:30 p.m. interurban train could cover the distance between Renton Junction and Kent in a shorter time than the big orange trains; however, to do so it had to roll better than sixty miles an hour all the way.

On its limited train, passengers would travel from Seattle to Tacoma in one hour and fifteen minutes; on the local the time was one hour and thirty minutes. By early 1906 the PSE was operating thirty-four trains daily, each of two or three cars and leaving terminal cities at hourly intervals. Most of the way the roadbed was double-tracked.

On December 12, 1908, the PSE opened its Puyallup Short Line, and within six months it had purchased the Old Puyallup Line from the Tacoma Railway & Power Company, which had operated it for many years. The Puyallup Short Line was originally planned to continue on to Orting, but only a portion was built, and that part discontinued and removed in September of 1919. Interurbans went into a decline about them.

By the early Twenties, with strong competition of private autos and a bus line, the PSE decided to discontinue its Puyallup interurban line altogether in 1922.

The PSE business peaked in 1919 then sagged badly. It was primarily a passenger system, yet it was also deeply involved in hauling coal, logs, lumber, farm produce and manufactured products. Twenty percent of its business was hauling freight. The interurban had its best year for both passenger and freight service in 1919. Then, World War I and Camp Lewis brought the system's passenger business to 3,000,000 fares. By 1928 the total had fallen to 1,000,000 passengers. Its freight business dropped just as precipitously. The decline, of course, was due to the addition of paralleling paved highways for autos and trucks. These vehicles used public roads, were flexible to go anywhere and had low capital investments. To the PSE it was a losing battle.

In its life span of about 25 years the PSE came into being as a lively confident enterprise, grew in stature and vitality, then almost abruptly died.

The end of the PSE came in 1928. It had lost heavily in the Twenties and went bankrupt in 1927. The last train rolled between Tacoma and Seattle on Sunday, December 31, 1928. The receiver of the line had attempted to rehabilitate the interurban's earnings but was forced to admit defeat late in 1928.

Then at a Receiver's Sale, February 25, 1929, the Puget Sound Power & Light Company, with an offer of $348,208, was the highest bidder for the right-of-way and operating equipment of the Puget Sound Electric Railway.

At once rumors spread that the power company might resume operations. They were scotched by Mr. A. W. Leonard, president of the Company, who said:

The power company had absolutely no intention of resuming rail operation, it merely needed the

right-of-way because its main power lines between Seattle and Tacoma were on it . . . the tracks would be torn up at once.

Harsh as was this termination of a once great interurban line, and as vituperative as was some criticism heaped upon the heads of management as being unsympathetic, it is this suddenness of the line's demise which had spared it a lingering decline and preserved a special nostalgia for it.

It began in the sweetness of favor, grew secure in a firm style, then met rejection and the debilitating anxieties of outworn usefulness.

A fitting commentary at the time was written by the *Tacoma Times,* December 29, 1928, under the caption: INTERURBAN GOES WAY OF STAGECOACH.

One last spark on the fearsome third rail, a dying screech from the brakes, a final glare from the headlights, a dismal clanging of the crossing bell, and the Seattle-Tacoma interurban will have gone the way of the stagecoach.

At 11:30 p.m. Sunday the interurban car will pull out from Yesler Way in Seattle bound for Tacoma, as usual. At the same time a car will leave the Tacoma Station bound for Seattle. Neither car will go over the route again. Each will be the last passenger cars to run over the rails, since they were laid down in 1902.

Perhaps two motormen who have been with the road since it was established will be selected to make the last trips. There are four of them: Howard Wellman, D.M. Dingwall, F. H. Andrews, and F. J. Dunn.

The old road will sing its swan song and missed it will be when it is gone. Although passengers are few in number, it used to carry hundreds. Long strings of cars were run to accommodate the travelers. Now one car runs and it is nearly empty.

The interurban was the way of the swift and fastidious, back in say 1908. It played many parts in the drama of lives. Run-away couples, persons rushing to death beds, traveling salesmen with stories that are yet being told, preachers of gospel going to new pastorates, fleeing absconders, school children on picnics, loggers with their bundles, pickpockets, families bent on outings, condemned men headed for the gallows, and intrigued little boys who became the railfans of today were in the human freight that filled the interurban cars. Now it is being relentlessly shoved aside by the motor busses and private automobiles, but its memory will never die.

Bellingham Sponsors Interurban Railway

Vitality and prosperity seemed to have eluded Bellingham in the early 1900s. So in 1910 enterprising and loyal citizens started a movement for an interurban electric railway to give Bellingham passenger service to nearby towns. Its businessmen consulted Stone & Webster, who were managing the Seattle Electric Company, as to the feasibility of building the electric trolley line. As a condition for Stone & Webster to undertake the construction, the Bellingham men raised $400,000 in subscription of stock.

A golden spike was driven on November 10, 1910, to mark the beginning of the work and to start a new era of prosperity in Bellingham.

The line was built under the corporate name of the Pacific Northwest Traction Company and was successfully operated until 1928, when auto stages were substituted.

The route was selected with but little friction. It touched Burlington, Mount Vernon, Sedro Woolley and small communities of Skagit County and connected them with tidewater for a line thirty-three miles in length. The scenic Bellingham-Skagit interurban electric railway was opened for business August 31, 1912, with ceremonies held at all towns.

This railway had several spectacular structures. There were five miles of trestle work with some stretches upon water along shorelands. Highbridge over Chuckanut Creek was 130 feet above the riverbed and 700 feet long. The Skagit Bridge near Mount Vernon was a steel drawbridge over 800 feet in length with a 240-foot middle span and 1,300 feet of trestle approaches. There were many cuts and fills along its scenic route.

The interurban was operated as a branch of the Pacific Northwest Traction Company, which also owned the interurban electric railway between Seattle and Everett; therefore, the new Bellingham-Skagit railway could draw on the experience and facilities of the Everett firm. As expected, the electric interurban became a real stimulant to business, even in some strange ways.

It did well with an unusually good evening passenger business. This evening business was due to "local option" (liquor prohibition) in Bellingham, so the trains to Burlington did a rush business after 5 o'clock and until midnight, for the towns of Sedro Woolley and Burlington were wide open and "wet."

The interrelation between the two interurbans should be explained. In 1908 Stone & Webster had acquired the original Everett & interurban Company which Fred E. Sanders had incorporated on May 29, 1902. Sanders had planned to build an electric interurban line from Seattle to Everett. It was a slow, difficult job for him. Within three years he had extended his line fourteen miles, in heavily timbered land, to Lake Ballinger and did well with hauling freight, mostly logs.

Then Sanders' line was taken over by Stone & Webster, who rebuilt the roadbed with heavier rails and succeeded in extending it all the way from Seattle to Everett at about the same time that the golden spike had been driven at Bellingham to signal the start of the Bellingham-Skagit line. The completion of the Everett line was a cheering event, then on August 31, 1912, the Bellingham-Skagit line was finished with equally as proud a moment.

Both systems, being Stone & Webster managed, were merged with the Pacific Northwest Traction Company as principal stock owner. In addition this company owned all the stock of the Puget Sound International Railway & Power Company of Everett, which in turn controlled the local water supply and practically all the lighting and power business in the City of Everett.

Nostalgia for the Bellingham-Skagit electric trains was just as poignant there as that of the Seattle-Tacoma line. For example, Andy Loft, born in 1898 in Bellingham, became a conductor and grew up with the line. At 14 he was told by his father, "Tomorrow your mother will fix you a lunch pail and you will get your first job at the shops, to sweep, clean and polish railroad cars — your wages will be 50 cents a day." This was in 1912 when the Bellingham-Skagit line had its first run (also in 1912 Puget Power acquired area-wide facilities).

At 21 Andy became a conductor. He had many vivid experiences. Later, because of his deep understanding of people he was given many sales positions with Puget Power, as well as leadership roles in the community. Retiring in 1963, among other interests, Andy Loft produced a slide-show of his railroading days, of terse events, for fascinating shows before audiences and other buffs. Andy is still amusing and alert. In his retirement, whenever there was a political issue, he would report and with the old-time charm of a conductor, ask, "Boss, can I help?"

PART FIVE

ERA OF WELL-BEING AND HOPE: 1910-1920

There was no television or radio in 1910; but, Edison's phonograph was a popular home entertainment. There was less ear-splitting noise, the air was sweeter to breathe and there were fewer people (only 92 million to our 238 million of 1985). More than half of the people lived in the country.

In the big cities there were no stop-and-go lights, although traffic might build into a shouting, bumping tangle of horse-drawn delivery wagons, trolley cars, a few autos, and every other type of vehicle. Trolley cars were the busses of 1910.

Since the dawn of the auto age in 1896 when the first Duryea Motor Wagon was built, the first million American motor vehicles had been produced by 1912. The early success of the automobile in America resulted from its rapid transition from a high-priced luxury item to a low cost family work-horse. Even so, a car was seldom seen on the open road and there was rarely an airplane in the blue yonder.

Men walked, bicycled, or took the trolley to their jobs. A 10-hour workday was not considered too long. Men worked all day Saturday and in some cases two Sundays a month. Payment of overtime was still to be invented.

The year 1910 had one special feature that made it unique. It came in the midst of a period of hope. People really believed in a rosy future. Americans had come to this country from Europe determined to create a new world better than the old. True, some immigrants in the sweatshops of big cities labored harder than ever, but even they had faith that their children would live a better life. It was an era of well-being. Americans considered themselves the luckiest people who ever lived, with native know-how, go-getting spirit, and general optimism.

Some people not only thought about their own problems but of those of the world about them. There were crusades against child labor, against cruelty to animals and against spitting in the streets.

The Boy Scouts of America were incorporated in Washington, D.C., on February 8, 1910, with their emphasis on a good turn, good citizenship and physical and spiritual fitness. Scouting took root almost instantly. For example, Tom Martin, a three-term treasurer of the State of Washington, was born in Hoquiam, became a scout Tenderfoot in 1911, later an Eagle and during his lifetime was an active scouter for more than 60 years.

Henry Ford had begun to manufacture his Model T car by assembly line methods, and it was aimed at the poor man rather than the rich. Other items like pianos, soap, phonographs, candies and perfumes suddenly became available to the average families. Autos and electricity were just around the corner for all to use.

Nine states had voted for women suffrage; nationally, women could not vote until 1920. There also was a rising tide of temperance sentiment, with battles between "wets" and "drys" in the state legislatures.

In the year 1913 two constitutional amendments were adopted. Congress was given power to lay and collect an income tax, and the election of a United States Senator by state legislatures was changed to the election by the people of his state, a more democratic method.

During the debate on the federal income tax, one congressman had exclaimed, "Gentlemen, in time this tax may go as high as 5%!" It would have boggled his brains to have realized that some fifty years later the middle class taxpayer of America would be taxed 25% of his income and the wealthy up to 70% to drain off results of our individual initiative.

Puget Sound Traction, Light & Power Company

In these times of hope and self discipline to excel, and when men in a lively way tasted the sharp sting of competition, the electric companies were lifting the country out of the horse and buggy days.

We should remember that outside of the cities roads were the old territorial trails. They were dirt, unimproved and suitable for horse-drawn wagons and buggies. The electric trolley roadbeds, on the other hand, were built for speed, with fills, cuts, trestles, bridges and tunnels to provide straight runs and gentle grades. A passenger riding a trolley from Seattle to Tacoma could make the trip in one hour and fifteen minutes; by horse and buggy, with a sweating horse, it would take him half a day.

Electric trolley systems produced the biggest revenues for the electric companies. Lines had been built so that electric trains were now running between Seattle and Tacoma, between Seattle and Everett and from Bellingham to the Skagit cities of Mount Vernon, Burlington and Sedro Woolley. Trolleys were revenue builders. Moreover, trolley systems were served by power lines and step-down substations, which further provided electric power to the in-between towns and cities. These distribution centers were supplied by major hydro and steam plants. The concept of central station power became firmly rooted.

Jacob Furth, president of the Seattle Electric Company, had transformed from a fragmented conglomerate of nine trolley companies in Seattle in the short span of ten years a coordinated successful electric system. And now in 1912 he took the next step to put under one management the plants, railway lines, substations, power lines, distribution systems and personnel, by an area-wide consolidation of electric service improved from the resulting economies of centralized engineering, load dispatching, purchasing, accounting, sales and financing, together with diversity in operation. For this purpose the Puget Sound Traction, Light & Power Company was incorporated in 1912 under more favorable laws of Massachusetts.

Purchases and Stock Acquisitions

With strength, persistence, patience and compromise, the new company purchased the Seattle Electric Company, the Seattle-Tacoma Power Company, the Pacific Coast Power Company, the Puget Sound Power Company and the Whatcom County Railway & Light Company. These five companies carried with them the combination of four hydro electric power plants, Snoqualmie Falls, Electron, White River and Nooksack Falls and an integrated transmission line network.

Additionally, the Puget Sound Traction, Light & Power Company acquired all or substantially most of the stock in the Puget Sound Electric Railway Company and the Pacific Northwest Traction Company.

The Puget Sound Electric Railway Company owned and operated the interurban electric railway between Seattle and Tacoma and controlled the entire railway and a portion of the electric power business in the City of Tacoma through ownership of all stock of the Tacoma Railway & Power Company and all stock of the Pacific Traction Company. Its principal office was in Tacoma. L. H. Bean was the manager.

The Pacific Northwest Traction Company, D. C. Barnes, manager, owned and operated an interurban electric railway between Seattle and Everett, and also the interurban between Bellingham, Burlington, Mount Vernon and Sedro Woolley. Pacific Northwest also owned all the stock of the Puget Sound International Railway & Power Company which controlled through a ninety-nine year lease the street railway, the water supply and practically all of the electric lighting and power business in the City of Everett, where the principal office was located.

Officers of the New Company

Jacob Furth, who had been president of the Seattle Electric Company, became the president of the Puget Sound Traction, Light & Power Company. Vice president and manager was Alton W. Leonard, who, upon the death of Jacob Furth in 1914, succeeded him as president. F. S. Pratt of Boston and R. T. Laffin of Seattle were vice presidents, Henry B. Sawyer of Boston became the treasurer and A. S. Michener of Seattle was controller. Leslie R. Coffin remained the manager of the Bellingham property and H. T. Edgar the manager of the Seattle system.

Progress, War, Peace

The decade 1910-1920 began in an era of hope and progress for the American people. This soon would be clouded by European conflicts that broke into war in 1914, and by violation of American neutrality through sinking of merchant ships the United States too was drawn into the conflict. It announced its declaration of war on April 2, 1917. Eventually thirty-two nations were involved in a global battle, World War I. The armistice was signed on November 11, 1918, bringing peace again; though war had overturned the world.

For the first time the United States had sent an expeditionary force to Europe: 2,000,000 men of which 350,300 became casualties. Altogether 4,355,000 men had been called to duty. America had made a massive effort to supply new ships, airplanes, material, food and manpower.

Fortunately the Puget Sound Traction, Light & Power Company had its start in the era of well-being with a few years to mold an efficient company. It became a major factor in the country's war effort. Those were busy years.

The merits of a large electric system were quickly revealed to its users. With multiple plants, a network of lines, centralized management and good morale, electric service was given with new dispatch and at reduced rates. Now, though newly organized in 1912, it eyed the towns east of Lake Washington with the intent to serve them with central station power. In 1913 it tapped its nearby Everett line originating at Snoqualmie Falls for extensions to Kirkland, Bellevue, Tolt, Duvall, Redmond and Bothell. Some were already being served by isolated local power plants; these were purchased as noted below.

Even as early as 1909 a farm line extension was built near Lynden. It was the first farm line in the nation, one and one-quarter miles in length serving fourteen farmsteads. Customers had furnished the poles and dug the holes.

More Properties Purchased

In contrast, there still were many smaller electric companies in outlying places wrestling with financial problems and the worry of how to meet peak demands. They sought to sell their systems to the larger company. During the period from 1912 to 1920 the following were purchased by Puget Power:

Lynden Mill & Light Company (1912)
T. S. Bird property at Tolt (1913)
Gray & Barash properties in Bothell (1913)
Gray & Barash properties in Kirkland (1914)
Buckley Electric Company (1914)
Enumclaw Water & Light Company (1915)
T. S. Bird facilities in Duvall (1917)
Tacoma Railway & Power Company, in part, (1917)

Personnel Encouraged

In the overall growth of property there was inherent also the need for special attention to new people coming with property mergers to absorb them into the scheme of things of the whole company. Both Jacob Furth and his successor as president, Alton W. Leonard, were men with a genuine interest in people.

To communicate with their employees the Company began from its incorporation in 1912, to publish a monthly magazine, the Electric Journal. Through this magazine employees participated as reporters and as subjects of stories. There were many other activities; a year-round one was the Electric Club which held excellent monthly meetings of entertainment and lectures. There were baseball teams, tennis matches, pep bands, quartets, smokers, annual picnics, contests and always the yearend, gala, family Christmas Party.

In 1915 the editor of the Electric Journal, E. A. Batwell, attended a convention of the Electric Railway Association

ALTON W. LEONARD

at Atlantic City. He was instructed "To see how the other fellow did his work." Batwell discovered that his own publication was widely quoted, due largely to the success of the various programs. He had good copy. The Electric Club meetings, for example, opened with musical numbers followed with speeches by outstanding men and ended with snacks. The editor printed the talks in full.

Talent was evident all about him. Good singing voices, as well as some excellent ones, abounded among streetcar motormen who used their voices all day long calling out street names. For example, one meeting of the Electric Club was reported as beginning with "marvelous work on the violin, followed by some barbershop chords." The quartet sang their own arrangement of "Die Schnitzelbank:"

Ist das nicht der King Kilo-watt?
Ja, das ist der King Kilo-watt.
Ist das nicht ein Ocean yacht?
Ja, das is ein Ocean yacht.

Ist das nicht ein Jitney bus?
Ja, das ist ein Jitney bus.
Ist das nicht ein horse on us?
Ja, das ist ein horse on us.

Horse on us, Jitney bus, Ocean yacht,
King Kilo-watt. Oh die Schnitzelbank.

Ist das nicht der Rheumatism?
Ja, das ist der Rheu-ma-tism.
Ist das nicht Syn-chro-nism?
Ja, das is Syn-chro-nism.

(and so on, for fourteen verses.)

Ideas Solicited

Employees were also invited to lend their ideas. For example, in July 1912, suggestions were solicited from employees for ideas for a suitable electric sign to be placed on the roof of the White River Plant. The power plant was situated along the East Valley Road near Sumner. It was noted that this plant was in full view of travelers on six railroads as well as those on the electric interurban line running between Seattle and Tacoma.

The accepted idea was submitted by W. N. Gordainer, superintendent of the Electron Plant. It was a sign 200 feet long to be placed on the roof of the powerhouse which read:

Reliable Power
Bellingham Everett Seattle Tacoma
Light Service
PUGET SOUND TRACTION,
LIGHT & POWER COMPANY

Gordainer had arranged the cities reading south to north: "Tacoma-Seattle-Everett-Bellingham." A. W. Leonard, then vice president, suggested the towns be reversed in order so that their first letters, when lighted separately, would read "BEST." The background of the huge sign on top of the White River Plant was a myriad of electric filaments depicting a waterfall and a boiling effect of water at the bottom of the falls, realistic and beautiful.

Large use Brought Reduced Rates

By 1912 the City of Seattle had become a serious competitor of the private company, and it had also become rather vocal about its claim that it was forcing the private company to reduce electric rates. To set the record straight the private company obtained the following figures, as of October 1914. They showed the decrease in the cost of electricity from 1905 to 1914 for twelve cities in the United States:

Portland	55.6%	Minneapolis	36.6%
Detroit	46%	Atlanta	35%
Boston	45%	Seattle	33.1%
Los Angeles	45%	Salt Lake	33.1%
Chicago	40.6%	Milwaukee	28.5%
Butte	37%	Omaha	38%

With the exception of Seattle and Los Angeles, there was no municipal competition in these cities. There were large cost reductions in all the cities. There were many reasons for reductions in rates, of course, such as expansion in the use of electricity, improved methods in generation and transmission, and a greater diversity in service. With larger use the cost per unit was brought down.

During this decade when consolidations of area-wide electric service took place, millions of dollars had been invested in the acquisition of little independent properties, in the rebuilding of these systems, in providing a reliable and adequate supply of power and in the extension of rural lines from each small community into the surrounding suburban and farm areas.

Furthermore, with the critical demand on industry during the World War I period, the electric system of Puget Power was greatly enlarged. Without centralized management and all that it means, and with the credit advantages of a going concern, it is doubtful that the job could have been done.

SIGN ON WHITE RIVER POWER PLANT

The decade 1910–1920 witnessed the growth of general use of electricity; however, it also saw the decline of electric railway patronage, yet the Company displayed fine flexibility in meeting its problems.

Traction Strike, Discord and Sale

Problems that left deep scars and a tangle of financial worries for the next thirty-five years to come, were brought on by pressures of a municipal ownership faction and a three-faction fight in Seattle over the operations of the electric streetcar system.

The three-faction fight was a battle among the mayor of Seattle, the president of the private power company and striking streetcar men, and it was triggered by competition, loss of trolley patronage and wartime rise in prices.

Events leading up to this conflict, the strike, and the eventual sale of the private traction system to the City of Seattle are discussed on the following pages, with a review of the steps that focused public opinion towards public ownership which erupted into front-page newspaper debates. There was no compromise, and disruptive arguments continued until the end of the railway operations in 1940 when new rubber-tired busses hit the streets of Seattle.

Seattleites Go for Public Power

By 1900 the municipal ownership faction, though far from power and influence, was able to put strong pressure on the City Council when Jacob Furth, as agent for Stone & Webster, applied for a franchise for city-wide streetcar operation when he was untangling the chaotic street railway system.

A Committee of One Hundred was hastily organized, and though unable to block the granting of the franchise, these men were able to write a number of conditions into the franchise, including transfer privileges, rate regulation, minimum wage provisions and a 2% tax on gross earnings.

A decade later the municipal ownership idea was rapidly gaining respectability and public support. On September 13, 1912, the city fathers did take the plunge into the street railway business when they began to build a four-mile loop of tracks with money authorized by the voters in 1911. The line was promptly dubbed, "The line that began nowhere, ran nowhere, and ended nowhere."

Then the City accepted as a gift a 14-mile line from its original builders, the Highland Park and Lake Burien Railway, but the catch was that a tremendous slide had wiped out nearly a mile of road. Restored, it became a lucrative business.

The City of Seattle had shown its muscle even as early as 1905, when it took over street lighting.

In 1919 it obtained the voters' consent to purchase the electric street railway system from the Puget Sound Traction, Light & Power Company. Now it would own all of the street railway business. The purchase of the railway system was completed on March 31, 1919. In payment the City of Seattle gave bonds, constituting a first lien on earnings of the railway system. High emotions, harsh accusations, and irruptive events precipitated the sale.

Irruptive Events Led to Sale

During the early years of the Seattle Electric Company's management street railway service had improved marvelously. It was a decade known as the Golden Era. In the second decade there was polarization of political factions, and the political climate bade ill to any big business.

So, leading up to the take-over of the private street railway business by the City, the private electric company faced urgent and tangible problems in its streetcar operations in a climate of opinion scarcely conducive to any favorable consideration even in matters in which it had legitimate grievances against the City.

Capitalists and monopolists were the current favored whipping boys in almost every part of the American population, and traction companies and railroads were looked upon as sinister, to be detested as moneyed interests.

Understandably, by 1917 in this political atmosphere, the president of the private power company, A. W. Leonard, and the mayor of Seattle, Hiram Gill, now both operators of competing street railway lines, disdained each other with undisguised hostility.

Also the Company's image was further tarnished through some of its own neglect. There were railway lines in bad repair. These were lines that had been originally built by real estate speculators at the fringes of the city which, when consolidated with other lines, should have been abandoned. But in the depression of 1907 they had been left just as they were.

By 1917 complaints about their slow, erratic service reached City Hall and the columns of the newspapers. It was unfavorable publicity, and with continued deterioration the city authorities began to treat the private company as "poor relations." On other problems the City could have helped, but it smugly looked the other way.

Jitneys

An example of one of the problems preceding and during World War I was the favorite sport of "Jitneying." Private automobiles and busses fitted with passenger seats would drive ahead of streetcars and pick off riders for a low fare. They skimmed off the cream of the traction company's business. The City could not be persuaded to pass an ordinance against this action. Finally a Court Order was obtained for an injunction against the jitney operators, declaring them a public nuisance. It never went into effect, pending an appeal.

Streetcar Employees' Strike

Scarcely three months had passed since the United States had entered the war, and the electric trolley company was confronted with a streetcar operators' strike. Workers were feeling the effects of inflation and a wage squeeze. The air was charged with discontent and talk of strikes. The lumber workers declared a state-wide strike in mills and the woods. When the private trolley company was denied by the City a request to raise trolley fares, the emotions of streetcar operators were further stirred up. Elsewhere there was a newly-established street railway workers union. Two

Company men joined this union. A strike was precipitated by the dismissal of these two union men.

So on Tuesday, July 17, 1917, 1,500 street railway employees of the Puget Sound Traction, Light & Power Company in Seattle went out on strike.

The strike was well-timed. With the mayor and the company president at odds it became a three-faction fight. The strikers stood firm, the mayor issued a steady series of directives to restore service and threatened to revoke the Company's franchise unless service was restored, and the Company's spokesmen countered with threats and entreaties.

Only the jitney operators provided a haphazard semblance of transportation service.

On Friday, July 20, president Leonard and general manager A. L. Kempster announced that the Company would attempt to run ten cars with strikebreakers. They asked the City for police protection. The next day, Saturday, two cars manned with strikebreakers, began to edge downtown. A mob of strikers met them. Mayor Gill had sensed the ugly mood and half-heartedly sent a squad of police to the scene.

As the cars pressed near, bottles and rocks begin to fly. Twenty persons were injured and about a dozen rioters were arrested. The cars had been nearly wrecked and were hauled back to the barn.

On Monday, July 23, the union strike committee offered to submit questions at issue to arbitration. This was rejected by the Company still highly incensed over the events of the preceding Saturday.

On July 25, a contingent of strikebreakers that had been rounded up from the East arrived on a special train. More came the next day. All were started in training to run streetcars.

On July 27, the Federal Labor Department put pressure upon the Company to end the strike. The mayor too pressed for an end, threatening anew to revoke the franchise.

On July 29, president Leonard yielded to the proposal to submit the points at issue to arbitration.

On August 1, under a tentative agreement, the strike ended, men returned to work and streetcars began to run. The Company gained an open shop, the discharged workers were reinstated, and the strikebreakers were sent packing.

Also, in the settlement the jitneys were restricted to routes other than those served by the traction company by having the original prohibitive Court Order put into effect.

By 1918 the City and the traction company were involved further in irresolvable litigations in which the Company sought relief from some of the obsolete franchise obligations for the duration of the war. One was permission to raise the 5 cent fare following the union strke when wages were raised.

Purchase Negotiations

With this impasse, negotiations were begun which finally resulted in the purchase by the City of Seattle of all the Company's municipal railway business in the City.

The purchase negotiations were charged with heavy political overtones. President Leonard announced that his company was willing to sell the entire property to the City for $18,000,000, a figure based on the consideration that about $19,000,000 had been spent to rehabilitate the original lines in 1900. Seattle's new mayor, Ole Hanson, made an offer of $15,000,000, basing his estimate on what the City had paid for construction of its lines. There was no appraisal of the facilities.

The City Council made up its mind on the $15,000,000 figure and the four daily papers, *The Times, The Post Intelligencer, The Star and The Union Record,* were all outspoken in favor of the sale and apparently printed very little in opposition to it.

Two councilmen, Erickson and Lane, contended the property was only worth $5,000,000.

On November 5, 1918, the people of Seattle voted on an advisory proposal regarding the purchase of the railway holdings for $15,000,000. It was carried by 13,000 For and 4,000 Against.

On March 31, 1919, the entire street railway property of the traction company was deeded to and turned over to the City of Seattle. The agreed price was $15,000,000, financed by a 20-year utility bond bearing 5% interest. $833,000 was to be paid annually on principal and $83,000 on interest. No cash was paid; the City had none.

The Company Changed its Name

With the sale of its street railway properties in Seattle, the Puget Sound Traction, Light & Power Company changed its name to the Puget Sound Power & Light Company.

Debate Continues

The public power faction that in 1917 had treated the private company with derision as "poor relatives," now as the years slipped by they too earned that epitaph. From the start of the newly acquired electric trolley system the City could not accumulate funds for rehabilitation or maintenance, and a number of routes, some even duplicating others, soon were losing money. So the transit debate in Seattle never subsided for the next twenty-five years.

Why was the transit system now in such a tight financial bind? First, it was operating with old equipment in changing times which reflected competition of the private automobile and taxi that caused loss of patronage. Then, for political expediency, the fare was kept at 5 cents, the same as in 1900. Moreover, the venture was unsound for the obvious classic economic tenet that you cannot start a business without cash and still hope to pay back the total borrowed capital out of earnings from the business. Nor could the transit system dip into the City's general fund.

Unlike the 1911 bond issue of $800,000 with which the City had financed its first own street railway line, and which was repaid from general taxes, a Court decision in 1920 enjoined the City from dipping into the general fund for its interest and principal payments on the newly acquired transit properties.

So the managers of the muncipal railway made heroic efforts and did hold the system together, making do with what they had, and through requested moratoriums extended payments on the bond held by the Puget Sound Power & Light Company. After fifteen years only $6,664,000 had been paid on bond retirement, leaving a balance due of $8,336,000. The total term of the bond was twenty years.

Then in 1937, John F. Dore, the mayor, in a flamboyant style, garnered the railway fares for payroll and deliberately passed up both interest and principal payments without asking for extensions. This threw the system into bankruptcy. And Dore died suddenly.

Solution to the Dilemma

The new mayor, Arthur B. Langlie, without acrimony found a solution. One of his first acts as the newly elected mayor, when Langlie took office on April 27, 1938, was to face the final crisis of the municipal railway, now bankrupt.

Langlie sought a Reconstruction Finance Corporation loan from the federal government to carry out recommendations of John C. Beeler's organization of New York, which already had made two studies of the Seattle transit system. It was to be rehabilitated with trackless rubber-tired trolleys and gas busses.

A loan of $10,700,000 was granted in September 1938. Then, with a desire to give constructive aid in this situation, the Puget Sound Power & Light Company, now headed by Frank McLaughlin, settled for a $3,250,000 cash payment of the long-standing agreement.

A condition of the RFC loan was that a three-man transportation commission should be set up to remove the management of the transit system from politics. The commission was to be appointed by the mayor and the city council. Donald H. Yates, Evro M. Beckett and William Paddock were selected. They in turn named Lloyd Graber as secretary and Lt. Col. M. D. Mills as general manager. Then the council changed the transit's name to The Seattle Transit System. Now there truly was a new look in Seattle's transportation business.

On January 6, 1940, the new busses hit the streets for scheduled operation. Mills converted the Transit System to rubber tires, then was called to active duty with the Army after Pearl Harbor. Lloyd Graber succeeded him as general manager. The war-worker load of the transit system swelled from 48 million passengers in 1942 to 131 million in 1945. Additional equipment was scrounged from other cities, junk yards and federal agencies.

Graber laughingly recalled, "We did things that probably were illegal, immoral and unethical, but we kept things moving both day and night."

During the summer and fall of 1943 the old streetcar tracks were torn up and used for steel in World War II. This marked the end of the street railway era for Seattle.

RUBBER TIRED 1940 TWIN COACH

PART SIX

FINANCIAL DIFFICULTIES DURING WORLD WAR I

Edwin S. Webster, of the management and engineering firm of Stone & Webster, delivered a talk before utility managers and executives at Boston, October 18, 1921, in which he gave a broad historical sketch of the financial situation of his firm during World War I. Below is this talk essentially as delivered.

It provides interesting insights into the courage, patience and sturdy character of these two business leaders, Stone & Webster, who, having "rounded the corner" in 1921, with restored confidence moved forward again making heavy investments in electric utility operations during the Roaring Twenties.

EDWIN S. WEBSTER

To go back, up to 1913 our business had progressed very rapidly. We had taken on new properties from time to time and the number was increasing. They had grown rapidly. We had some ups and downs, but financial conditions by and large were good and we were able to provide the money that was required for the properties. We were able to make any extension to any property that we thought would be profitable, and, either through the banks or through our own securities department, the securities were placed.

Lots of banking houses were all the time after us, wanting to know if we could not get out a new issue. In that way, from a financial standpoint, we had placed in the vicinity of $200,000,000 of securities. A good part of them were placed through banking houses but a great many through ourselves. They were placed with people who had confidence in the public utilities business and confidence in Stone & Webster.

In 1913 business commenced to slow up and we had about as quiet a time as we ever had. Then the European War was declared, and what little business there was left pretty much disappeared.

Our earnings then showed a very decided slump, and on top of that came the trouble with the jitneys (automobiles driving ahead of streetcars and at reduced fares skimming off profitable business from the trolleys). The net of a great many street railways absolutely disappeared.

We kept hoping that that would not last. In the beginning we said, "Well, this is not an economic thing," and we told different bankers and banks that had made inquiries that we thought it was temporary, and would go very soon.

But when it lasted month after month and our earnings instead of going up went down, all of these $200,000,000 of securities we had sold commenced to decrease in value. They would go down from month to month, and we would have to explain to the banks, and you have no idea of the number of inquiries that came to us from presidents of banks.

The different companies were at that time borrowing from the banks about $10,000,000 as floating debt. Stone & Webster as a firm was also borrowing money, and it certainly looked for a while as if all the properties would be taken out from under us and we would be almost entirely out of the public utility business.

A lot of people said that the street railways were a thing of the past, that the gas engine was going to replace them, and you can't imagine the situation we were in.

There were all these security holders who had been our friends, instead of having profitable investments every one of them had big losses, all the way from 25 to 80 percent of the money they had invested through Stone & Webster had gone, and an unfortunate thing from our standpoint was that after the first six or eight months the industrial boom started, in which the same people who had lost so much money in our securities were making a lot of money out of industrials. A large number of people told me that I was a damn fool to stay in the utility business.

We could not possibly have gone through it if we had lost our courage for an instant, because while the situation in itself was bad enough, it looked worse because every other thing was so good. All the industrial companies were good. But we never lost courage, for we were optimists.

One of the most interesting things, however, was that though we had a number of inquiries we had no criticism that were more than expressions of opinion; we never had one request from a single stockholder for a change in management, nor was there a single statement that we had deceived anybody.

The reputation which we had acquired and stuck to of telling the plain straightforward facts, was the thing that carried us through. I think, in fact I know, that the banks and the bankers never lost confidence in the organization. They absolutely lost confidence in the street railway business—temporarily. And they partly lost confidence in all kinds of utilities, and they did say they could do better in something else.

We had to sit there and take those inquiries and some of the joking sneers of people in the industrial line. We never got any particular sympathy. And that thing lasted for nearly three years before we could see the corner. About a year ago we could begin to show figures that the corner had been turned.

I will not attempt to trace it step by step, but it is enough to say that confidence has been restored almost entirely in public utilities. Confidence in electric light and water power companies is absolutely reestablished, they perhaps would stand at the top of the list now. The street railways stand well up.

And now that the whole thing is over, you can look back and see that although the earnings did slump everywhere, and particularly on street railways, yet if you add them all together there wasn't any business of any kind that came through better, relatively, then the public utility business.

The result is that our reputation, which we never lost, is increased still more. If the people to whom we sold the $200,000,000 worth of securities (they could cash them in for what they paid) had put that $200,000,000 into anything else, they would have lost so much more, so today they are a happy lot. I think there is not a firm that has a more satisfied lot of customer and financial connections than Stone & Webster.

During the whole of that time I do not think that any company loan was really called by the banks. We had all kinds of special things; for instance, the Puget Sound Company, where our earnings were still very good, had borrowed two or three million dollars from the banks and it looked as if we might need more. The banks said, "You are paying six percent dividends on your preferred stock, if you cut it to three we will see you through."

Well, that was a pretty hard thing to do, and some of the shareholders did not take it very kindly. But that was one of the disagreeable things we had to do for the good of the cause, and we did cut it to three percent. It is now re-established, I am glad to say, and the banks will carry us through.

I tell you all these things to give you a general idea of the sort of hell we have been through in the financial line since the beginning of the war, and I would not tell them to you if it were not for the fact that the corner is really turned.

I think there has been a feeling among some of the younger men that perhaps they are in the wrong business, that the public utilities business had gone by, that there is not any future in it. That feeling was accentuated during the industrial boom. Anybody engaged in any kind of industry was apparently making a lot of money. The story is different now.

We told all our investors who were in industrials that, of course, they would make money then, but that we believed that they would see the time when they would not make hardly anything. They said, "We are making 100 percent, we can't drop down to anything like any ordinary return, we will make 40 percent anyway." But those companies which made 100 percent, are losing it all now, and they have learned a sorry lesson.

For ourselves I really think we can look forward with confidence to an absolute re-establishment of a broad investment market for public utilities securities.

Part Seven

THE ROARING TWENTIES

The decade 1920-1930 was known as the boom-bust era and as a dizzying time of change. On the surface there was fluff and playfulness, while underneath there were deep-rooted social stirrings. Americans were assertive in serious as well as in pleasant and satisfying ways.

This was the golden age of American sports, of Babe Ruth in baseball, Bobby Jones of golf, Big Bill Tilden and Helen Wills of tennis, Jack Dempsey of boxing and Red Grange and Knute Rockne of football.

Holding public attention were feats of endurance which ranged from Charles Lindbergh's solo flight across the Atlantic and Gertrude Ederlie swimming the English Channel to ridiculous marathon dancing, flagpole sitting and cross-country walking.

Women's skirts climbed higher and higher, reaching the knees. Flappers were bobbing their hair and rolling their stockings.

There were Victrolas in the parlor, crystal radio sets with earphones, and newly published popular sheet music for group-singing around the piano. It was the jazz age. In vaudeville and in movies it was the era that prospered with stars like Al Jolson, Ben Bernie, Bill Robinson, Sophie Tucker, Charlie Chaplin, Jackie Coogan, Harold Lloyd, Lon Chaney and Douglas Fairbanks.

The deep-rooted stirrings were the "wet" and "dry" issues, women's suffrage, inflation, the boom-bust economy after the War, wrenching and displacement caused by the War and apprehension of the "Bolshevik" menace creeping across the United States. Moreover, only a few years past the State of Washington had been near the core of world-shaking events such as the woodworkers' strike of 1917 that closed down just about every lumber camp in the State, the Seattle streetcar strike of 1917, and the 1919 Seattle general strike, called in sympathy with 35,000 shipyard workers, in which 60,000 men walked off their jobs, grinding to a standstill a whole city, the first general strike to ever take place in the North American continent. Also, before the voters was the move for public ownership of electric utilities.

Then, like an explosion that shook the country to its core, the stock market crashed on Tuesday, October 29, 1929. It brought the greatest losses in all financial history. It was a traumatic shock. Variety Magazine gave it a headline in the mood of the times, "Wall Street Lays An Egg."

As surging and as expansive as the decade began, just as suddenly the market crash signaled the end of an era. A very different America was to take shape at the turn into the Thirties.

For the electric industry, the decade 1920-1930 had been a time of consolidation of extensive holdings. The Puget Sound Power & Light Company had acquired holdings from the north border of the State of Washington on the Coast, south to properties in the State of Oregon, and from the Peninsular area of Bremerton and its vicinity east to Wenatchee and towns in Central Washington.

Puget Power Becomes Leader

The Puget Sound Power & Light Company, having survived the financial pressures put upon utilities during the years of the European War, had its house in order by 1920 and looked upon a future of the light and power business as its predominent field of endeavor.

In the decade 1920-1930 it embarked on an unprecedented program of extending power lines to power-short areas, of building new power plants (Baker, 1926; Shuffleton, 1929; and Rock Island, 1930), and from a position of strength acquiring ailing electic properties throughout nineteen counties of Western and Central Washington.

Sound planning, good financing and competent engineering preceded any property purchase. Proof of ability to provide good electric service was first established with the extension of power lines to the area. For example, in 1919 a power line extension was built from its Tacoma power line to DuPont and on to Olympia to provide a firm power supply to the Olympia Light & Power Company. This line was further extended to Tenino in 1924 to allow shutting down a slabwood steam plant there and also to close down the old steam plant at Chehalis. Further, in 1921 the Company made plans to build a 110,000-volt line across the majestic saw-toothed Cascade mountains to bring central station power to the power-deprived Wenatchee country. (This unusual line is described separately on following pages.) Having provided sources of electric energy, the Company was in a position of favor to negotiate purchases.

By 1924 the Puget Sound Power & Light Company embarked on astonishing expansion. This was the time of the Roaring Twenties. In one year it bought the properties of the North Coast Power Company, the Washington Coast Utilities, the Olympia Light & Power Company, the Anacortes based Washington Power, Light & Water Company, the Tacoma Railway & Power Company (in part), the Everett properties of the Puget Sound International Railway & Power Company and the Pacific Northwest Traction Company (interurban lines which later became bus lines between Seattle-Everett and Mount Vernon-Bellingham.)

In succeeding years this pace of purchases of ailing systems continued. Small systems serving little communities had attained their limits of usefulness as isolated operations. Now under one management they were shaped into one large interconnected network. Rates were lowered and quality of service improved. By 1930 the service area of Puget Sound encompassed nineteen counties. On the following pages are noted more particularly the small predecessor companies and their date of acquisition. Each possessed a historical aura of its own.

Many Systems Reached Their Limits

The pioneers in the electric business were at first dazzled just as much as were their customers by the glamour of electricity. With a flick of a switch the lamps burned brightly and without smoke; besides there were no wicks to trim and no need for cans of such fuels as kerosene. But they had not reckoned with an immediate surge of growth.

Thirty-watt lamps in the home were just a beginning. Next to be added would be a 1,000 watt hand iron, or a 1,200 watt electric space heater — and the wires and generators would begin to heat up and burn out. Besides, the plant manager was asked to switch from night-time operation only to both day and night service. He needed to double his staff and provide standby boilers and generators.

So like the story of beginnings of electricity in the cities of Seattle, Spokane, Tacoma, Everett and Bellingham, the isolated operations in hundreds of communities elsewhere also reached their limits of capabilities and funds. Now distressed they began to consolidate and merge, first in two's, three's, four's and five's. This was not enough. So during the European War, with its shortages in materials and inflated prices, these clusters were driven by sheer survival towards massive mergers.

It is of interest to trace this phase of early mergers that preceded the final moves towards a single integrated system, the Puget Sound Power & Light Company. The Twin City Light & Traction Company evolved by the merger of:

Centralia Electric & Power Company	(1909)
Chehalis Light & Power Company	(1909)

The Independent Electric Company began with the merger of:

Hillsboro Water, Light & Power Company	(1910)
The Haines Electric Power Company	(1910)

The Wenatchee Valley Gas & Electric Company was a merger of the following:

Wenatchee Electric Company	(1910)
Entiat Light & Power Company	(1910)
Valley Power Company	(1910)
Brown Electric Company	(1912)

The Northwest Electric & Water Works acquired:

Montesano Light & Water Company	(1912)
Mountain Spring Company	(1912)
South Bend Electric Company	(1912)
Tenino Water Company	(1914)
Elma Light & Power Company	(1916)

The plight of the systems still had not changed much for the better. So more substantial mergers took place to further consolidate the management of the small systems. Two of the larger ones were the Washington-Oregon Corporation and the Washington Coast Utilities. The Washington-Oregon Corporation was organized on December 8, 1910, with its place of business at Vancouver, Washington. Its president was Issac W. Anderson. In the following year, 1911, this company purchased the following utility properties:

Twin City Light & Traction Company	Centralia
	Chehalis
Centralia Water Supply Company	Centralia
Kelso Water & Electric Company	Kelso
Vancouver Traction Company	Vancouver
Vancouver Water Works	Vancouver
Tenino Light & Power Company	Tenino
Kalama Electric Light Company	Kalama
Independent Electric Company	(Oregon)
Rainier Electric Company	(Oregon)
Independent Light & Water Company	(Oregon)
Lay Water Plant Company	(Oregon)

This was a time when electric traction companies were most profitable, so on May 7, 1912, the Washington-Oregon Corporation decided by resolution "to construct an electric railway from its existing line in the City of Centralia in Lewis County to the present terminus of the Olympia Light & Power Company's railroad in Thurston County." It proceeded to obtain the necessary right of way, but the tracks themselves were never laid, for times were changing and automobiles began to show on city streets and country roads. On October 14, 1915, the Washington-Oregon Corporation changed its name to North Coast Power Company, and some years later, on May 22, 1923, it changed its principal place of business to Seattle, Washington. This was a prelude to a subsequent larger merger.

Another company, with its principal place of business at Arlington, Washington, the Washington Coast Utilities, was organized on August 17, 1916. Its president was Charles E. Shepard. This company too proceeded to acquire utilities, struggling small systems, in the hope of a profitable operation of them. These were:

Jim Creek Water, Light & Power Company	(1916)
Stanwood Light & Power Company	(1916)
Vashon Telephone Company	(1917)
Edmonds Electric Light & Water Company	(1917)
Port Townsend Properties	(1919)
Vashon Light & Power Company	(1921)
Wenatchee Valley Gas & Electric Company	(1921)
Central Washington Gas Company	(1922)
Northwest Electric & Water Works	(1922)

Neither the North Coast Power Company nor the Washington Coast Utilities had been able to build major power plants as a backup to its distribution systems. So, understandably, they were looking for a sale of their investments.

In 1924 all holdings of both the North Coast Power Company and the Washington Coast Utilities were purchased and consolidated by the Puget Sound Power & Light Company, which by then had demonstrated stability and resources to build the essential central station power plants. Puget Power rebuilt and integrated these holdings in a dramatic manner. The scope and depth of this new operation in the electric utility business in the Northwest is further developed on the following pages.

A Nudge and a 110,000 Volt Line Was Built

The beginning of a vast network of new electric power lines to hundreds of small communities in Western and Central Washington was highlighted in 1921 by the plan to build a big line across the mountains. This expansion began with a nudge from a neighboring electric utility, the Washington Coast Utilities. It served Arlington, Stanwood, Edmonds, Richmond Beach, Vashon, Port Townsend, Montesano, Elma, South Bend and Tenino.

The Washington Coast Utilities in effect proposed that if Puget Power would build a 120-mile line extension to Wenatchee and deliver 5,000 kilowatts, then the Coast Utilities would go ahead and buy the financially embarrassed, short of power, Wenatchee Valley Gas & Electric Company. This was done.

The transmission line was actually designed to deliver 25,000 kilowatts, the power company having an eye on selling electricity to towns, mines, farms and sawmills along the route and to electrify railways as well.

Preliminary work was done by Magnus T. Crawford, engineer of Puget Power, who in 1921 toured the available mountain passes looking for the route of the electric line and gathering data. He also initiated surveys. All towers in the mountains were to be steel, and the wires on the lower levels were to be supported on poles in pairs with spacing spans of 500 feet.

Engineering and construction was done under the direction of Stone & Webster construction firm. This brought back to Seattle the personalities of Sam Shuffleton and W. D. Shannon, engineers of the firm. Shuffleton had been noted before as the construction engineer of the Electron Hydro Plant, and Shannon, equally colorful, was described by an associate as:

"A person who had no regard for hours of the day or night, when it comes to getting things done. Physically he is built of steel wires and fiddle strings and has dynamite in his blood, that is why he is able to run up and down cliffs and jump over rivers, gorges and canyons."

Shannon was in actual charge of the line constuction. Work was begun on June 22, 1922, and the line was contracted to be finished with delivery of power in Wenatchee by July 1, 1923.

Four hundred men were engaged in the project, working out of six camps. Each camp was located at a fresh water source for living quarters, cookhouses and barns. Horses were the primary motive power requiring barns, grain, hay and care. Construction in the mountains was pushed to completion before winter snows would interfere, and the work on the lower levels was carried on through the winter months. The line was actually put into service a month and a half ahead of schedule on May 14, 1923. The closing of the switch took place at Wenatchee.

At 2:45 p.m. of that day, Acting Mayor George W. Coburn closed a switch that connected the two systems of the Puget Sound Power & Light Company and the Washington Coast Utilities.

Among those present besides Mr. Coburn were the secretary, Vaughan H. Clearman, of the Wenatchee Commercial Club; president, C. Harry Whiteman, of the Rotary Club; president, George C. Jones, of the Lions Club; and several other citizens. Also on hand to see that the program went through without a slip were manager, Ray U. Muffley, of the

W.D. SHANNON

Washington Coast Utilities; district manager, O. M. Carter; district superintendent, Frank Walsh; and foreman, G. E. Bergman.

At the appointed time Mr. Coburn stood ready with a firm grip on the switch at the switchboard of the Wenatchee Steam Plant awaiting the signal from Mr. Muffley. The latter was carefully noting the dial of a synchroscope which indicated the speed of both the white River Plant and the local Washington Coast Utlities Plant.

When the dial ceased revolving and showed a tendency to remain fairly stationary, indicating that both plants were synchronizing, a wave of the hand from Mr. Muffley sent the switch into place and electric energy flowed smoothly along the 120-mile stretch of copper wires without a jolt or a ripple to show that anything unusual had happened. The only change observed about the plant was that the dial of the indicator remained absolutely motionless, telling the expert that there was no variation in the speed of either of the generating plants.

Next followed the shutting down of the steam plant, which had been in operation for some time. This plant would be maintained for emergency purposes, but it was hoped that it never would be necessary to start it up again.

Wenatchee Had Been Long Suffering

The 110,000 volt power line brought much needed electrical energy to Wenatchee, the largest city in Central Washington, and to the large apple orchards, for irrigation and spraying.

Wenatchee had been incorporated in 1892, when lights were coal oil lamps and tallow candles. And for the ensuing thirty years, when electricity seemed in good supply on the Coast, there was an enduring dearth of electric power in the Wenatchee Valley. There never was enough power for pumping water to irrigate the orchards, let alone domestic needs. in 1921 electric ranges could not be used in any of the communities outside Wenatchee, and some customers could not even use irons or appliances. The existing equipment was necessarily turned off in rotation during peak hours.

The story of electric power began in 1893 when L. V. Wells, Wenatchee's lone druggist (he and his wife were the only two school teachers), decided to install an electric generating plant on the bank of the Squilchuck Creek. His firm was incorporated as the Wenatchee Electric and Power Company. It served the community for several years, however, even though its water source was just a trickle of a stream.

The firm was sold to the Wenatchee Electric Company headed by Arthur Gunn, who spent a quarter million dollars between 1904 and 1910 building a steam power plant and a distribution system.

Another company, organized in 1908 by J. H. Stout and associates, the Entiat Light and Power Company, built a hydroelectric plant on the Entiat River, extended a transmission line to Wenatchee and built a steam plant there. This company also built a distribution system to serve parts of the townsite.

Also in 1908 the Dryden Hydro Plant was built, using water from the Wenatchee River by way of a diversion canal with the canal doubling as an irrigation canal. The power firm was known as the Valley Power Company, and its transmission line extended to Cashmere.

A fourth hydroelectric plant was installed for transmission of power to the town of Waterville. Built by George H. Gray and his son, its site was on the Entiat River downstream from that of the Entiat Light & Power Company. In 1909 the plant was sold to the George D. Brown Electric Company.

A major consolidation of the various systems took place in 1910 when the Wenatchee Valley Gas & Electric Company acquired the Wenatchee Electric Company, the Entiat Light & Power Company and the Valley Power Company. In 1912 this firm also bought the George D. Brown Electric Company. Still there was a power shortage.

In 1918 the Chelan Falls Power Company was started by George D. Brown. Most of its output of 1,000 kilowatts was delivered to the Wenatchee Valley Gas & Electric Company, and still it could not meet the demands of irrigation pumps.

In 1921 the Wenatchee Valley Gas & Electric Company was declared bankrupt. Its receiver contracted with the Great Northern Railway for 1,000 kilowatts from its Tumwater Plant, built to drive electric trains through the Railway's tunnel across the Cascades. Still the power supply was inadequate. It was then that the Washington Coast Utilities purchased the bankrupt Wenatchee Valley Gas & Electric Company, and in 1923 the 110,000 volt power line was finished by Puget Power. So now there was an adequate supply of electrical power for the Wenatchee Valley area.

In July 1924, the Washington Coast Utilities sold its entire Western and Central Washington properties to Puget Power. The thirty years and more of power shortage had ended.

Today, this area is "The power belt of the State of Washington," as Rufus Woods, the founder of the Wenatchee Daily World, repeatedly declared. In 1921 no one ventured to suggest that the Columbia which flows through the City of Wenatchee should be harnessed; however, in 1930 the Puget Sound Power & Light Company built the first dam to span the mighty Columbia at Rock Island, eight miles south of Wenatchee. From this beginning the full potential of the Columbia has now been harnessed, and Rufus Woods' "power belt" includes Rock Island, Grand Coulee, Chief Joseph, Rocky Reach, Wells, Wanapum and Priest Rapids hydroelectric developments. All are within 100 miles of Wenatchee.

Power Network in Central Washington

In a spirit of assurance and drive, Puget Power, upon acquiring the Washington Coast Utilities properties in 1924 and its ailing collection of electric systems on both sides of the Cascades, set about to rebuild them and build tielines. Its responsibility for electric service in Central Washington now embraced portions of Chelan, Douglas, Grant and Kittitas counties.

Orchardists in days prior to 1924 had had rough times with electric pumps. During the irrigation loads the frequency would drop from sixty cycles to fifty-four cycles, and voltage, too, would sag correspondingly. This created a bad situation, for centrifugal pumps driven by induction motors would continue to run but would not develop sufficient head to pump water. With the construction of the new 110,000 volt line across the mountains bringing a large block of energy from the Coast, frequency was held at sixty cycles, and further, through improved distribution lines and new substations, the voltage was kept up.

In all towns a vigorous program of reconstruction was carried forward. New substations were built at Leavenworth, Monitor and Sunnyslope, and major improvements were made at the hydro plants of Entiat and Dryden. At Dryden an additional generator of 1,200 kilowatts was installed.

Twelve existing substations were rebuilt with higher capacity and new protective devices. At Wenatchee the pole lines were removed from the main streets and put into alleys, and at Leavenworth the entire distribution system was rebuilt.

At Kittitas, Thorp and in the area surrounding Ellensburg, all lines were rebuilt to conform with State Standards. A 33,000 volt line was built from Cle Elum to Ellensburg, a distance of 30 miles, which was connected by a loop around the City to all rural lines. This gave Ellensburg and the surrounding communities service from the main system of the Company.

Prior to the building of this line, service was cut off from rural lines whenever the Ellensburg plant could not supply the peak load, and only those customers having an interest in the mutual lines could get electric service.

After 1926 a line extension policy was put into effect by Puget Power so that anyone wishing electric service could get it. Unrestricted electric service was available to all.

Whatcom, Skagit and Island Counties

Before 1924 the following areas were served by nine separate companies, all of which were acquired by Puget Power subsequently as noted:

Washington Light & Water Company	(1924) Anacortes and environs
Oak Harbor Lighting Company	(1925) Part of Whidbey Island
Coupeville Lighting Company	(1927) Part of Whidbey Island
Island Light & Power Company	(1930) South Whidbey Island

Langley Light & Power Company	(1930)	Langley and environs
Whatcom County Power Company	(1926)	Custer and Ferndale
Acme Lighting Company	(1930)	Town of Acme
Baker River Light & Water Company	(1925)	Town of Concrete
Puget Sound Pulp & Timber Company	(1929)	Town of Clearlake
Alger Light & Water Company	(1931)	Town of Alger
Rockport Electric System	(1931)	Town of Rockport

Residents may well recall the service of the days prior to 1924. The area of Oak Harbor was served by a small generating outfit run by a steam tractor. It was inadequate for the demands put upon it. Interruptions were frequent. The plant was operated only from dusk until midnight, except on Monday - washday — when service was available from one o'clock in the afternoon until midnight for washing and ironing. No ranges or appliances could be used because of limited capacity of the system. Complaints were handled at the convenience of the lighting company.

At Anacortes, a small steam-electric plant served the town and surrounding area up to 1924. Interruptions had not been frequent, but when repairs were necessary on the plant, service had to be curtailed because no alternate power supply was available.

At Concrete, where power had been obtained from the Superior Portland Cement Company, voltage fluctuations were very pronounced due to the character of the load at the cement plant. A similar voltage condition existed at Clearlake where customers were served by a pulp and timber company. There the distribution facilities were too small to allow the use of ranges and other heavy appliances.

At the community of Coupeville electric power was supplied by a fifty kilowatt generator driven by a tractor. Breakdowns were often, and sometimes outages were months in length.

Mr. M. S. Mortenson of Langley wrote: "During the time of the old company, the lights winked at 10:45 p.m. as a warning that they would be turned off at 11:00 p.m. and in the midst of any party, or entertainment, a mad rush was made to get either kerosene or gas lights ready. Chicken house lights were on from six to eight in the evening during winter and during that time no reading or close seeing could be done. There was no current on in the daytime except two hours, just two days of the week at that, for washing and ironing. If that was not done on those two days, washing had to be done by hand."

With the acquisition of the independent properties, which were the pioneers (and much credit should be given them for that fact), Puget Power immediately launched upon a program of reconstruction of lines and standardization of service. Plants were dismantled. New lines and substations were built. In 1926 a new hydroelectric plant was completed on the Baker River and all service on Whidbey Island, Skagit and Whatcom counties was of high order, in contrast to the original local service.

Rates, too, were drastically cut. Before acquisition the top rate in Island County was 12 cents per kilowatt hour; in Whatcom and Skagit counties outside Bellingham the rate was 9 cents. In Bellingham it was 7½ cents for the top

rate bracket. Uniformly lower rates soon followed in Pierce, Thurston, Lewis, Grays Harbor, Mason, Pacific, Cowlitz, Clark counties and Parts of Oregon.

Small utility firms had been built throughout the area by pioneers, each with daring dreams and buoyant expectation of a bonanza. In their articles of incorporation they had boldly proclaimed all-inclusive objectives, to give gas, electric, water, telephone and railway services.

In retrospect, through a quarter of a century of starts and mergers of these struggling utility firms established in isolation, few of their dreams were realized. In the course of time they ran smack into the harsh realities of lack of funds, deteriorated facilities and unfriendly public moods.

Water lines laid in acid peaty soils would corrode fast, wooden poles, untreated against decay, would rot at the ground line within eight to ten years, and wires for electric conductors rusted quickly in the damp and often salty air. Moreover, these small companies had been built on stretched credit, so they were always short of funds for repairs and replacements. Customers became sensitive, unhappy, and the second generation of utility leaders were perplexed, distressed and depressed.

In this atmosphere came the Puget Sound Power & Light Company with offers to buy their properties and to update them with new equipment. It was like opening a door of a musty building and letting in a breath of invigorating fresh air.

Beginning in 1924, the following utility properties were acquired by Puget Power, with the year of purchase and area served noted:

Olympia Light & Power Company	(1924)	Olympia, Tumwater, Lacey
People's Utilities Company	(1924)	Oakville, Littlerock, Rochester
Washington Coast Utilities	(1924)	Montesano, Elma
Washington Union Coal Company	(1924)	Tono
North Coast Power Company	(1924)	Tenino, Bucoda, Chehalis, Littell, Adna, Ostrander, Kelso, Kalama, Woodland, Vancouver - and in Oregon: Rainier, Beaverton, Hillsboro, Forest Grove and Gaston
Washington-Idaho Light & Power	(1924)	Winlock, Vader, Napavine, Castle Rock, Toledo
Avery Public Utilities	(1926)	Roy, Pe Ell, Doty, Dryad
Thurston County Utilities Co.	(1926)	Yelm

It was soon realized that the properties in Oregon and in Clark County were far away from the executive offices of the Company, and furthermore these properties could not readily be integrated with the transmission system.

So after a year and a half of operating a headquarters office in Portland, the Puget Sound Power & Light Company sold its Oregon properties, as well as the railway and water systems in Vancouver, and the electric distribution systems of Kalama and Woodland. The personnel were taken over by the purchasing companies, and the Portland office closed.

In the operations of predecessor companies, interruptions of electric service had been frequent, poles were short, crossarms light, power was limited and iron wire was used extensively. No heavy appliances were possible under these conditions. In most communities power had been available only after dusk until midnight, except during one day — washday.

At Dryad, no service was available when the mill was not running. In all systems the electric rates were high, on the average ten cents per kilowatt hour.

Following the consolidation by Puget Power, the distribution systems in nearly every community were rebuilt to State Standards. For example, in the towns of Winlock, Napavine, Vader, Toledo and Castle Rock, it was necessary to set 500 new cedar poles and run 225,000 feet of primary and secondary circuits. Then each little town reacted with pride by demanding new street lights, and over 225 new lights were installed.

In Olympia, the hardware dealers who sold pumps begin to drop in at the power company office to express their appreciation of adequate voltage. New pump motors no longer burned up, and sale of water pumps was brisk.

Improved voltage and service was only possible by building transmission lines between towns and building new substations. With these done, unlimited power was brought to the customers.

True, this was considered a giant leap forward in the 1920s. In the light of quality of service of the 1980s — sixty years later — with the resources of the Northwest Power Pool to back up Puget Power and with total underground wiring to bury the electric system from view, in time the quality of service would be further improved.

Snohomish County

Prior to 1922 the following communities were served by various systems in Snohomish County which subsequently were all acquired by Puget Power:

Washington Coast Utilities	(1924)	Arlington, Edgecomb, Florence, Sylvana, Stanwood, Edmonds, East Stanwood and Richmond Beach
Sultan Electric Company	(1926)	Sultan, Startup and Goldbar
Mountain States Power Company	(1927)	Snohomish and Monroe
Skykomish Municipal Plant	(1927)	Town of Skykomish
Darrington Light & Power Company	(1930)	Town of Darrington
Index Municipal Plant	(1931)	Town of Index
Granite Falls Electric Company	(1922)	Town of Granite Falls

These predecessor companies, using small hydro plants,

encountered their own kind of difficulties in giving electric service. During low water, service had to be curtailed. Outages were frequent. Minor trouble at the plant, or the water supply, or in the electric lines necessitated shutdowns. It used to be a common occurrence to give the excuse that salmon got into the wheel at Granite Falls. Power would then be off for one-half day or sometimes a whole day.

This was also the character of service at Sultan, Startup, Goldbar, Arlington, Stanwood, and Skykomish. Speaking of the service at Granite Falls, Mr. Joe Mueller, a local resident at the time, said, "Prior to the purchase of the electric system in Granite Falls by the Puget Sound Power & Light Company, I was asked many times by the Granite Falls Company to shut down my ice machine when it was time to start the movie picture show, as the system was not able to carry both loads at one time."

Mr. M. A. Fulcher, of Sultan, told this story, "The Sultan Electric Company's hydro plant ran twenty-four hours a day, except during low water periods. Then it was necessary to close down the hydro plant during the day to save enough water to run the plant at night."

These small companies had served their communities separately and independently as best they could. Great strides were made by Puget Power to provide tie lines between towns, to give alternate sources of power and to improve and enlarge all facilities. Existing power supplies were extended and reinforced. Rural electrification was carried forward with vigor and in earnest, following the Company's establishment in 1925 of a farm electrification department to serve all its farms.

Electric rates were pushed down. Even as late as 1929 residents were paying 14 cents per kilowatt hour in Darrington, 12 cents at Arlington, Edmonds, Richmond Beach, Stanwood, Granite Falls and Sultan, and 10 cents at Skykomish and other parts of the county. Following acquisition by Puget Power, they were uniformly reduced.

The Olympic Peninsula

The Olympic Peninsula received central station power from Puget Power's network through underwater cables in 1926. The Peninsula, the most westerly land of the Northwest, is reached mosly by boat or ferry. Discovery of the Peninsula was by sea. On April 29, 1792, as his ship the Discovery was probing its way along the coastal waters of a new and strange land, the English explorer, Captain George Vancouver, saw this land of rich scenic splendor and made a terse entry in his logbook. The Captain wrote:

"The most remarkable mountain we had ever seen presented itself. Its summit, covered with eternal snow, was divided into a very elegant fork, and rose conspicuously from a base of lofty mountains clothed in the same manner."

The mountain is now known as Mount Olympus, and the land was the coastal area of the Olympic Peninsula which jutted into the Pacific Ocean. On the far side of the mountain range, after entering through the Straits of Juan de Fuca, there lay an 80-mile-long sheltered inland sea, to be named Puget Sound.

As our forefathers moved westward they found this peninsula remote and intriguing. They built homes and industries along Puget Sound, and the glacier-clad

Olympics, as viewed by Captain Vancouver, would later be set aside as a National Park. With typical energy and enthusiasm electrical men also sought to provide electricity for the townspeople of the various communities. By the 1920's these electric systems had reached the limits of their capabilities. They needed central station power.

A Bold Decision

To extend electric power to the Olympic Peninsula, separated by an inland sea, was no less as bold an undertaking as had been the construction in 1923 of a 110,000-volt power line across the majestic saw-toothed Cascade Mountains that stood like a dividing wall between the Coast and the power short City of Wenatchee. In 1926 Puget Power made the decision to purchase the separate electric systems on the Peninsula, and, as was its custom of providing a major power supply immediately, it further concluded to span Puget Sound with four-mile-long submarine power cables laid deep under salt water of the Sound.

Laying Submarine Cables

Following the announcement that Puget Power planned to lay submarine cables across the waters of Puget Sound, excitement ran high among engineers and citizens. It would be breaking all world's records considering the combination of length, power capacity, voltage and depth of water. There would be two cables, each capable of carrying 10,000 horsepower.

Okonite Company of Passaic, New Jersey, would manufacture the cable; total length was 46,800 feet, weighing 15½ pounds per foot. It was armored with spiraling stainless steel strands as an outside sheath, and total diameter would be four inches, having three conductors embedded in high-insulating material to sustain 13,000 volts between conductors. It would be manufactured in seven lengths to be delivered on eighteen gondola freight cars, on which the cables would be loaded in S-loops spanning two gondolas per loop. Delivery point was dockside at Edmonds. The total estimated cost installed was $350,000.

On recommendations of Col. J.D.L. Hartman of the Signal Corps, U.S.A., permission was granted by the Secretary of War at Washington, D.C., to use the U.S. Cableship *Dellwood* for laying the cables. It had been assigned to the Alaska Military Cable System.

The *Dellwood*, 375 feet long, was splendidly fitted for handling all kinds of cable work; however, the usual sub-

Taking Cable into Hold of Dellwood

49

marine telegraph cable was not over two inches in diameter, so, in order to enable the *Dellwood* to handle the four-inch power cable, new sheaves and a larger drum on the paying-out machine had to be installed. The ship's crew was a capable, well-trained crew accustomed to their work. They took charge of laying the power cables.

A large complement of equipment was needed for removing the cables from the gondolas to the hold of the *Dellwood,* for splicing the seven lengths, beaching one end at Richmond Beach Substation, keeping the *Dellwood* on course, and finally securing the cable at President Point on the Peninsula.

Once the cable had been spliced and transferred to the hold of the ship, the hold was flooded with water and the cable tested for 14,000 volts.

In laying the cable, a line between landing points on each shore was clearly marked by large targets, so that the Master of the vessel could hold the ship on course. When near the opposite shore the ship's course was changed to follow parallel with the shore until all the cable was laid in shallow water for the distance needed to bring it ashore to its terminal.

The end was picked up by a scow with a power-driven reel on which the cable was slowly wound until a point on the original course was reached, then the scow headed for shore. Two cables were laid on different courses spaced 500 feet apart across the channel.

Power was delivered July 31, 1926, substations and transmission lines having been previously built to link the Company's transmission system, including power from the Baker River development.

This was the beginning of under-water electric power transmission. In 1928 the ship *Wm. Nottingham* was bought by Puget Power and fitted with cable laying gear, with an eye towards expanding electric service to other islands, such as Mercer, Vashon, Bainbridge and Whidbey. In 1947 the *Wm. Nottingham* was replaced with an Army Surplus vessel and was named the *Puget Power.* Through the years Puget Sound Power & Light Company had racked up an impressive total of over 25 miles of submarine cable laid in water depths down to 840 feet in places.

Pioneer Systems on the Peninsula

The beginnings of electric service in each town on the Peninsula is part of the local history. Some had received electricity from small steam plants built in the 1880s. For example, at Port Townsend, when on March 23, 1889, the first spadeful of railroad dirt was turned over, land values soared. The town grew by leaps and bounds, and before the year ended more than 7,000 people had come to Port Townsend. Only a short six months earlier, in the fall of 1888, the Port Townsend Electric Company was founded by W. J. Grambs, S. Z. Mitchell and E. B. Downing. The generator was driven by a steam engine fueled by slabwood. Grambs and Mitchell had been classmates at the U.S. Naval Academy at Annapolis, and upon completing two years sea service, they came West to seek their fortunes.

Bremerton, too, was supplied with electricity produced at a sawmill by steam power in the early days. Sawmills located on the Sound were dumping their mill refuse into the Sound. Laws were passed prohibiting this, so Bender's

Mill at Bremerton, in 1901, was confronted with the alternative of either buying a refuse burner or utilizing the fuel for making more steam to operate an electric generator. It was decided to do the latter, and that was the beginning (1901) of the light and power business in Bremerton.

Then in 1912 construction was started near Port Angeles of a hydroelectric plant on the Elwha River, to produce 20,000 horsepower. Thomas T. Aldwell, who became known as "number one citizen of Port Angeles," was the father of this project. In his book, *Conquering the Last Frontier,* he gives a graphic story of pioneers who saw the potential of hydro power and set about building a big dam to harness a river.

The Elwha River Dam was Aldwell's. He provided the site, the leadership and also money to the limit of his resources; then, with support of local townspeople and the trust of prominent men, he persuaded Chicago investors to provide the rest of the funds to build the hydro project. To his dismay, it was beset with misfortune and financial troubles.

When the water was impounded behind the dam, the questionable underpinnings of the dam blew out. It was a massive blow to the project. Then the dam was successfully repaired, with a dent in the funds, and on December 2, 1913, the *Olympic Leader* of Port Angeles jubilantly ran the headline: "Elwha Juice in Town."

A 110-mile transmission line to Bremerton was part of the project. On January 23, 1914, this line was energized, and power from Elwha reached the Puget Sound Navy Yard at Bremerton. By fall, power was marketed in Port Angeles, Port Townsend, Bremerton and other small towns in the area. The Elwha plant had proven its merit.

A covetous glance was cast at the Elwha plant in 1915 by J. D. Ross, superintendent of Seattle City Light. He began negotiating seriously to buy the power plant for $1,750,000. A City Election intervened, and with a change of administration in Seattle the purchase was set aside.

By 1919 Zellerbach officials of San Francisco were interested in building a pulp mill at Port Angeles, and to assure themselves of electric power they bought the Elwha properties. Their new mill, known as the Washington Pulp & Paper Company, then set up a subsidiary, the Northwestern Power & Light Company, for distributing power to Port Angeles, Port Townsend, Sequim, Dungeness, Bremerton and intermediary territory.

With these added demands in the winter when the water was low at the Elwha River, the Bremerton load and loads en route taxed the capability of the hydro plant to its limits. The Elwha plant now was the major supplier on the Peninsula. Voltage was low at the end of the one 110-mile line to Bremerton. Faces brightened and the reaction of the citizens was most cheerful in 1926 when Puget Power seriously considered taking over the facilities of power distribution. Their plan was to raise voltage and bring unlimited electric power to the Peninsula.

Puget Power bought the transmission line and the separate independent electric systems. Below are noted these companies, their service areas and their date of purchase:

Northwestern Power & Light Company	110 miles of power line	(1926)
Washington Coast Utilities	Town of Port Townsend	(1924)

50

North Pacific Public Service Co.	Bremerton, Manette, Port Orchard and Bainbridge Is.	(1926)
Sequim Light & Power Company	Sequim and Dungeness	(1926)
Hub Electric Company	Chimacum, Hadlock, Irondale	(1927)
Poulsbo Light & Power Company	Poulsbo, Pearson, Lemolo, Keyport and Suquamish	(1927)
Silverdale Light & Power Company	Silverdale, Brownsville, Bangor, Chico and Tracyton	(1928)

With the acquisition of the electric properties in this region, the service was now in the hands of a company whose primary interest was the electric power business. So improvements were made as fast as possible to give the best electric service. Vast improvements were made, oil switches were installed so that faulty circuits could be isolated in case of trouble, several new substations were built, and the Olympic transmission line and whole distribution systems were gone over, new insulators added and wires cleared of trees and brush.

A contract was signed to sell wholesale power to the City of Port Angeles, giving this city a second source of electric energy. Additional cable crossings were also put in at Hood Canal. No money was spared to improve service and voltage conditions on the Peninsula.

Part Eight

NEW POWER PLANTS OF THE TWENTIES

While the acquisition of many small electric distribution systems in isolated towns marked the character of the growth of Puget Power in the 1920-1930 decade, equally important was the Company's heavy financial investments in new electric generating plants. These were: a hydro project on the lower Baker River built in 1925, a major steam plant built on the shores of Lake Washington in 1928, and a hydro dam of bold dimensions on the Columbia River planned in the late 1920's for a completion date of 1933.

Lower Baker River Development

The Lower Baker Plant has a history of being built (1925), enlarged (1960), knocked down by a massive earth slide (1965), and again rebuilt with a slide-proof profile (1967). Significantly, the site for the power project had been filed on many years before, in 1912.

The initial development, completed in 1925, had two units for a plant total of 40,000 kilowatts. At the time it was the fifth major power plant to be operated by Puget Power. The dam and powerhouse are located on the Baker River in Skagit County, and the project's eight-mile reservoir extends north into Whatcom County.

The entire development lies in a deep canyon about one half mile upstream from the confluence of the Baker and the Skagit Rivers. The arch-type dam has a height of 293 feet above bedrock and impounds a lake that reaches back into the mountains where it reflects the beauties of the snow capped peaks of both Mount Baker and Mount Shuksan. The site is particularly good in that it is an area of heavy rainfall and where the runoff occurs at times when rivers farther south are not affected.

Site Selected in 1912

The original filing of water power rights on the Baker River was done by the Seattle Electric Company, a predecessor of Puget Power, on October 10, 1912. At the time other water powers, some on the Skagit River, had been filed upon and were ultimately surrendered because of low stream flow and high development costs. The Skagit River sites are now owned by the Seattle City Light, which did find development costs high. The two potential sites on the Baker River are now fully developed, as are the three on the Skagit.

Estimates of the Lower Baker project gave a construction cost of $9,000,000 for 60,000 horsepower, or $150 per horsepower. The White River development of Puget Power's had cost less than $100 per horsepower.

The City of Seattle found its Skagit development much more costly. In 1922 the City began to build the Gorge Plant, estimated to cost $4,500,000 for 50,000 horsepower. By 1924 the cost stood at $11,000,000. This was a cost of $220 per horsepower, without a dam for water storage. Without water storage half of the time the streamflow would be reduced to 20,000 horsepower. Building the Gorge Dam the cost per horsepower would reach $400. This is why the private company originally surrendered its Skagit River sites but valued its Baker River sites.

Construction

The elapsed time for the construction of the Lower Baker Project was nineteen months. Begun April 1, 1924, delayed by a strike and hampered by one of the most severe winters on record in that part of the country when flooding waters of the river erased progress time and again, the completion of this plant was regarded as one of the outstanding feats of engineering in the Northwest. The basic work was done by steam donkeys, dynamite and manpower. The contractor was Stone & Webster with W. D. Shannon in charge. In 1922 he had been the engineer for the construction of the 110,000 volt power line across the Cascade and Wenatchee Mountains to extend power to the Wenatchee Valley, a job which he completed in less than a year.

The Baker project included a dam, powerhouse, connecting tunnels, ninety-two miles of 110,000 volt lines as well as two substations, one at Sedro Woolley and another at Beverly Park near Everett.

One thousand men were employed at the peak of the Baker River Project. Most of the materials were purchased in Washington State, and a large part of the project was financed by the sale of securities within the territory served by Puget Power.

Fish Trap and Fish Taxi

A special feature of this hydro plant was the design of a fish trap and other facilities for catching and elevating migratory salmon up and over the dam. During 1927 as many as 2,200 salmon a day were trapped and elevated over the 293-foot Lower Baker Dam.

Through the years, fisheries scientists, from this country and from Canada, have used the Baker River Dam as a research area for handling adult salmon going upstream, as well as for a study of the fingerlings migrating downstream. This information became useful in the designs of other dams, both in our country and in Canada.

In 1957, when the Upper Baker Dam was built (94,400 KW), new fish handling facilities were installed at the two Baker dams at a cost of $2,200,000. They comprise a facility for collection of adult salmon at the Lower Dam, tank trucks for hauling them, artificial spawning areas upstream above the Upper Baker Dam, as well as facilities at both dams for attracting and passing fingerlings uninjured downstream over the dams for their migration to salt water.

An average of 12,500 native fish a year are trucked by the

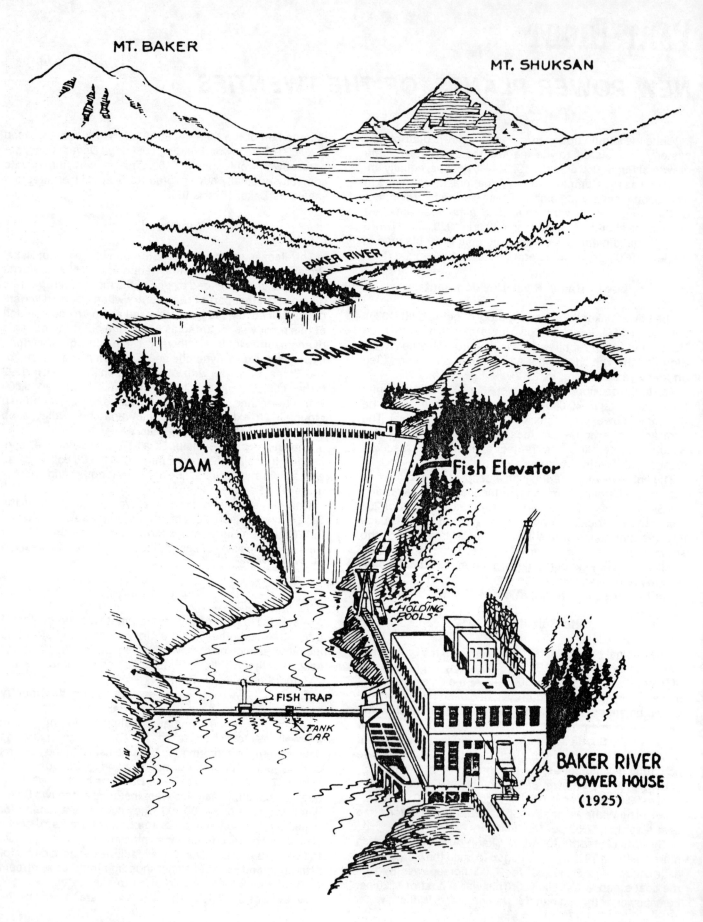

MT. BAKER

MT. SHUKSAN

BAKER RIVER

LAKE SHANNON

DAM

Fish Elevator

HOLDING POOLS

FISH TRAP

TANK CAR

BAKER RIVER
POWER HOUSE
(1925)

54

MT. SHUKSAN

TO
CONCRETE

FISH
BARGE

BAKER
LAKE

FISH PIPE

POWER
HOUSE

UPPER BAKER RIVER
DEVELOPMENT

LAKE
SHANNON

"Fish Taxi" to the upper lake. The bulk of them are silver salmon, and the rest are chinook, sockeye, humpback and steelhead. The newborn number about 300,000 a year; some remain in Baker Lake a year before they head out to sea. Most salmon from here migrate to Alaska. Three or four years later they return to spawn. The fish taxis are busy from June to December. Tests by State Fisheries experts have shown that the returning salmon reach their destination in better shape than when they went up river before the dams had been built.

New Unit Added Then an Earth Slide

The Lower Baker Power Plant was enlarged with a third generating unit of 64,000 kilowatts placed in service September 1960.

When work was begun on this third unit, little did the project builders realize that the powerhouse would in time be damaged by an earth slide. The builders of the powerhouse in 1925 anchored the back wall to the granite cliff of a canyon. The wall was three feet thick. There was no evidence of unstable earth in the surrounding terrain above the powerhouse site. Virgin timber, fir, stood on the hillside in 1925 with trunks four feet across which, when cut, showed growth rings of trees that had stood for 200 to 300 years. True, with roads established above the rim of the canyon, there had been some seepage from the hillside, for which drainage channels had been provided, but no slide threat existed. By 1960 a sizeable stand of second growth timber covered the slopes amid the old stumps.

In 1965 two blows struck the area. First an earthquake severely shook the countryside, and then within less than a month there erupted a flow of mud and earth from the hillside above the powerhouse.

At the time of the quake, April 29, 1965, workmen driving by in a pickup truck on a roadway near the top of the hill stopped for two men to climb out and walk the hillside on a routine inspection of the drainage ditches. The driver of the truck remained at the wheel, and when the quake struck he felt his pickup wobble, shake and rattle. His first thoughts were that his fellow workers were spoofing him by bouncing and shaking his vehicle. The men were on-the-spot observers of the quake's violence.

Then, within less than a month, on May 18, 1965, there erupted a flow of mud and earth from the hillside triggered by the quake. It was likened to the flow of grain pouring from chutes. It began abruptly, and for the next 24 hours unremittingly poured its weight against the upper walls of the powerhouse and then upon the roof until it collapsed. The mud filled the interior until the steel-reinforced concrete walls bulged outward.

The two older generating units were damaged beyond repair. But after the hillside was stabilized and the debris and earth cleared away, the third, the larger unit, was found salvageable. No life was lost, and insurance covered the damage.

Unique Geology of the Slide

Though not an avalanche catapulting down the hillside, this flow of mud was equally devastating and very unique. Its explanation provides intriguing reasoning.

There was no tilting strata under the overburden of the hill to start a slide. The earth rested upon a rock plateau, which extended from the canyon at an elevation of about 300 feet above the riverbed in a level manner.

It was reasoned that the outpouring of mud was due to the heavier earth mass at the high point of the hill, pushing

EARTH SLIDE oozed tons of earth, destroying half of the Lower Baker powerhouse, May 18, 1965. BELOW, rebuilt, 1967, with a slide-proof profile.

the thinner and saturated overburden outward at the edge of the canyon.

Additionally, there was a strange geology, an evidence of glacial silt which showed as oval cores of white silt when the debris had been cleared away. They were hard compacted cores, about ten feet thick, which, when intact, tilted upward and tended to hold the softer earth from moving.

Broken by the earthquake, this glacial silt absorbed water and when wet flowed like a fine emulsion the consistency of soft ice cream and was carried away by seepage, leaving cavities for more water to collect. It was reasoned that this freak in the geology, disturbed by the quake, was the contributing element in the disastrous flow of mud and earth.

SHUFFLETON STEAM PLANT

The Shuffleton Steam Plant is located in the City of Renton at the south end of Lake Washington. Built in 1928 it was isolated; today, it is somewhat over-shadowed by the Renton Boeing areo-space complex built around it.

The site was selected because of the excellent quality of water of Lake Washington which is fed by mountain streams needed for the condensers of the plant, and because ocean-going fuel tankers can navigate the lake.

When built in 1928 it was planned to give economic balance to hydro-power and insure standby capacity during dry seasons. Today it is a valuable standby power plant of the Northwest Power Pool.

Construction began in November 1928, and the first unit of 40,000 kilowatts after testing was immediately pressed in service in August 1929, to meet hydro deficiencies of a low water year. The cost was $5 million.

With the second unit added the Shuffleton Steam Plant is rated at 80,000 kilowatts, and at the time was the largest single power plant of Puget Power. Its value was proven from the time it was first fired up. In 1929, taking the year as a whole, the rainfall was but 20.03 inches compared with normal rainfall of 34.05 inches. So the timely addition of the first 40,000 kilowatts enabled Puget Power to cope successfully with acute hydro shortages.

The municipal plants of Seattle and Tacoma had to curtail use of electric service. The City of Tacoma requested the use of the airplane carrier *Lexington* to make up its deficiency.

Rock Island Dam, The First To Span the Columbia

Leslie R. Coffin was the father of the Rock Island Dam, the first dam to span the wide, turbulent, deep-flowing Columbia River. Coffin was a native of Denver, Colorado, and a 1907 graduate of Harvard. In 1910 he was the manager of the Whatcom County Railway & Light Company in Bellingham, Washington, where he proved himself a personable and able manager.

In 1917, during World War I, Stone & Webster asked him to a wartime construction job at Hog Island in the Delaware River, where this firm was building the largest shipyard in the world. It was recognized as one of the greatest engineering feats of the war days. Later Coffin had charge of construction work in all parts of California.

Shuffleton Steam Plant

In 1927 he returned to join the Puget Sound Power & Light Company as manager of its Wenatchee district. His office was right by the mighty Columbia River. The big river fascinated him, and with the eye of an engineer and one accustomed to huge projects, he studied the river for a potential power site. The Rock Island site, thirteen miles downstream from Wenatchee, became his absorbing hobby.

For many centuries the Columbia River had been plowing its rockbed, and at this site it split its course to leave a rock island. Rock Island, he reasoned, would be the key to diverting the mighty river for construction of a power dam. Coffer dams would divert the water, first past one side of the island, then past the other side.

The finished dam would extend from the east to the west bank of the river. From the east bank within the dam for a considerable distance would be the powerhouse structure. Spillways would occupy all the available space between the powerhouse and the west bank of the Columbia. Fish-ladders would be part of the installation.

The finished dam would be sixty feet in height and one-

LESLIE COFFIN

57

half mile in length. The lake created behind the dam would extend to the City of Wenatchee. This is essentially how the Rock Island Dam was built.

Engineering surveys and investigations of the site began in 1928. Exhaustive studies of the needs of the Company's system had been projected ten years ahead, and they indicated that the Rock Island development, in successive steps would provide the cheapest available program.

A Federal License was issued on January 21, 1930, and on the following day a contract involving $15,000,000 was awarded to the Stone & Webster Engineering Corporation covering the construction of the dam and the first unit of four generators for a capacity of 80,000 kilowatts. Provisions were made for additional units of a full development of 250,000 kilowatts.

The Federal License was issued to the Washington Electric Company, a subsidiary of the Puget Sound Power & Light Company, set up specifically for the Rock Island Project. Leslie R. Coffin became the manager of the Washington Electric Company.

At the peak of the construction 2,500 men were employed, working day and night. By December 1930, the powerhouse structure of the dam was taking on form to the point where a person could readily see that a hydro plant was being built and water wheel parts were being erected.

By December 1931, two of the generator units and the station service in the powerhouse were ready for testing and adjusting, and the pouring of concrete on the west spillway, which had been started October 1, was substantially completed during the month of November.

Visitors were coming from all parts of the United States at the rate of 2,500 a month, and their remarks indicated that they were greatly impressed with the magnitude and possibilities of the undertaking.

Many, watching from vantage points, were overwhelmed to the point of silence. A thousand men were working everywhere, cranes were swinging, drills clattering, and trainloads of concrete and gravel on trestle work came hurtling with noise and speed — all this heard high above the roar of the river. Before them, a magnificent, colossal epic in concrete and steel was rising from the rugged rock bottom of the diverted streambed of the turbulent Columbia River.

ROCK ISLAND DAM, 1933

PART NINE

CHANGES ON MANY FRONTS IN THE TWENTIES

The excitement, the novelty, the importance, the ingenuity of an industry that was 35 years old by 1920, now somewhat more mature, still was brimful of creative ideas for continued re-structuring to fit changing times.

Bus Lines

As a matter of history one of the objectives of the electric company in 1900 was the unification of nine small street railroads within the City of Seattle to become the Seattle Electric Company. So it is of more than passing significance that during the 1920's the Company engaged in a similar activity on a much larger and more important scale, thereby supplanting railway lines. It successfully consolidated and unified ten independent stage lines into an excellent motor coach system and operated it as a subsidiary, the North Coast Lines.

By 1929 the North Coast Lines had extended their service from Vancouver, B.C., through Seattle, Tacoma and on to Portland, Oregon. It was fed by many branch lines serving the entire Puget Sound territory. This meant building terminals, shops and garages in all of the principal cities and acquiring a fleet of large, high-powered coaches suitable for long-distance travel.

Fares were reduced and service improved to develop travel and to increase revenues. Results amply justified this radical departure from prevailing customs. During 1929 the bus company averaged about 5,000 passengers daily. Inasmuch as the Company was switching operations from the declining electric railway system to bus service, it needed to think and act creatively.

Trolleys On Way Out

Rail operations reflected competition of private automobiles. So, one by one, the electric trolley lines were phased out or faced bankruptcy. The Tacoma Short Line to Puyallup was discontinued in 1922. The Everett-Snohomish line had suffered washouts after a torrential rainy season and was operated only until 1921. In 1927 the Puget Sound Electric Railway went bankrupt, and its last run between Seattle and Tacoma was made on December 31, 1928. Also in 1928 operation of passenger service over the Bellingham-Mount Vernon interurban was discontinued and auto stage service substituted. The Centralia-Chehalis railway was discontinued and the property sold in 1929. The Company disposed of its city transportation system in Olympia on December 1, 1933, and the Everett City system gave up its ghost on January 1, 1934; both operations were not self-supporting. The Seattle-Everett line, which had its right of way quite some distance from a paved highway and thereby was serving small communities, continued to operate until 1939, when Seattle, too, converted its rail system to trackless trolleys. The era of electric trolleys came to an end.

Hires a Farm Specialist

In January 1926, Puget Power hired John C. Scott as an agricultural engineer with the duty to apply electricity to farming.

John Scott had the distinction of being the first specialist in the Northwest engaged in seeking practical solutions to problems connected with rural electrification. His training included a degree in animal husbandry from the Washington State College at Pullman, manager of a stock and hay ranch in Idaho and a stint as a county farm agent.

Scott faced a vast farming area with diverse soils and crops, including some of the richest lands in the United States — the tide flats of Mount Vernon. There were rich strawberry fields at Marysville, cranberry and blueberry farms at Olympia and in Grays Harbor, miles of orchards of apples and soft fruits in the Wenatchee Valley and many small farms devoted to poultry, berries, truck farming and dairying.

JOHN SCOTT

How well did John succeed? "Happy" Scott pioneered, devised, explored, taught, worked with farm groups and college students, wrote and delivered radio programs, prepared pamphlets, advertised ideas, enlisted aid of research laboratories, prepared fair displays, held demonstrations and within eight years copped a national award — the Thomas W. Martin Rural Electrification Award of 1934. He never engaged in politics; consequently, he had good rapport with all farm groups. He also sang as a hobby. He called himself a businessman who enjoyed singing and was regularly heard on his farm radio program. In meeting with farm groups, he was invariably asked to sing before the evening was over.

He applied his zeal and thoroughness in many ways. For example, under his guidance, there was established the Company's Research Laboratory at Puyallup. From it have come many profitable ideas. These were necessary to apply electric service to farming. Some ideas have created new industries, such as soil heating cable for electric hotbeds, now also used for panel heating of houses. These cables are sold the world over. Another development, the forced draft electric brooder for chicks, is now sold by national manufacturers. Hundreds of devices, from burglar alarms to electric eye counters for field crops have been developed.

Through the years, Scott's stature grew as a farm leader. Requests for information addressed to him have come from many foreign countries — Prerov, Czechoslovakia; London, Canada; Murchison, New Zealand; Melbourne, Australia; Paris, France; London, England; Auckland, New Zealand; Sidney, Australia; Buenos Aires, Argentina; Haiti Mauri; and so on. Ideas are powerful stuff.

In 1942 John Scott retired. On March 20, 1951, Governor Arthur Langlie named him to serve on the Board of Regents of Washington State College, so with a wealth of experience he returned to his Alma Mater.

Start of a Home Service Department

To carry the daily message of how best to use electrical appliances into the home — the vital spot which is the heart of all community life — a home service department was established by Puget Power in 1926.

Mrs. Edith Rauch, a thoughtful, wholesome, comely person, was selected to head this new department. She was well versed in the art of cooking, understood the use of

EDITH RAUCH

electrical appliances and also was an able and patient teacher.

Edith Rauch soon averaged a hundred calls a month by telephone; she attempted to come to the home of each caller and new owner of an electric range to teach the homemaker its best use. Moreover, she concocted special recipes, conducted cooking schools and managed displays at fairs.

Only those who knew her fully appreciated the extent of her impact in promoting sales, in helping keep those appliances sold and in nurturing and establishing goodwill towards the Company. In time Edith had a staff of a dozen trained girls busy consulting with customers and working with youth groups, community clubs and schools. To reach many more homemakers, Edith Rauch also conducted a radio program, known as the Highlight Hour.

Sincere friendliness and a free, clear, sweet expression of personality plus hard experience in merchandise sales, lighting, home economics and homemaking, in time gave to Edith a distinction enjoyed by few professional women.

Appliance distributors and manufacturers across the nation, time and again, honored her by soliciting her opinions and advice. At her retirement in May 1960, she had proven the soundness of the Company's decision in 1926 to hire a woman to help homemakers use electricity.

Employee Pension Plan

On October 1, 1926, after a thorough investigation of many forms of industrial pensions and insurance plans, Puget Power adopted a pension plan for its employees. In brief, it provided life insurance, disability income and pensions. The cost was partly borne by the employee and partly by the Company. It was a new and a popular plan. Within four years there were about 2,000 individual policies in force. Of course, many improvements in subsequent years were made upon this original pension plan, and other fringe benefits provided.

Securities Department Formed

In 1923 the Puget Sound Power & Light Company organized a Securities Department. Its purpose was to encourage its employees and its users to become stockholders and thereby partners in the business. Through political barbs it was becoming painfully aware that 90 percent of the people actually believed that Stone & Webster owned the Company. It held less than 4% of the stock. Stone & Webster, in reality, was the manager under contract of the utility, which insured expert technical talent combined with strong financial connections.

Most of the investors in Puget Power at the time the Securities Department was formed were living in the New England States. There were 10,000 stockholders and about 35,000 bondholders. So a vigorous campaign to sell stocks and bonds locally was begun. It was effective. The first $1,000,000 had been sold in eleven days. Salesmen were told: "Everyone who has a dollar to invest is a prospect for some of our stock."

By June 1926, the Company's shareholders had increased to 26,000, of which 8,000 lived in the Puget Sound area, holding an investment of $9,500,000. At the end of 1929

Preferred Stock was held by over 11,500 investors in the Company's service area and valued at over $15,000,000.

Also a more friendly and tolerant attitude by the consumer became evident. Stocks were purchased by doctors, lawyers, architects, retired capitalists, loggers, auto mechanics, government employees, teachers, veterinarians, merchants, restaurant proprietors, steamship captains, farmers, chicken ranchers, salesladies, mining engineers, ship builders, streetcar conductors, managers of industrial plants, tin workers and many other people. Local stock sales financed much of the expansion and maintenance of Puget Power facilities.

Looking to Other Sources

The year 1928 had been one of the most speculative years in the history of the country from an investment standpoint. Even so, the Company had been able to market a conservative investment in this highly speculative market.

In 1928 the Company made several prudent arrangements. It was about to begin construction of the Shuffleton Steam Plant, and plans were advanced on the Rock Island Hydro Plant on the Columbia River. So, upon completion of a new hydro plant by the Washington Water Power Company at Chelan Falls, Puget Power built a 110,000 volt transmission line for an interconnection to this plant and made a power purchase contract for 20,000 horsepower. The second arrangement was to enter into an agreement with Engineers Public Service Company for sizeable funding on October 5, 1928.

By this agreement Puget Power sold to Engineers 300,000 shares of Junior Preferred Stock for $7,500,000. Also, holders of Puget Power's common stock were invited to exchange their stock with common stock of Engineers Public Service Company. A satisfactory number did so, and Engineers became the owner of a majority of the stock of the Puget Sound Power & Light Company. The significance of this agreement was that financing for the construction of the Shuffleton Steam Plant and of the Rock Island Hydro Plant were assured.

Moreover, with this change the responsibility for efficient and satisfactory management was placed on the local officers of Puget Power. The Stone & Webster management contract was terminated in 1931.

1920-1930 Growth and Officers

In summary of the decade 1920-1930, the "Roaring Twenties," Puget Power surely made vast gains in its corporate growth. The number of customers served by all departments rose from 55,784 in 1920 to 156,135 in 1930. Sales of electrical energy jumped from 467,371,000 KWH in 1920 to 980,325,000 KWH in 1930. Gross earnings were $10,000,430 in 1920 and enlarged to $17,056,347 for 1930.

Puget Power's officers and top executives were:

Alton W. Leonard,	President
William H. McGrath,	Vice President
S. P. MacFadden,	Vice President
F. W. Brownell,	Treasurer
E. L. Crider,	Assistant Treasurer
H. J. Gille,	General Sales Manager
G. E. Quinan,	Chief Electrical Engineer
W. H. Somers,	Traffic Manager
N. W. Brockett,	Director of Public Relations
H. G. Winsor,	Personnel Officer
W. B. Donaldson,	General Purchasing Agent
Leslie R. Coffin,	Manager Central Division (Seattle)
R. C. Saunders,	Manager Southwestern District (Chehalis)
Frank Walsh,	Manager Northeastern District (Everett)
H. B. Sewall,	Manager Northern District (Bellingham)
Louis M. Shreve,	Manager Eastern District (Wenatchee)
A.S.J. Steele,	Manager Western District (Bremerton)
A. M. Chitty,	Manager Southern District (Olympia)
George Newall,	Manager North Coast Lines
W. J. Grambs,	Manager Diamond Ice & Storage Co.
Dwight Ware,	Manager Securities Company

Part Ten

POLITICAL PRESSURES MOUNT

We have seen how in the early 1900's more and more industrial workers were joining unions to fight for improvement of their conditions. The bulk of the middle class distrusted labor unions, but the excesses of some business leaders brought about distrust of big business too. For example, the railroads, in their internal struggles for control, earned the enmity of the very farmers who had settled on the land along the railroad lines. Such excesses led many voters to turn to politicans who criticized big corporations.

Theodore Roosevelt became President in 1901, and later, when he ran for re-election, his reputation as a "trust buster" led wage earners, farmers, small businessmen and many other groups to support him eagerly. This naturally was the cue to lesser politicians to speak out boldly too.

In the Puget Sound area there was still another political front. It was the public power movement led by the two largest cities in the State, Seattle and Tacoma. They had built their own electric light and power systems and were promoting public power ownership outside their city limits and actively trying to take over the private power companies which had pioneered the electric business.

J. D. Ross, superintendent of the Seattle lighting department, was an effective campaigner. He wanted to extend lines outside the City to help finance the City's expensive Skagit project, which he hoped to do through the State legislature. Inside the City his slogan was, "Duplicate lines are costly and unsightly."

By the 1920's there was a polarization of public opinion on the power issue. Feelings had run high during World War I, when in 1917 there was a state-wide lumber workers strike and also a local streetcar strike. Then in 1919, when the City of Seattle purchased the private trolley system, the move was interpreted as a victory for the public power advocates.

Cities Ask Legislative Action

In 1922 the cities took the legislative route to reach for state ownership of electric utilities. They originated Initiative Measure No. 44. It would give the cities the right to engage in practically every line of business. This measure was considered so radical that it failed to obtain a place on the ballot.

The same group organized the Washington State Superpower League to initiate a so-called Erickson Bill. This measure also was repudiated by the taxpayers.

Then in 1922, Homer T. Bone, an attorney from the City of Tacoma and a fiery orator, was elected to the State Legislature as a farm-labor representative. In his talks before various farm groups he directed a veritable barrage of charges against the private power companies. His theme at every Farm Grange appearance was, "Water power is a God-given resource that belongs to the people."

The Reed Bill

In the 1923 legislature Homer T. Bone proposed a power bill; however, the Speaker of the House pushed to enactment a more moderate bill, subject to a referendum clause, granting to the cities the right to sell their surplus electric power outside their city limits but imposing a gross earnings tax of 5% in the event the cities should exercise the right granted by this law. It became known as the Reed Bill.

Moderates in the legislature had much to say about the bill. They pointed out that under our laws, cities only have such powers as are granted them by the state legislature. To construct and operate plants for furnishing water and electricity to their own citizens, cities were given separate legislative grants. They cannot engage in banking, wholesale or retail business or any other line of business activity.

When the cities of Seattle and Tacoma demanded the right to sell electric energy outside their own city limits, the members raised the objection that this was not a governmental function, that the cities were in fact seeking to engage in the light and power business, and that there was no necessity for granting this extraordinary power.

The members asked for a report from the state department of taxation which showed that the light and power companies were paying in taxes an average of $9.60 out of every $100 gross revenue they collect and in addition were subject to state regulation.

The legislators therefore decided that, if this extraordinary privilege were to be given to the cities, insofar as taxation was concerned, they should be treated just like any other power company. However, they did not impose as severe a tax upon the municipal plants as the one borne by the private utilities. But the Reed Bill did place a 5% occupation tax on gross sales.

Discussions were far-ranging. Members of the country districts raised the point that the waters of the State of Washington belonged to all the people of the State, and that when they were developed by a private utility, the entire State received a rental for the use of these waters in the form of taxes paid by the utilities, which, as stated before, were 9.6% of their gross revenue. So the cities had no more right to the waters than the private utilities, and likewise should pay a tax.

The 1924 Bone Power Bill

An Initiative Measure No. 52 was petitioned to be placed on the ballot. It had been anticipated to be the Reed Bill and was sponsored by members of the League and Homer T. Bone; actually it was not the measure as passed by the legislature. The Ballot title of the initiative read in part: "An Act authorizing cities and towns to purchase, sell and dispose of electric current, inside or outside their corporate limits, without the payment of any tax thereon . . ."

Also two sections had been added which, in essence, empowered the cities to acquire, either by purchase or by condemnation, all of the existing light and power properties in the territory into which they might extend their lines. Petitions were circulated for signatures to place this initiative on the ballot of the 1924 general election.

The initiative measure traveled under the title "Bone's Free Power Bill." Many signed the petitions to place the initiative on the ballot without reading it.

The private power companies were first stunned, then they alerted their employees and through them obtained approximately 3,000 withdrawals in Seattle and Tacoma alone within the limit of three days. Even so, the necessary 50,000 signatures were obtained and Initiative Measure No. 52 was on the ballot.

A Strenuous Campaign

The proponents of the initiative had adopted the "Free Power" slogan to catch the eye of the people. It was said that every municipal light employee was engaged in promoting the initiative measure.

And the employees of the private industry felt that they had the same right to present the truth of the controversy as they saw it. Alton W. Leonard, president of the Puget Sound Power & Light Company, took the position that his company alone was paying annually one million dollars in taxes in this district. If the Bone Power Bill should become law and the cities exercised the rights granted them, all this property would become tax exempt. This would, of necessity, raise the taxes on all remaining property.

To his employees he said, "We have a splendid working force, if we will all do our part the people will be given the true facts so they can vote intelligently. There is no compulsion about this work. I am simply asking for the same cooperation so well expressed by Kipling, who said, 'It ain't the individual, nor the army as a whole, but the everlasting team-work, of every blooming soul.'"

The voters, on November 4, 1924, decided that Seattle and Tacoma should not extend their electric lines out into the country and take over private power. The vote was: Against - 217,393; For - 139,492.

The 1928 District Power Bill

Homer T. Bone was not quitting. He had felt the pulse of his supporters, made some adjustments, and settled on a new campaign of cultivating the farmer vote. It was an astute conclusion. Farming was the nation's largest industry. It employed more than the public utilities, steel and the automotive industries combined. Furthermore, the farmers were discontented. Overproduction had plagued them since World War I when a boom-bust cycle had started.

He found Albert Goss, Master of the State Grange, and Fred J. Chamberlain, its legislative representative and Deputy-at-Large, eager to join him in his drive for public power. They became a slashing political team. In time the Grange News took on a tone which must have shocked many a gentle soul.

The *Grange News* printed muckraking, vituperative and slanderous articles. It ran lurid caricatures. All were intended to arouse strong feelings against the private power companies. The Puget Sound Power & Light Company, being a Massachusetts based company, was pictured as a cow standing across the map of the United States, fed in the State of Wasington and milked in Boston. Other times the private power companies were labeled "The Power Octopus."

Bone re-shaped his public power bill. Cities were not in the new script. This time it was a district power bill in which the counties — the farm areas — would be given the rights to purchase or to condemn private properties. He also used adroit timing. His public power bill was ready when the stock market crashed and when confidence in business was badly shaken.

The District Power Bill was filed in the office of the Secretary of State on October 25, 1928. It was submitted to the Legislature January 21, 1929. The Legislature failed to take action on the bill February 1, 1929, which automatically referred it to a vote of the people at the next general election. Then, before the general election, the stock market crashed on October 29, 1929, signaling a very different America in the years to come.

On November 4, 1930, the District Power Bill was passed by a vote of the people: For - 152,487; Against - 130,901. The Act is now identified as Chapter 1, Laws of 1931.

A New Direction

The passage of the Public Utility District Bill was a devasting blow to the private power companies. It spelled dismay and dismemberment. And Homer T. Bone, now called "the father of public power," was elected to the United States Senate in 1932. As a Senator, he often publicly thanked the Puget Sound Power & Light Company with sardonic humor for "electing me to the U.S. Senate."

There, as a New Dealer from the State of Washington, Bone embraced the federal government's full development of the Columbia River and was instrumental in setting up the Bonneville Power Administration. Senator Bone was intent on knocking out all private power ownership in the State of Washington.

A Body Blow

Alton W. Leonard, president of Puget Power, realized that the 1929 stock market crash had seriously hurt investors in his Company, especially those in the East. However, he found that business held up with good resiliency on the West Coast. Upon learning of the results of the vote on the District Power Bill, the Eastern owners of the Company interpreted it as a body blow. They begin looking for a new president. Effective April 1, 1931, Leonard resigned as president and went into retirement.

Frank McLaughlin Succeeds Leonard

Frank McLaughlin, a young man of 36, born on a farm near Hingham, Massachusetts, was selected to replace Leonard as president of Puget Power. McLaughlin, in his leaderships of other utilities, had achieved a brilliant record through his policies and ideals of reversing public opinion from that of hatred and distrust, under old management, to that of

HOMER T. BONE, Democrat candidate for the U.S. Senate, in a speech at Wenatchee in 1932, blasting the "Power Trust" and Insull interests. **(Post Intelligencer** *photo).*

confidence, trust and helpful cooperation. His was to be a shattering experience of matching his metal against the ravages of a devastating depression and of socialistic efforts towards dismemberment of his Company on a local level as well as by the federal leadership of a four-term president of the United States, Franklin D. Roosevelt. It took twenty years for the sun to again come over the hill for Puget Power.

Homer Truett Bone

With such a political following, what manner of a man was Homer T. Bone? He was born in Franklin, Indiana, on January 25, 1883, and came to Tacoma, Washington, in 1899, where as a youth he became a postal clerk. Young and impressionable, as well as intelligent and intense, his sympathies tended towards the common people. He dreamed of leadership. He began to "read law" in the long nights and passed the bar examination as a self-taught attorney.

Bone was strongly motivated. He became a fiery orator, and, though self-taught, he was looked upon by his peers as a legal giant. In 1922 he was elected to the House in Washington State as a farmer-labor representative, and in 1932 he was elected to the United States Senate. In the Senate he served continuously until 1945, when he received the appointment to become a judge of the U.S. Circuit Court 9th District in San Francisco. There he was a tireless researcher and a competent judge. In his term on the 9th Circuit Court of Appeals he never had his decisions reversed.

He had unusual traits and an intense drive. To his listeners he projected considerable charm, both as an orator and as a person. He was not particularly interested in making money and said so. This, of course, made him attractive to laborers and farmers. He was of the old school, polite to old women, knew people by their first names — and these were legion — including train porters. He had a fabulous memory for faces and names.

With a stong sense for the dramatic and a flair to strike the right pose he could captivate his audiences. In his speeches he would roar his barbs, yet for the clincher of his arguments he would drop his voice to a whisper, with listeners bending forward to catch each word. Addressing farmers at their Grange Halls he made solid impact with his delivery and the Grangers would ask repeatedly for him to come back. Bone's political formula was to pick a critical goal and never compromise.

For example, in his whole political career his thesis was that the water power of the world was a resource that belonged to the common people. Pounding away on this theme, he brought about the passage of the Grange Power Bill and the Bone Power Act under which public utility districts could be established, then as Senator he became a leader in advocating a Columbia River Authority and the Bonneville Power Act. He became known as "father of public power."

As a New Dealer and an effective orator, he also embraced such concepts as old-age pensions, unemployment compensation and a shorter work week. All his life he was a pusher, a vital force, until his death in March 1970, at the age of 87. He left major marks on regional and national history.

Book Section Two

The subsequent chapters are written in the first person, because the writer's experiences parallel the years covered in the book.

Editor's note

PART ELEVEN

BEGINNING YEARS OF A CAREER

On June 16, 1930, I reported for work to Puget Power as a cadet engineer. I was one of two electrical engineers accepted from the graduating class of the University of Washington. We were the third-year group of student engineers of a course begun by Puget Power in 1928 for in-company training. Graduates previously selected were: Lawrence Karrer, John Wallin, Wallace Quistorff, Howard Park, Charles Butt, Wallace Joyce, W. Hockersmith, Emmett Kelley and Lawrence Palmer. Reginald Plymire and I were the latest cadets.

Most of these men later distinguished themselves in positions of leadership. In the plan, each man was to spend two years at a variety of jobs as training towards a niche in the company best suited to his skills and temperament.

So began my career in the electric business. It had been determined obliquely in 1925, when, as a graduating high school senior, my ambition "to throw sparks" was noted in the school annual. When the inquiring class reporter had asked what nibbles or bites I had towards a career he was told that only the summer before I had been shocked with a three-inch static spark from a windmill as I grabbed the handle to set its brake in a high wind. This happened at my home on a wheat ranch in Lincoln County. Like Ben Franklin with his experiment of drawing sparks from a kite string, a mighty spark gave me a foretaste of my future work.

At the University, the seniors had been interviewed by industry men. Mr. Magnus Crawford, general superintendent of Puget Power, interviewed us. Looking over my grades and dossier, he asked, "Why didn't you choose to go East as others had, to work for General Electric, Westinghouse, Allis Chalmers or Bell Telephone?"

My reply was to the effect that most of my friends had been staying at home to attend college, and now only wanted an excuse to get away from home. I, on the other hand, had lived on a wheat ranch in a dusty, windy part of Washington, and having once seen the lush forests, the Pacific Ocean and the snow-capped mountains all about us, considered the Puget Sound country to be unsurpassed and wished to stay here, and that the Puget Sound Power & Light Company looked like the firm I was best suited to work for. I was hired.

Mr. Crawford then said that he too had left his home at Louisville, Kentucky, as a young man to come to the Sound. (He was the same lad who, at eight, upon seeing the World's Fair in Chicago in 1893 and Edison's electrical displays, likewise yearned to "throw sparks.")

A Two Year Tour

So in June 1930, at the age of 22, I reported for work at the engineering office of Puget Power and was assigned as a helper at the construction of a new substation in the Laurelhurst area of Seattle. The salary was $120 a month.

Though some impact of a depression was evident, the Company continued with its construction program

My first job was not hard work as on the farm. The hours were only eight a day. Just out of college, where the faculty had let up on pressures during the last week leading up to commencement exercises, then let us walk solemnly in cap and gown, and finally reminded us of our responsibilities of directing the affairs of state and nation, I reported to my first job wondering how to apply this recently nurtured sense of importance. My first few days were spent pushing a wheelbarrow.

So it was easy to shake off sentimental things. The $2.50 rental refund of a cap and gown were used to buy a pair of overalls and a tin lunchbox. Now I was mentally ready so the Company could use me.

In a few days I was a helper to an electrical installer, Fred Faucett, who used trigonometry to figure the angles and bends of copper bus drops and runs. I was impressed. Actually, in the course of building the substation, there was much to learn in the practical work of wiring circuits, switchboards, relays and electrical apparatus. In time my work would be at other substations and at power plants; having been introduced to this work there I felt quite at ease.

In an emergency we were pulled off the Laurelhurst job to make repairs at the industrial Massachusetts Street Substation where lightning had struck. The lightning caused the main busses inside the building to melt — porcelain insulators were melted to gobs of white masses, and copper was gone except for a few droplets of metal. Moreover, concrete cubicles in horizontal alignment had spurted their heat and flame forward into one end of the control room, burning the fronts of switchboards and leaving the station dark. Now blackened, the interior revealed the vivid reality of Nature causing a flash-over.

Before the first year of my cadet training had passed, I had traveled with engineers busy at planning lines and services for new customers, assisted salesmen both in their contacts and in their office routines, and had also done very practical work in the Company's service departments. I had traveled with cut-in trucks, at times as the driver and at times riding the end-gate. A wholesome spirit was evident in our areas of work. We young fellows were welcomed to share in the work.

We gained a profound admiration for these men. They were competent. They were men who would calmly light their pipes, and after coaxing the smoke to rise just right, then take up their work with hot lines. The lesson we learned was that to do a job was to do it right.

A New Boss

On April 1, 1931, with the country staggering from the depths of the Great Depression and the Pacific Northwest the focal target for government ownership of electric utilities, the Puget Sound Power & Light Company secured a new president, Frank McLaughlin. He was thirty-six, an impressive figure of positive, vigorous bearing, in the prime of life, with a knack of getting the ear of the public.

The 3,000 employees of Puget Power at first did not know what to expect of their new boss. They would see massive pressures placed upon him. He experienced more than two decades of desperate struggle to save a private company from engulfment by public power. It was a long and taxing fight, the details of which are many and varied and often astounding. All employees would feel deep involvement.

Whatever was wrong, McLaughlin had to make it right. Farmers had nothing pleasant to say about the power company. Power lines along farm lanes were few, though Puget Power, more than other companies, had been seeking to develop rural customers. Service and rates were in the experimental stage. Another source of ill will was the approaching vote on a District Power Bill for public operation. Puget Power stocks had lost almost all market value, taking the savings of many people. The old president was out, the new was at the helm. Said he, "We are turning over a new leaf; if the slate isn't clean, my job is to clean it!"

FRANK McLAUGHLIN

Training Tour Continues

The new president of the Company, Frank McLaughlin, would soon take decisive action as the depression was deepening. Business conditions were decidedly unfavorable. By 1932 it was estimated that for the year the entire payroll of the State dropped 50% under the 1929 level. We engineers of the cadet course, however, were given continuing assignments.

In June 1931, I was sent to the Electron Hydro Plant located on the western slope of Mount Rainier on the Puyallup River. A room fitted for emergency use of the superintendent at the forebay became my sleeping quarters. Meals were provided at a mess hall similar to dining halls at lumber camps; this one, however, was for men doing maintenance work on the flume. We ate like loggers.

At the forebay, which had an elevation of 871 feet above the powerhouse, the view of Mount Rainier was magnificent. At sunset it glowed in red and pink colors, and after sundown the mountain was a chilling blue. At this elevation

the air was clear and summer haze or fog was below us.

My work was special assignments in the plant office and the powerhouse. When night work was needed I became a member of the crew. A special job rich in plant information was that of sorting and binding in hangers a mass of original blueprints of the plant dating back to 1903. The drawings and lettering were made by true draftsmen and were the finest examples of skilled work.

Unanswered questions are ever present at a power plant. These intrigued me. For example, at the Electron Plant there is a "beat" in the normal hum of sounds. My watch timed it at exactly 100 pulses per minute. The blueprints yielded the answer. One of the four original water turbines had been replaced with a machine of higher rating. The beat was due to a difference in buckets per wheel. So with fixed speed of the drive shafts to provide 60 cycle per second alternating current, the pulse or harmonic, when calculated, turned out to be exactly 100 per minute as confirmed by a stop watch.

Many things piqued a young man's curiosity. For example, how fast does the water travel through the 7 inch diameter nozzles just before it impinges on the water wheel buckets and looks like a stick of hard glass, at which point it is under a static head of 871 feet; and is the same water that at the top at the forebay began its fall in an eight-foot diameter penstock. Calculations showed the answer to be about 500 miles per hour. Such questions were real posers.

One morning, after a lightning storm had relayed out one transmission line, the hydro operator called our attention to the bright metal band that capped each pole piece of one of the generators which now had the colors of the rainbow as brought about by white heat. Why? These poles were not linked to the alternating current; they were separately excited by direct current. A discussion of electrical surges, traveling waves and magnetic and electro-static energy changes known as electrical transients followed. Such traveling waves have broken insulators miles away from a fault. It was concluded that the cause of the heat coloring was a surge of high frequency lightning energy which passed through the transformers and generator windings and, in a rather bizarre way, momentarily heated the bright metal bands by induced currents.

Under the tutelage of J. R. McClymont, the plant superintendent, I gained much insight of power plant operation. In September Magnus Crawford of the general offices requested I should report to him. From then on my career took on a decidedly new direction.

Helper and a Masters Degree

The note from Magnus Crawford read: "I believe your assignment at Electron is over September 1, 1931; there may be a helper job available to fill a place vacated by a man sent to Rock Island when that plant starts up. If so I will try and get this for you." Jobs were getting scarce.

After beginning to work at the substation another fellow employee came to me with a proposition. He said if we would split that helper job he would not be laid off, and we could both enroll at the University to study for a Masters degree. To this I agreed. Graduate study was attractive to me, inasmuch as I already had accumulated extra credits.

So we worked alternate periods of two weeks each on the four o'clock to midnight shifts, at the Massachusetts Street Substation. The operator, D. C. McCabe, was a former Navy man with exacting requirements for records and house-keeping. Other than that, he was a most understanding man and insisted we use our spare time in study.

Though short on sleep in two week periods, and on a Spartan diet of rice, beans, bologna and milk because of our restricted salaries, we did pursue college studies. They were mind-stretching and also gave insights into how academicians viewed the outside world of private enterprise, the utilities, government and politics. Besides working on electrical research as a thesis, I enrolled in classes of labor problems, public utilities, philosophy and German.

My thesis was quickly decided upon, for, during an interrupted fifth year at college, I had assisted Dr. Carl E. Magnusson, the dean of the electrical engineering department, on some of his research devoted to Lichtenberg Figures (also known as Electric Figures). So my thesis subject was: "Experimental Study of Electric Figures."

Dr. Magnusson carried on a correspondence with a coterie of scientists interested in electric figures, including men in Germany, Sweden, Japan and on the continent, and particularly his old friend Dr. Steinmetz, the Wizard of Menlo Park, with whom he frequently had worked during summer vacations. It was Steinmetz who had urged him to write a textbook on electrical transients.

Electric Figures are imprints of a spark formed upon the surface of a plate. We used glass photographic plates on which the sparks ionized images that were photographically recorded. They were produced under varying conditions, and one could read into them the whole theory of electrons, ions, magnetic and electri-static pheonomena. Dr. Magnusson was probably ahead of his fellow scientists.

So I was given some of the sticky, unsolved aspects for my thesis. Fortunately I stumbled upon an answer which had bugged the dean. Upon seeing my sketches, his eyes bulged out and he exclaimed, "Now I can write Pedersen!" (Pedersen was a fellow experimenter in Sweden.)

Prophetic Profs

Dr. Carl Magnusson had a sharp intellect and many interests. For example, he was an authority on the Columbia River. His published bulletins on potential power developments on the Columbia preceded by at least ten years President Franklin D. Roosevelt's interest in Bonneville and Coulee. Credit should go to Magnusson for calling attention to each of a dozen power sites. Electrical engineering students were required to take his three-month seminar on the subject, and each had to select one site and make a comprehensive report. The potentials on the whole stem of the Columbia River were well documented.

In opening his course, Dr. Magnusson would step to a large relief map of the State and, with a sweep of his arm, speak in a clipped voice, "Here on the Coast from Bellingham to Portland will be one continuous city of people — and here at the Big Bend of the River will be a million acres of irrigated farms to food them."

Politically, the campus was devoid of serious agitation. Professors were mostly conservative and cautious. Dean Tyler of the civil engineering department, having been in Germany in early 1932, came back worried about Hitler and fearing war. He was right.

Another professor did throw a verbal bombshell, and he missed his mark. I was in his class. He was James K. Hall, a lecturer in a course in Public Utilities. He was distinguished as having been the youngest attorney to graduate from Stanford University. I felt he directed his remarks at me, a graduate student and an employee of Puget Power. Rather dramatically he marshalled his facts on stocks, bonds and maturity dates of Puget Power, and pointedly said, "This power company has watered stock and will go under." He was wrong.

Years later I related this to Fred Brownell, treasurer of Puget Power, who had sauntered into my cubbyhole of an office on a quiet Saturday morning, sat down and put his feet on a corner of my desk to chat. When I said it, both his feet hit the floor. "I regret," he said, "that Mr. Hall did not know the first thing about a company's good will. Yes, a bond issue was due at that time, and consumers were in arrears by at least one million dollars, so I had asked my cashiers and collectors to explain that the Company had to meet a cash payment on its bonds, would they please pay cash — dimes, quarters, dollars, whatever they could spare — the response was amazing."

Hard Times

One late afternoon, while I was raking gravel at the back door of the substation, a man came by, walking the railroad tracks, and stopped to watch me. I spoke to him, and for conversation asked where his home had been. He said, "Chicago, where I was a jeweler. The depression drove me West."

"Riding boxcars?" was my next query.

"Yes," he answered in a flat tone.

"Tell me," I pressed, "are you left unmolested on the trains?"

"The trainmen are all right," he volunteered, "but your guard is always up, you sleep lightly and with all your clothes on, buttoned up tight and your shoelaces knotted, otherwise, someone may strip you."

"Where are you headed?" was my next question.

"I'm staying where many of us are living a few blocks from here at a shacktown we built from packing cases. We call it Hooverville, and the City Dump is only a half mile south of here which we work over daily for salvage and even for food." With this rather lengthy statement he stiffly walked away.

The next day I discovered thay my friend had cased the substation and through the open back door had noticed the wash basin and toilet facilities; on my rounds I became aware that they had been used. Three neatly lettered calling cards were propped up at the mirror. They read: "Thanks! Herbert Hoover's Hungry Hordes."

After that we were instructed, for plant safety, to keep the back door latched, and within a week a protective fence was installed at the backyard. However, understandably, the Company never did fence its huge coal pipe at the Georgetown Steam Plant, a friendly gesture to the down-and-outers.

Panhandlers

Panhandlers, men who surely at one time had held respectable jobs, now became a common presence uptown. Times were tough. College graduates were also pounding the pavements for work.

Dave, a young graduate of Whitman College and an old friend of mine, came to Seattle to look for a job. I invited him to stay at my place. After a month of looking, he came home one night and wryly reported that he almost had been clobbered by a panhandler. The man had approached him with, "Can you spare a dime for a cup of coffee and a doughnut?" Dave eyed him coldly and leveled with: "Look, Bud, get over to your side of the street. I'm working this side!" After a tense moment they parted. Dave left Seattle and in time landed a job in a clothing store in Yakima.

The Great Plains Drought

Nationally, conditions were worsening. On top of the economic depression, there also came a drought and talk of a dole. With the stock market crash less than a year old, a heavy stillness had enveloped the land. The weather had turned hot, hotter than anyone could remember. A drought was settling across a swathe of the middle states from Chesapeake Bay to the Rocky Mountains. In Arkansas, during one forty-three-day stretch, the thermometer reached 100 degrees or more on all but one day. In Petersburg, Indiana, a grocer opened up his shop one morning to find a newly hatched chick hopping on top of a basket of eggs, incubated by the heat.

This drought brought crop failures and a water famine. Streams dried up. The Great Plains were entering one of their uncommonly dry periods, bleak as never before, and the skies were the color of the earth caused by endless months of dust storms. Homes and farms were abandoned. This plight of the farmers later was dramatized by John Steinbeck in his Pulitzer Prize book, *The Grapes of Wrath*.

The Great Depression reached bottom in 1932. The price of wheat dropped to 32 cents a bushel. My wages had dropped to $100 a month, and management had voluntarily cut its salaries.

Going Up a Pole

In June 1932, I had finished my stint at graduate study at the University and was reassigned to a full time job in the Company's inspection department. Here men took load checks on substations and feeder lines, oiled and polished blades of pole top switches and made spot tests on highline insulators. Since it was summer our primary work was that of testing insulators on the Snoqualmie power lines.

We worked on hot lines. The 55,000 volt conductors were mounted on pin-type insulators. We were looking for defective disks on the insulators. The pin-type high voltage insulators are now obsolete and have been generally replaced with suspension or post type insulators, so explaining the testing is purely historical.

We tested as a three man crew, with one man staying on the ground with a clipboard to record readings as called by the other two men who had climbed poles. Readings were obtained with an "Eiler Stick," a small radio amplifier energizing a meter and fitted with a prong as an antenna. This small assembly was mounted at the end of a six-foot wooden stick, dry and waxed. When we placed the prong at the bottom of the insulator, the reading was zero; when we placed it under each successive disk (petticoat, as it was then termed), higher readings were indicated, and when the prong was on the conductor, it read at the top of the scale. If a reading was the same above and below a disk then we would conclude that the disk had a crack or was defective, and the insulator would be marked for replacement. This was preventive maintenance.

My first day with the inspection crew was spent writing down the readings as called down to me. Then, at lunchtime, I wanted them to show me how to use climbers and safety belt. I practiced climbing. By the end of the week I had my own hooks, safety belt and leather gloves, and was taking turns at climbing.

The poles were 65 feet high with a two-pin telephone crossarm attached about 30 feet above the ground. The telephone crossarm was a rest stop and morale builder. So we would climb without safety belt to the small crossarm and the rest of the way use the belt, flipping it upward as we climbed. Then with a handline we hauled up the Eiler Stick. Going up the pole was easy. Coming down was a lonely walk.

Near the end of the week, two bosses, Clyde Millar and Billy Dick, drove by and saw me at the top of a pole. It was an old pole and its butt was sound and had not rotted much because it was in swampy ground; its surface, though, was badly weathered and rotted to a depth of an inch or more, so my descent was halting — each hook was driven deeply, step by step. Clyde and Billy were shocked to see a green kid climbing, but they conceded my method was safe. I continued to climb all summer as we worked our way from Snoqualmie to Seattle.

PART TWELVE

HOW DID PUGET SQUEAK THROUGH?

Frank McLaughlin ran a tight ship. Puget Power's most pressing problem was how to offset revenue losses. First, funds were conserved by suspending dividend payments on common stock, done immediately in 1931, though dividends were still being paid on Prior Preferred and Preferred stock.

In the next year, 1932, gross earnings continued to sink. They were 14.1% under 1931. These losses were offset in a large measure by cutting operating expenses by 21% through salary and wage cuts. Again in 1933 earnings dropped 7% under those of 1932, so on January 15, 1933, dividends were deferred on all classes of stock. By 1936 the Company could again resume dividend payments.

Also helpful in reducing expenses was a 99% KWH output produced by Puget Power's own hydroelectric plants. The new Rock Island plant had been put into commercial operation on February 1, 1933.

Though by the last half of 1933 the country in general showed an upturn in business, the Company's progress was throttled by added burdens through punitive regulatory expenses and taxes singled out especially for private utilities — municipal systems were exempt. So again, on January 1, 1935, decreases were made in salaries of principal executives and several eliminations effected in management personnel.

Up by Its Bootstraps

At this point, the Company, having abundant power potential, set about to lift itself by its bootstraps. It put together an excellent sales department and effectively broadened electric sales through reduced rates, attractive merchandising and promotional effort. Featured were the load builders — the automatic water heater, the electric range and the refrigerator. Then also came the Better Light Better Sight Campaign. Handsome floor lamps could be purchased at one dollar down and one dollar a month at a total price of $12. Locally staged radio programs were beamed towards customer and community service. Through promotion and sales Puget Power pulled itself out of a hole. This is a rousing story in itself.

Two Years to Set Feet Firmly

As acute and as searing as the Depression had been to business, still another siege was being leveled at the Puget Sound Power & Light Company. It was a political assault by men of tremendous zeal who pulled out all the stops. Their purpose was to choke off funds, demoralize management by condemnation suits, impose rate cases, invite offers of purchase by cities, the state and federal agencies, and to conduct an awesome campaign directed at the dismemberment of a private utility. It began when young, liberal, socialistic office holders were elected and appointed to positions in State and Federal government. They set off tremendous waves of controversy and excitement.

Frank McLaughlin had had at least his first two years as president of Puget Power to set his feet firmly and to obtain a measure of success.

Public Power Moves Checked

When Frank McLaughlin came to Seattle, in 1931, it was assumed that he was to make a last-ditch effort to salvage heavy investments in Puget Power. Local businessmen found him a strong and decisive leader who scoffed at reports that Puget Power would not survive. To one of his new acquaintances, Christy Thomas, he declared firmly:

"Many of my Seattle contacts seem to think this company is ready for burial, but they're mistaken. With good teamwork by our officers and employees, reasonable community cooperation, and earned public confidence, it will become strong again, and an important factor in city and state industrial and agricultural expansion."

Soon the policies of the new management struck a responsive chord with the public in increased confidence reflected in turndowns of public power at a dozen local elections.

A vote in Bremerton in 1931 to extend the company franchise for ten years was significant, because in June 1929, the people had voted for municipal operation. Also in 1929 the City of Puyallup had brought suit for condemnation of Puget Power's service system, to which negotiations led to an agreement in April 1932, to dismiss the suit. Initiative measures to create so-called "power districts" in Snohomish, Whatcom, Skagit and Island counties, were defeated in November 1932 elections. Likewise, voters in the City of Bellingham decisively defeated a proposition to establish a municipal power plant at an election held on December 2, 1933.

What were the new policies of Puget Power that now succeeded in checking the flood of politically inspired elections? Frank McLaughlin, the new president, wrote, spoke and traveled. And business-like, delivered on his statements. His first objective was to build a record of outstanding service and confidence in the Company. Rate reductions became a key endeavor.

Numerous rate reductions were made for fairness and uniformity. Regarding rates, he said:

"Our new residence and farm service rate with its initial block of 40 kilowatt hours at 5½ cents represents a material reduction for previous rates and is one of the lowest in the country. Our new water heating rate of 0.8 cents per kilowatt hour designed for the storage type heaters is the lowest rate in the whole country."

For water heating the Company had researched an entirely new concept, the automatic and insulated electric

"WHAT ARE YOU DOING?" was asked of some workers.

"LAYING BRICK," one replied.

"MAKING TWELVE DOLLARS A DAY," answered the second.

But the third, gazing upward at the rising majesty of the mighty pile, replied:

NEW ROCK ISLAND PLANT

"Building a Great Cathedral!"

THE HUMBLE WORKMAN VISIONED THE GLORIOUS WHOLE; SUCH IS OUR IDEAL IN BUILDING OUR ORGANIZATION FOR BROADER AND MORE CONSTRUCTIVE PUBLIC SERVICE

By FRANK McLAUGHLIN, *President*
PUGET SOUND POWER & LIGHT CO.

WE, too, are carrying bricks; we, too, are engaged in the business of earning a living, and like the third workman, we feel that we are also "building a great cathedral." Ours is an ever rising structure of public service that brightens lives, increases happiness, multiplies man-power and motivates industry throughout the rich and rapidly developing territory which it is the privilege of the Puget Sound Power & Light Company to serve.

Not alone for today, not alone for next year must our plans be laid to meet the electrical needs of our domestic, commercial, industrial and agricultural customers. Far into future years must this program be charted to care adequately and efficiently for an increasing population, growing industries and a greater public service.

We in this organization fully recognize this responsibility, which is placed squarely upon our shoulders. Our management must become the active, vital force which takes men, money and materials and puts them to work to render a useful service for the benefit of the public who buys, of the investor who advances the money, and the

employe who labors for the success of the enterprise. Recent changes in management add new points of view and new ideals of public service to the experience of more than 30 years.

Successfully fulfilling our obligation means that:

The people we serve should obtain courteous, prompt, reliable and efficient service at the lowest possible cost;

Those who put their money in the enterprise should receive a fair return on their investment;

We should have employees who are fairly compensated for the work they do, who have the necessary technical skill, who are in complete sympathy with our ideals of public service, who are good citizens and whom you will be delighted to have as neighbors and friends.

This is the cathedral we would build. And as we build we join with the people of the entire state in constructing another cathedral —a greater state of Washington—a mighty edifice of rich resources, of great industries and of useful institutions, the home and playground of a happy people.

PUGET SOUND
Power & Light Company

water heater. Originally its tank was of monel metal, heavily insulated, and its electric elements were thermostatically controlled. It was designed and built to Puget Power's specifications, guaranteed to last twenty years.

The rate discussions carried conviction. Their merits were talked about in many ways, as in this statement:

"Uniform rates in all rural territories were adopted (1932), including street lighting and municipal water pumping schedules. The Company's residence and farm customers today pay on an average less than 3 cents per kilowatt hour. This is a decrease of 70% as compared with the average rate paid for similar service in 1913. During the same period, the per capita tax burden in the State of Washington increased 150%."

In the short span of just two years, Frank McLaughlin had evidence that he was getting through to his customers. His Company's image began to change under wise guidance. Puget became a living organization close to and respected by the people it served. But this was to be short-lived.

A Scapegoat

At the elections of November 1932, socialistic and New Deal elements took over government at the Statehouse as well as in the National Capitol. At this point, in the depths of a depression, private power became the scapegoat.

Local municipalities took their cue from these men. Political assaults by the City of Tacoma to remove all facilities of Puget Power from its streets were intensified when Puget's franchise expired in 1930. The history of Tacoma's electric system began in 1893 when voters dis-satisfied with their water service decided to purchase both the water and light properties of the Tacoma Light and Water Company. In time the City built dams on the Nisqually and Cowlitz Rivers and set a goal of having the lowest electric rates in the nation for homeowners. Its rates for businesses remained competitive. Puget Power was unable to compete with the low residential rates due to tax inequities, but continued serving some fifty business firms. On January 20, 1932, now without a franchise, Puget Power agreed to sell these remaining contracts to the City. This marked the end of the private company's electric service inside Tacoma's city limits.

His Basic Philosophy

In facing destructive opposition McLaughlin never swerved from his basic philosophy. He believed in the fairness of people and in the honesty of his fellow man who would recognize character, idealism and good sense; and that honest, candid treatment with service of the highest order was his obligation to his customers and his fellow employees. These ideals he expressed through newspaper advertisements and public statements.

For example, a "Cathedral Ad" portrayed the parable of the workman laying bricks. The illustration was the outlines of the new Rock Island Dam slanting to the future, with a cathedral towering in the background and a lowly bricklayer explaining, "I am building a great Cathedral!" As a subscript was this statement: "The humble workman visioned the glorious whole; such is our ideal in building our organization for broader and more constructive public service."

PART THIRTEEN

THEN CAME THE BIG FIGHT

When the legislators convened in 1933, for Puget Power it was the big fight and a terrific challenge. The issue was private versus public power. Emotionalism took the place of reason and logic. Legislation, license, regulatory acts, and news headlines were used with a passion against the private utilities. Much went into the pot for a bitter brew.

Tax Bias

The newly elected public power advocates in government began with a program of shifting substantial costs of government to private utilities through specific tax increases. Puget's taxes for 1934 totalled an increase of 28.4% over 1932, 63.2% over 1930, and by 1933, 122% over 1930. This bias showed also in the enactment of a state occupational tax in 1933 of 3% on electric energy, contrasted with ½ of one percent for manufacturing industries and retail sales.

On the national level a 3% federal tax on electrical energy was transferred from the consumer to the utility on September 1, 1933. Municipal utilities were expressly exempt.

Cities Permitted to Extend Lines Outside City Limits

Though repeatedly turned down by legislatures and voters during the 1920's, now laws were passed in 1933 to enable cities to extend their electric lines outside their corporate limits, free from taxes and unregulated. The act was known as the "Bone Bill." It was approved by a state referendum.

State Too Tries to Go into the Power Business

Also in 1933 a constitutional amendment was proposed for the State of Washington to engage in the electric power business, though postponed; however, in 1935 it was passed by the legislature. When referred to a vote of the people in 1936, it was defeated. This was the first setback of the public power proponents since 1933.

Regulatory Pressures

Other harassments devised by the 1933 legislature were new regulatory laws and bold moves by the State Department of Public Service. For example, it entered objections to specific items in Puget Power's 1934 budget. This was contested in Court on the grounds that the Department's action went beyond the scope of proper regulation and was an intrusion in matters of management. The Court ruled in favor of the utility.

In subsequent rate cases initiated by the Department, two were appealed to the Court and the Company's appeals sustained; these were rates for wholesale power to the City of Port Angeles and irrigation and spray pumping rates company-wide. In a South Bend water case the Department found that the property was yielding only a 4.2% return and took no action on rates.

Furthermore, in 1933 the Department ruled that its expenses in pursuing rate investigations should be paid by the subject utility. Its purpose was to carry on company-wide rate investigations and saddle the utilities with expenses.

Company-Wide Rate Case

Forthwith, the Department put into the field a corps of engineers and accountants engaged in making an appraisal of Puget Power's electric property for the purpose of a major rate case hearing. For its defense, Puget Power did likewise.

So by March 1933, in a hubbub of politically inspired rate cases, Puget Power was forced to divert engineers, clerks and accountants into the preparation of a physical inventory of its properties. Henry L. Gray, a consulting engineer, was hired to head up this project. Company engineers and linemen teamed up in pairs, driving in cars and walking, with tally sheets and rolls of maps. They listed every pole and facility, counting every piece of hardware, wire, pole and structure, complete with sizes, weights and measurements.

As an apprentice engineer, I found this to be another door that was swinging wide for me. While we men in the field took inventory of the physical property, clerks and accountants in the office tallied the field notes as fast as we turned them in. In time, each of us engineers got specific work to do, such as a separate inventory of the private telephone system serving the load dispatchers office, the wires inside conduits of the Baker River Plant, or feeder lines and control systems at the Snoqualmie Power Plant.

When the field inventory was done — for the Company to have evidence of its own — the Company transferred most of us to the executive offices to prepare this mass of information for rate case hearings under the direction of Samuel P. MacFadden, vice president. This is where we became painfully aware of the heavy pressures placed upon management. In design the overall rate case was a harassment. Much evidence revealed that the Company was not earning a return of 6% on its investment as permitted by law, as witnessed by deferred dividend payments, stringent economies, extraordinarily high taxes, voluntary rate reductions and higher costs for labor and material, and of course, the cost of the inventory.

Then in 1935 a Supreme Court ruling finally jarred the Department. In the South Bend water case the Department had brought action to force the Company to pay the Department's cost of $3,183. This was brought to the Supreme Court which sustained the Company and ruled that the statute under which the cost was assessed was unconstitutional.

So at this point the major rate case was called off. On July 26, 1935, the Department entered an order suspending further action if the Company would make effective certain rate reductions, file the appraisal and original cost study of its electric property and pay expenses incurred in the case assessed against the Company. A compromise was accepted, though altogether the cost to Puget Power in inventory and expenses was more than $1,500,000. It was the end of that intensive and expensive regulatory harassment.

Strategy and Pressures

As would happen, other executives took a shine to some of us young engineers, and at this point I began working for Lamont A. (Bill) Williams, who had been coaxed by president Frank McLaughlin to leave his job with the Seattle Chamber of Commerce and work for Puget Power. Bill was setting up the Company's advertising department.

It is strange how small encounters determine your life's course. I met Bill in a very casual way. While spending long hours on the rate case preparation, one evening on my way out for dinner I stopped to greet him. He was alone. I was struck by Bill's engaging manner, his pleasant smile and his cheery voice. So when the rate case was called off, he asked that I help him in his office.

That is exactly how a young engineer was introduced to a career in advertising. For Bill we analyzed media records, tallying the circulation of metropolitan dailies and local weeklies for each city and town, to arrive at costs of how best to spend advertising dollars. It was not surprising to learn that the Seattle Dailies held almost an even count of subscribers in each small town with that of the local weekly paper.

As an engineer with a flair for writing, the field of advertising was exciting. From our viewpoint, too, the potency and effect of political pressures on the Company hit us like a ton of bricks. We met this assault with down-to-earth efforts. Also, in the institutional field we used personalized photographs of satisfied customers giving testimonials on low rates which for solid impact were beamed for each locality. Groups of customers were selected from each of the nineteen counties Puget Power served.

It was felt Puget Power was getting through to its customers for they were buying the company's services. Additionally the Company sponsored three radio programs, the Greater Washington Hour, the Highlight Hour and a Farm Show. Telling the story of electric service was a better strategy than arguing toe to toe with an adversary over ideology.

we spent a busy five years in vigorous advertising and sales work, then when World War II brought the United States into the conflict after the bombing of Pearl Harbor, December 7, 1941, all sales efforts were brought to a standstill. All priorities were directed towards the war effort. My attention was again directed back to engineering, to the Division of Power Supply, where one of the most spectacular achievements before us was the formation of the Northwest Power Pool.

While Puget Power was busy with vigorous advertising and sales work, its adversaries were also directing campaign after campaign directed at Puget.

J. D. Ross Opines to Buy

J. D. Ross, superintendent of Seattle's municipal light department, proposed in October 1934 to the mayor and the city council that his department should acquire Puget Power's electric system in the city, predicated on his statement competition and duplication was wasteful. It made news. No real offer was made to the private company.

In 1937 he proposed a somewhat more concrete plan. Now a committee was appointed by the council to explore Ross's offer, which now was $37,370,000 for Puget Power's Seattle system together with the Shuffleton Steam Plant, the Snoqualmie Falls Plant and the White River Plant. Headlines again hit the local papers. The committee did not discuss this plan with the private company.

Later in the year the plan died. Mr. Ross left town. On October 9, 1937, Ross was appointed administrator of the newly enacted Bonneville Project Act. He had been appointed to implement the federal act. The first federal hydro plant on the Columbia River, Bonneville, was placed in operation on July 9, 1938, with two generators installed to produce 86,400 kilowatts.

(By 1944 all ten generators planned for Bonneville were in place with a capacity of 518,000 kilowatts. The Bonneville Dam was the first of a federal super power era. Forty-five years later, a second powerhouse was dedicated at Bonneville, in 1983, with an added capacity of 558,000 kilowatts, which marked the end of the era — for in this powerhouse was the last set of generators to be installed at power sites on the Columbia to utilize water storage benefits of three Canadian dams.)

So with the removal of Mr. Ross from Seattle, in 1937, his plan for purchase of Puget Power's properties died for lack of a sponsor.

Holding Company Act of 1935

A federal public utility act of 1935 had as its purpose the curtailment of holding companies such as that which had been pyramided by Insull and came toppling down in the stock market crash of 1929. To Puget Power this Act was a death sentence to financing. Puget Power was registered as a subsidiary of the Engineers Public Service Company, which had been a powerful financial contributor to the building of both the Shuffleton and the Rock Island power plants. Now under this Act the Company would be subject to broad regulation by the Securities and Exchange Commission. It would be forced to live off its own fat. With threatened condemnation suits, investors were driven away. This was another way for public power advocates to drive the private power company to the wall.

Boeing Airplane Company Hit Too

The Holding Company Act also nearly struck down the Boeing Airplane Company. Bill Boeing had been successful. He had bid low and won a Post Office contract to carry mail from Chicago to San Francisco, beginning on July 1, 1927, and took this as an occasion to form a subsidiary to run this operation, the Boeing Transport Corporation. It was a commercial venture for testing long scheduled flights with new plane designs, and Boeing became innovative and showed profits.

In 1929 Boeing enlarged further, consolidating six companies as the United Aircraft & Transport Corporation. They built airplanes, engines, propellers, carried mail and operated passenger flights.

Then like a one-two punch, on February 9, 1934, President Roosevelt cancelled all airmail contracts, ordering the Army to carry the mail, and under the Holding Company Act, forced Boeing to split his corporation into three fragments. The weakest in capital funds and lowest in backlog was a remnant, presided over by Claire Egtvedt, comprising the

Boeing Airplane Company of Seattle, the Stearman Aircraft of Wichita and a small subsidiary in Vancouver, British Columbia.

Said Harold Mansfield in *Vision,* a history of The Boeing Company:

> Egtvedt was completely wrung out. The whole organization had been working from the heart making marvelous advances in airplanes. His men came from the shops to suggest a plan of alternating work, then when the plan was put into effect, a lot of them came down on their time off and worked without pay.

Seattle, alarmed, was fearful that all Boeing operations would be consolidated in Wichita. The Seattle Chamber of Commerce promptly embarked on a campaign to "Save Boeing." The Boeing Airplane Company stayed and soon was busy developing and building the famed Flying Fortresses.

Puget Power people, members of the Chamber of Commerce at the time, ruefully asked: "Why not a campaign to save Puget Power?"

Heat from Public Utility Districts

From all directions Puget Power was confronted with aggressive socialism and political agitation aimed at nothing less than the destruction of private ownership of electric power companies. PUDs being set up wanted preferential wholesale power rates for purchase of power from the private utilities.

The public power advocates were having good success in setting up public utility districts in various counties. They were impatient to wait even for the completion of the federal hydro project on the Columbia River at Bonneville.

So they turned to the State Department of Public Service, demanding that, through the regulatory process, Puget Power establish a wholesale power rate for Public Utility Districts. Under PUD ownership Puget Power should serve fragments of its own body.

So again regulatory matters were livened up in 1939. The Washington State Grange and certain public utility districts filed a complaint to the Public Service Department asking that Puget Power be ordered to file an electric rate applicable to public utility districts and that it be required to keep records on a county-wide basis and that the complainants have access to all its records.

The Department issued an order, it was appealed to the Court and Puget Power won this one. The order was set aside.

Puyallup Votes on Condemnation

During 1939 the citizens of Puyallup again voted down a proposal that the city condemn the Company's electric property inside the city. Puget Power had pressed hard that it was a good citizen. One of the ways used to claim attention was that of stuffing the weekly and monthly payroll dollars in individual see-through plastic envelopes imprinted with large red letters, "A PUGET POWER PAYROLL DOLLAR." This flood of dollars was taken good-naturedly and helped stem the political tide.

Bremerton, too, Makes Resolution

On January 16, 1941, the Bremerton City Commissioners passed a resolution favoring purchase of the Puget Power's system in that city. On November 28, 1942, the Commission dismissed the previous motion of the city.

Bonneville Sticks in Its Oar

On September 23, 1940, the Bonneville Administration stated that they desired to present a workable plan, backed up with evidence of ability to perform, for acquisition of the Puget Sound Power & Light Company, and in order to make such a proposal, the Bonneville Administration required certain information.

Consistent with past policy, Frank McLaughlin advised that his Company would furnish such information as would be necessary to enable Bonneville to make a proposal, provided satisfactory moratoriums were made as to condemnation suits.

On October 10, 1940, Dr. Paul J. Raver, then administrator of Bonneville, did secure such resolutions from various public utility districts and filed them under Puget Power. Discussions continued until February 16, 1941, when a representative of the public utility districts announced to the press that the districts would proceed immediately with the prosecution of their individual proceedings without waiting for conclusion of discussions between Mr. McLaughlin and Dr. Paul Raver. Also certain cities indicated that, if there was to be public ownership, they preferred municipal control to county control. Again the fat was in the fire.

Box Score by 1940

By the end of 1940 the electric operations of the Puget Sound Power & Light Company were in direct competition with municipal plants in the City of Seattle and certain adjoining areas, with the City of Tacoma and adjoining areas, with Centralia, Ellensburg and in and about the town of Milton.

The formation of public utility districts had been authorized by the voters in thirty of thirty-nine counties in the State and in sixteen of the nineteen counties (all except Island, King and Pierce) served by the Company. Condemnation proceedings, excluding major power plants and transmission facilities, were pending in six counties. These troubles all were politically inspired.

To manage its finances, from Janurary 1, 1933, to December 31, 1940, Puget Power had retired approximately $15,750,000 of outstanding debt and made expenditures for construction aggregating $12,100,000 with cash derived from earnings and from the sale of the City of Seattle Municipal Street Railway Bonds. (This long pending debt had finally been resolved when the street railway system was rehabilitated.)

As of December 31, 1940, there were cumulative dividends unpaid and undeclared of $3,025,000 on the Prior Preference Stock and $13,199,750 on the Preferred Stock. The Company was up against tremendous odds.

Since September 1939, further rate reductions aggregating $1,630,000 on an annual basis were made. Taxes increased rapidly, year by year, and the Company was forced to expend large sums to protect its property against public utility district condemnation suits. During the year 1940, were it not for increase in taxes and condemnation suits, the financial showing would have been better by $779,003.

Puget Power's territory was the most competitive across the nation. The competition was highly subsidized or favored by immunities not available to private business.

"Speaking personally," Frank McLaughlin said, "I have been greatly troubled when realizing the vast expenditures made in the name of preserving democracy in this and other countries, and, at the same time, view with concern the effect of forces which are trending towards the destruction of private enterprise in this country. I believe that the cause of democracy and that of private enterprise are fundamentally one and the same. If you destroy one you destroy the other."

Employee Morale Remained Good

Just as warmth, tenacity and backbone were traits of Frank McLaughlin, so also, by and large, these traits were evident in the rank and file of Puget Power's workmen. Their morale remained good. Each was sure of his skill and took pride in his job. For example, Cecil G. Judy, a drayage truck driver, was probably the happiest workman you could find anywhere. He had driven his trailer rigs over one million miles without an accident, and any rider would swear that Judy played his seven-speed gear shift like an organist played his keyboard, double-clutching on mountain roads so smoothly a rider would not feel the changes.

Morale Builders

The salesmen, too, were by nature animated and spirited and instilled a tone of good cheer about them. They had a club which gave them impish pleasure, The Sharpen Your Feet And Drive Them In The Ground Club. It existed for one purpose, to elect as its president one of their members who had made the biggest booboo or blooper during the year. When the choice was made, a humorous caricature of him was framed for his office, and at a dinner honoring him, his sole responsibility was to pick up the tab for the cocktails.

The Personal Development Committee, on the other hand, rewarded constructive talent. For a number of years I was its chairman under the direction of Leslie Coffin, vice president and division manager. We offered a range of academic courses, and a popular series of "Know Your Company" meetings, which featured top executives.

Of these speakers probably the most sanguine was Jack Clawson, then an assistant treasurer. He brought with him his "blue" report, a totally confidential report, and explained it with complete candor. Jack began with a disarming smile, saying, "As employees these things you should know." Years later, upon the retirement of Frank McLaughlin, Clawson succeeded him as president.

A Hobby Show

An Employees' Hobby Show, sponsored by the Personal

Development Committee, was considered a good morale builder. A committee of a dozen employees mulled over the idea and went right ahead with plans to have one.

The Hobby Show turned out to be a rare novelty, for the rarest glimpses of a man's true self are revealed in his hobbies. We rented a vacant store building for a weekend and started to set up late on the Friday afternoon of the show. In our enthusiasm we almost forgot to invite Leslie Coffin, the Division Manager for a preview. When he saw it he was delighted.

There were hundreds of collections, both whimsical and valuable, including brass spinnings, woodcraft, novelties, china, coins and stamps. The showroom was packed to the walls.

An outstanding collection was a velvet panel of ribbons and gold awards from local to international events won by Helene Madison, a remarkable swimmer and a 1932 Olympic Games Gold Medalist. Helene dominated the world of swimming as no swimmer before or since, including Mark Spitz and his seven gold medals won in the 1972 Olympics. The year Helene won in the Olympics she held all 16 women's world freestyle swimming records and 56 American records. In three years she had smashed American and world records 117 times. Helene was now the wife of Luther C. McIver, a Puget Power executive.

A novelty collection that provoked many a chuckle was a young lady's display of carefully arranged wishbones, dozens of them, in sizes from a half inch across to as large as a horseshoe. Not dainty, but loud and whirring, was a homemade family-size electric concrete mixer.

Altogether, whether from the enthusiasm of a large group of salesmen, the expertise of management or character glimpses through display of hobbies, the morale of the Company's employees continued high.

Organize Their Own Union

With new national labor legislation, by 1935 workmen of Puget Power sensed that the time was ripe for them to organize their own labor union. The National Labor Relations Act at long last gave workmen protection and leverage to set up their own union without coercion or interference from management. Besides, for Puget Power employees there were other compelling reasons.

They had a nagging concern about their jobs because of a fear of their Company's dismemberment through slicing political actions by public power zealots aiming at the demise of Puget Power. An immediate event that also aroused emotions was a violent wind storm that tumbled pole lines. Emergency repairs required line crews to work a straight thirty-six hour period to restore electric service, and as was customary in those days, the men did not receive overtime pay. Times were changing.

For many years they had watched with lively interest the pattern of the whole sweep of American unionism surging about them. They believed in union organization but they did not want strikes, violence, bitterness, or to be used by subversives who infiltrated union ranks. Puget Power employees were cautious men who, by training and experience with hot wires, believed in no-nonsense and in work integrity. So they had hesitated. True, many carried union cards, loners in an open shop, and further, Puget Power had provided a means for idea input from employees through its Employee Benefit Association, to which delegates were elected from all shops and headquarters of the company. However, neither a loner's union card nor MBA membership provided firm bargaining rights.

So in a climate of concern and with advantageous legislation, linemen and other operating men seriously visited fellow employees at their homes to discuss and organize their own electrical workers' union. Their goals were to improve working conditions and wages, shorten hours of labor, get pay for overtime, and set up rules of employment. Among them were enthusiastic leaders.

Outstanding in the drive were such men as George Mulkey, Scott Milne, Fred Bird, Earl Wyatt, Red Dakers, Dave Fink, Irving Pattee, Al Major, Art Kent, Ed Hadden, Archie Lennon and Slim Nichols.

The clincher to their argument was that if a majority voted to join, then all would be members of a closed shop protection through union negotiation, as provided by new national legislation.

They succeeded. Following a period of soul-searching, slowdown and militancy, these men, through the International Brotherhood of Electrical Workers, negotiated a labor union contract with the Puget Sound Power & Light Company. The agreement was signed on April 4, 1935. Once done, workmen and management alike were glad it was over, and now all could give full attention to their regular jobs.

The first agreement was brief, its primary purpose stating that the Company shall bargain collectively with the duly authorized representatives of the I.B.E.W. as the bargaining agency selected at the recent employees' election, and that all disputes shall be settled by direct negotiation.

A memorandum agreement of a few months later, dated July 25, 1935, enlarged on the original agreement, setting forth a schedule of wage increases and adjustments effective for the period of July 15, 1935, to July 14, 1936. As a union instrument these agreements were exploratory.

In the following year a new contract was signed, dated July 24, 1936, which spelled out specifics in a form that became standard for many years. It listed job classifications, rates of pay, and specific working conditions. For the first time the subject of overtime pay also became a part of the union agreement. The regular work period was an eight-hour day for a five-day week. Overtime for monthly men would be allowed the equivalent of straight time off. Overtime for hourly paid men would be paid as double time. Also for the first time the 1936 contract was signed by representatives of Local 77, International Brotherhood of Electrical Workers.

Through the years, the union men have been articulate and forceful in their negotiations and surprisingly loyal, too. They value their union and their company. Moreover, they regard their union's history with pride. They feel they are a part of the pattern of the whole sweep of American unionism which began with the dawn of the electric industry in the last half of the nineteenth century.

Unionism in the developing Far West, however, began in the twentieth century. Its history has a flair and flavor all of its own, so to understand our electrical workmen's feelings it is necessary to know this labor history.

Labor in the Far West

The Far West wrote its own style of labor history.

Unionism in the West began in the woods. The lumber industry, Washington State's greatest natural resource, was the first to feel the thrust of organized labor. Linemen felt a kinship with them, for many had worked in the woods as high-riggers and tree toppers.

Loggers, a rough and ready breed, were no longer content in the early 1900's to spend ten or twelve hours a day at dangerous work for $1.00 to $2.00. In 1903 delegates met in Everett to form the International Shingle Weavers Union of America. They were men with the most hazardous jobs, that of snatching cut cedar shakes away from huge saws. Within the same year sawmill workers also organized. The demands of shingle weavers and sawmill workers caught employers in the bind between rising prices of raw material and a declining price for finished lumber. They did not bend to the union's demands. There followed a swelter of strikes, the first in Washington State.

Then, beginning in 1905, there surfaced another faction, the International Workers of the World, or Wobblies, as they were called. They were anarchists who believed in world revolution and were at war with society. They were brave, ingenious and violent. In clashes in Seattle, Everett, Aberdeen and Chehalis some were shot and killed. By notoriety and intimidation the I.W.W.'s gained followers. So in time many loggers in Washington woods also carried the red card of the I.W.W.

In the spring of 1917 the biggest strike the Far West had known took place. The craft unions and the I.W.W. asked lumber operators for an eight-hour-day at $3.00 in the mills and a choice for the same in camps, or a nine-hour-day at $3.50. The operators refused and formed a Lumbermen's Protective Association. In July men walked out of nearly every mill and camp in the State. This was when the nation was at war, and the War Department took a hand in the dispute. As a result most of the demands of the unions were met. The men worked an eight-hour-day and were paid time-and-a-half for overtime. In addition employers had to furnish bunkhouses with clean bedding and change the sheets and pillow cases weekly.

In the settlement of the strike two strange new organizations appeared in the woods, the Loyal Legion of Loggers and Lumbermen and the Spruce Production Division. The 4-L's, as the Loyal Legion came to be called, was a "fifty-fifty outfit, half employer, half employee, half you-know-what." They signed a pledge to help the war effort "to stamp out any sedition or acts of hostility against the United States which may come to their knowledge." When the war ended the craft unions tried to fill the vacuum left by the Loyal Legion; they failed, and that left the woods to the Wobblies, who carried on their fight as before with violence.

Also, at the time of the big strike in the woods in 1917, 1,500 street railway employees in Seattle were striking for union recognition and higher wages. Management had brought in strike breakers, resulting in battered streetcars and arrests. A settlement was reached with an open shop and higher pay.

Then on February 6, 1919, a few months after the close of World War I, a general strike in Seattle was called in sympathy with 35,000 shipyard workers, and everything in town ground to a standstill. It was the first general strike that ever took place in the North American continent. Sixty thousand men walked off their jobs in Seattle. The shipyard workers struck and asked all unions of the city to support them by a general strike. Such a strike, as a political protest, was against the policy of the American Federation of Labor. It was a strike that the labor leaders did not want.

In writing about it, Anna Louise Strong, in her book *I Change Worlds,* said:

> The General Strike Committee, composed of more than three hundred delegates from one hundred and ten unions, met all day Sunday, February 2, 1919. They faced and disregarded the national officers of craft unions who were telegraphing orders from the East . . . Yet swiftly union after union violated its constitution, flouted its national officers and sacrificed hard-won agreements to join the strike. The conservative typographical union, the property-holding carpenters union, the weak hotel-maid union, the staid musicians, the fighting longshoremen and teamsters — swung united in line . . . so did I.W.W. organizations.
>
> Suddenly on the fourth day the strike was called off by a resolution which declared that there had been no defeat, but that everyone should return to work on the following day. It was a muddled resolution in which the only thing that was clear was that the strike was over, and that nobody could tell exactly why.
>
> Actually the strike could produce no leaders willing to keep it going.

The Seattle general strike had all the elements of dire and tragic conflict, but with this awesome potential nothing happened. Men Laughed: "Our first vacation in three years." Union leaders bragged: "Sixty thousand out and not even a fist fight.

Yet only nine months later, in the sleepy farm and lumber town of Centralia, tragedy did strike from I.W.W. conflict. Now with World War I over, the I.W.W. had carried on their fight in the woods as before. Feelings were running high. In Centralia, on Armistice Day 1919, an American Legion parade unit paused before the Wobbly Hall. Inside the Hall were armed men. Others were stationed in a hotel across the street. So when the Legionnaires stopped in front of the hall the whole town seemed to hold its breath. Then there was an exchange of gunfire. When the ugly business was over, three young Legionnaires were dead, and that night there was a lynching. This ended the I.W.W. era of violence. The local loggers did not want revolution.

Judging by the foregoing highlights, the Far West certainly was writing its own style of labor history. These raw events in the struggles for union recognition did serve to give direction to men such as linemen of Puget Power, who were to organize their union in 1935. They succeeded without undue bitterness and with no violence at all.

Part Fourteen

THE LOAD DISPATCHER

From the beginning of the winter of 1932, as an assistant in the Load Dispatcher's Office, though there less than a year, I continued to have a keen interest in its operation. By December 1941, at the outbreak of World War II, I again was assigned work in the area of the Load Office, making power supply studies and preparing the Company's weekly reports to the newly established Northwest Power Pool.

The Power Pool was the biggest phenomenon to take place in the Northwest in the electric power business, and the load dispatchers were the key men in its operation. They are a rare breed and deserve a place in the history of Puget Power.

The crew of dispatchers are a very wholesome and cheery lot. Back in 1932, as I recall, since it was wintertime and my work was from midnight till eight o'clock and then to bed, I hardly ever saw daylight. Lark Livermore and Harry Wille, the dispatchers on the evening shift, showed sympathy. With a twinkle in his eye Lark explained, "Art, in this job you are a night owl. As I now think about it, my twin boys were fourteen before I first saw them in daylight."

Scotty Ewart, a relief dispatcher and an old-country Scotsman, enjoyed telling of his boyhood. He had been a curtainboy for Harry Lauder, the renowned singing comedian. One evening at the finale of his show Lauder had finished taking his bow, but the curtain did not fall. Lauder looked in the wings, saw Scotty asleep on a high stool and promptly boxed his ears. Whereupon Scotty lost his balance and sprawled on the stage. As Scotty put it, "Then there was a real comedy!" His background showed in many ways. Once when I told him of a good buy (I had paid $325 for a two-year-old Chevrolet sedan with two spare tires in fender wells), Scotty abruptly reminded me: "When you drive a bargain too hard you're a thief." This was a terse reminder that in 1932 our nation was in a deep depression.

Between themselves the dispatchers maintained excellent rapport, when at his desk each man is pleasant but all business.

His Duties

The dispatcher's job evolved with the beginning of the electrical industry. Just as a steam engineer was in charge of a steam plant and an operator in charge of a power substation, so when these were linked by power lines, the load dispatcher was charged with the duty of coordinating all facilities. He must regulate the supply and the flow of power of an integrated electrical system. In electrical parlance, he proportions the "load" to the best advantage between power plants over a network of power lines.

His office is the nerve center of the system, the point of control. The dispatcher runs the command post for all switching orders to avoid duplications and conflicts. Also, in case of outages, he alone can quickly pick up loads through systematic switching orders. Power plant operators and substation men report to him hourly, and they report any change from normal immediately.

Working in isolation, he is a man of infinite forbearance and calm control. He is always alert to service failures, power interruptions, rush hour traffic, storm conditions, reservoir storages, switch outages, loads, over-loading, changes in voltages and changes in frequency. If there are interties with neighboring utilities, he conforms with contractual agreements.

Perhaps to an outsider the most interesting duty is to take care of sudden interruptions. Then indeed his place is the busiest in the building. Now he thinks and acts almost at the same time. Normally there are two men on a shift, and in case of storms as many as six men may be needed to handle all switching orders. The dispatcher can chart the path of a storm by the outages as it sweeps for miles.

The Tools of His Trade

Before him is a diagram board, extending from floor to ceiling and arcing the room, on which are drawn all power lines, color-coded for different voltages. Shown also are all switches on lines, in power plants and in substations. Moreover the miniature switches on the board are lighted, green or red to show at all times whether they are open or closed. Lines and switches are "tagged" on the board just as in the field when men are working on them.

Within reach and sight are multiple means of communication and metering. There are line-drawing meters for power loads, voltage, frequency, and barometric pressure. In the old days a Naval Observatory timepiece was a must, so that the 60 cycle current ticked off total number of seconds each 24-hour day; now the timepiece is a computerized IBM clock. Assisted by the tools of his trade, and with experience the dispatcher's mind is continually weighing the impacts upon the power network.

Telephone lines were the early day communications between the dispatcher, the power plants and the substations. The telephone wires were even more vulnerable to falling trees than power lines; so carrier-current telephone was added, using the high voltage wires themselves. More recently micro-wave and radio have become part of the network. Also, today, for each service area Puget Power has its own radio transmitters arranged in the "mother hen" idea, serving clusters of radio receivers in trucks and cars.

Communications extend to neighboring utilities, and each transmission line intertie is remotely metered, with telemeters mounted on the dispatcher's desk so he can monitor all outside tielines. And more, automatic supervisory control of whole power plants and switching stations center in his office. In 1985 these varied functions were con-

MODERN POWER DISPATCH CENTER of Puget Power, located at Redmond.

solidated in a computerized single system.

Computerized Energy Management System

In late 1985 dispatchers and system operators were given a computerized energy management system, so that the dispatcher will be able to sit at a console and know instantly what is happening on the transmission and power generation network, for accurate and fast response to system problems.

The facilities consist of four large computers and associated equipment, as magnetic tape drives, disc drives, and large memory units. Located throughout Puget Power's area are 18 consoles and more than 60 remote terminal units.

This energy management system provides many functions, as instant information of power flow, reactive power flow, line voltage, location of equipment failure, weather reports, energy scheduling and prompt accounting. Furthermore, the computer system will provide data to analyze specific parts of the network for surveillance of over-loading and for meeting future growth.

Planning this computer system had been in the works for a long time with input from many engineers and on the job personnel, in design, specifications and testing. It is a modern-day marvel.

Blackouts Need Not Happen

When the Electric Building became the headquarters in 1910 of the Seattle Electric Company, Room 601 on the top floor was the Load Office. Here the first group of load dispatchers hammered out plans and policies to cope with emergencies that were so soundly conceived they still are valid.

In the twenty years following, very practical rules were formulated by these pioneer dispatchers. These men were: Wiltse Mathis, Gould Mathis, Harry Wille, Lark Livermore, Claude Noble, William (Scotty) Ewart and Floyd Parker.

They had to cope with blackouts. Power blackouts were not new to them, for on dark days the voltage would sag, frequency slip, and circuit breakers pop open. One practical solution was to establish the concept of a "north" and "south" bus in Seattle. This way they split the system and prevented a total failure. In time, when the White River Plant was put into service and all power lines were brought there to a switching station, the switchyard at White River then became the "north" and "south" bus for the power network.

Eventually in the experience of these same men, interties were made with other utility systems, such as the Western Canada Power Company and the Washington Water Power Company of eastern Washington. They were called upon to improve their techniques. Finally, in 1942, with the creation of the Northwest Power Pool comprising interties between eleven utilities, both private and public systems, solid plans again were instituted for handling blackouts.

The proven technique is that today, in case of major power failure, each utility in serious trouble separates from the Power Pool; proceeds to shed load so it can build up its voltage to normal and frequency to 60 cycles; then it may get help from a neighboring system to pick up power loads; finally, it will again synchronize with its fellow pool members.

This plan has been severely tested, and it works. So today, through hard and harsh experience, the load dispatchers are convinced that the Northwest Power Pool members will never be subject to a massive blackout as occurred in New York, November 9, 1965, when cascading and uncontrolled relaying of power ended in a blackout, plunging much of the Northeast into darkness for 12 hours.

Following the New York blackout of 1965 the electric utilities in the eleven western states and British Columbia of Canada formed the Western Systems Coordinating Council, to set uniform operating practices; to continue studies on operating methods and improved technical plans so as to insure against the probability of massive power blackouts.

Special Pride

The Load Dispatcher corps is a proud and dedicated group of men. They plied their trade back in the late 1890s when central station power was first begun. In the ensuing years they pioneered techniques which enabled them to supervise the operations of a vast network of power lines and plant facilities, which in the Northwest Region is a power pool that spans across two time belts that had become by 1985 a pooled total of 37,666,000 kilowatts of instant surging electric energy.

From its beginning the load office has functioned every hour, twenty-four hours a day, every day including Saturdays, Sundays, and holidays, with men working the day shift, the night shift, and the graveyard shift, through wars and even earthquakes. They have a remarkable record of service.

Part Fifteen

COMPANY INTERTIES

In the Northwest, interties with other utilities date back to nearly the turn of the century.

Forerunners of the Northwest Power Pool

A Puget Power intertie with the Western Canada Power Company was cut in on August 4, 1916. The City of Tacoma was synchronized with Puget Power on September 13, 1916. The electrified Milwaukee Railway, being served jointly by Puget Power and the Washington Water Power Company, brought about a cross-state tie in 1919. A report on this interconnection said:

> At five minutes past four, on the 20th of August, 1919, the closing of a switch at Snoqualmie Falls, had sychronized Snoqualmie with Long Lake, and approximately 1,500 miles of transmission lines had been interconnected, extending from the eastern borders of Idaho to Olympia, and from Pendleton to Everett.

The significance is that in arriving at these distances, two other utilities also were intertied, the Washington Water Power Company and the Pacific Power & Light Company.

An interchange of power between Seattle City Light and Puget Power was provided for 30,000 kilowatts with the signing of a contract on August 3, 1937. Appreciable savings would be effected through efficient use of generating capacity from the combined systems by better use of surplus hydroelectric kilowatt hours.

Other systems too were interconnected. The Washington Water Power Company and the Montana Power Company were interconnected in 1923; the Northwestern Electric and Portland General Electric in 1925; the Utah and Idaho Power companies in 1928; the Northwestern Electric, the Pacific Power & Light and the Washington Water Power Company in 1930. In 1941 a major transmission tie was built between Montana Power and Utah Power, which brought together the above six utilities into a power pool. With their operation of one year before the larger Northwest Power Pool was formed, success was assured for the larger pool from the start. Bonneville also joined the cities of Seattle and Tacoma in 1941.

The Northwest Power Pool

In July 1942, kilowatt-hours were pooled in the Pacific Northwest for war. Without building a single power plant, 100,000 kilowatts of additional electrical generating capacity was made available for war industries through interconnection of all major power systems in a five-state area. This was a super power pool.

It was a war drama with peacetime implications. It was a pooling of 3,400,000 kilowatts generating capacity into one of the world's greatest power reservoirs and combining power resources of all private, municipal and federal systems in the states of Washington, Oregon, Idaho, Montana and Utah. The country was at war, so political animosities were set aside on power production.

Eleven power systems were intertied. They comprised 150 power plants, 130 privately-owned and 20 publicly-owned. These were:

Portland General Electric Company
Norhtwestern Electric Company
Tacoma City Light
Seattle City Light
Puget Sound Power & Light Company
Bonneville Power Administration
Washington Water Power Company
Pacific Power & Light Company
Montana Power Company
Utah Power & Light Company
Idaho Power Company

There were other important sources of generation such as Eugene, Oregon; Centralia, Washington; and a number of industrial power plants, including sawmills, pulp and paper mills.

One thing the European and Oriental mind did not understand was how we in this country, with our competitive enterprise system under democracy, could so quickly and cooperatively put over a great undertaking. Any diverse political opinions were subjugated to the one aim of winning the war.

Great Diversity

The diversity between hydroelectric power resources obtained by pooling was tremendous. On the eastern part of the Montana system there were plants located on the Missouri River, a stream which finds its way finally into the Gulf of Mexico. Its watershed lies east of the Rockies. Plants on the Columbia River — Bonneville, Coulee and Rock Island — responded to water resources that had two main forks, one rising in the Canadian Rockies and the other the Snake River, rising in southern Idaho. They were fed from areas different in rainfall and snowfall. Power plants on Puget Sound and the Pacific slope were in areas of heavy rainfall and deep snows on streams that flowed into the Pacific Ocean from the western slopes of the Cascade Mountains. The Coast plants had ample water storage from winter rains, the Columbia had its low stream flow in the winter, which, however, peaked in June.

So under the power pool, electric power is shifted back and forth across a vast network of power lines in such a

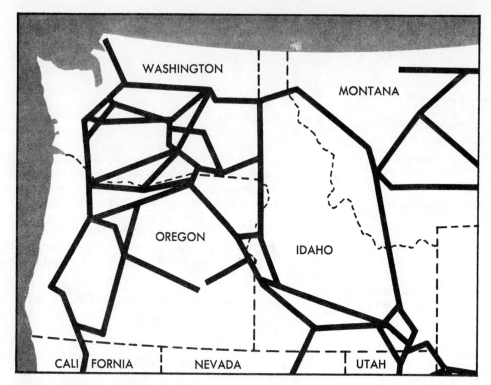

THE NORTHWEST POWER POOL
A network of high-voltage transmission lines connects all the generating plants in the Northwest with each other and with the areas where power is used. Cooperating utilities are then able to match power supply to power demand throughout the entire region.

way as to take full advantage of this great diversity in water resources.

Moreover, the pool enabled regions with little war load to pump surplus power into the 13,000 mile web of power lines and make it available where needed. It saved burning thousands of barrels of critical fuel oil and thousands of tons of coal by substituting hydro power. It was a good-neighbor deal, whereby all systems would pitch in and help another that might be in trouble, perhaps due to storms. Systematic scheduling of shut-downs for repairs were set up. Even the daily load peaks, which occurred near sundown, were relieved because of time-belt differences. The eastern part of Montana has a two-hour time difference from the Coast, so power reserves would flow east, then west, as the end of the day approached across the wide region. Darkness moves 1,000 miles an hour.

This diversity afforded an instant supply of 100,000 kilowatts in pooling resources, a saving of $25,000,000, which would have been the cost of building a 100,000 kilowatt power plant and transmission lines. This added power in pooling was immediately available.

Operating Organization

Matters pertaining to pool operations were placed in the hands of a committee composed of one man from each of the pool members. Each was given full authority by his management to act in all operating matters, an important factor in the success of the whole operation.

At monthly meetings special problems were discussed at length, and at an hour-long weekly telephone conference, reports on resources outlook, maintenance outages and current problems were raised. Weekly written reports prepared by each pool member were also exchanged.

To manage the smooth running pool, four full-time engineers located at a central office were kept busy with resources studies, making graphs and developing sup-

porting data, to determine critical years and set up basic philosophy of pool operation. Simulated line faults were made on calculating test boards to find bottlenecks and to remedy them.

Billing Power Exchanges

Energy billing of exchange purchases was unique. The pool did not buy and sell. It functioned somewhat as a stock exchange board. Members made their own contracts for purchases from each other; the transfer of power was on a basis of scheduling deliveries from the pool, such as "in" or "out" fixed amounts of electric energy for specific hours of the day or night.

It is dramatic to sit in the dispatcher office and observe the telemeters of interties as the peak comes on. Telemeters show all the individual tielines between neighboring systems and the net "in" or "out" on a totalizing meter. Curve drawing instruments trace a red line, exactly as automatic controls at power stations monitor power deliveries as pre-set by the dispatcher.

How Water Is Stored

As a basic philosophy of pool operation, no water is spilled that can be converted into electrical power. It is stored in a reservoir somewhere in the pool. For example, if Lake Shannon is full, which is the reservoir for the Lower Baker Plant, while Long Lake near Spokane is down, then the Baker plant is run at full load day and night, while generators at Long Lake are shut down or run at light load, permitting stream flows there to raise the lake level. A reservoir might have energy stored in it for the account of several pool members. For clarity we may think of the energy as being stored in layers of water.

Growth

The Northwest Power Pool has been truly one of the industrial wonders of the Pacific Northwest. Set up for war-time conservation of electric energy it has grown phenomenally, in both public and private power. In 1985 about 50% was federal. From 3,400,000 kilowatts of pooled energy in 1942, it totalled 25,000,000 kilowatts by 1975, and 37,666,000 kilowatts in 1985; though in 1985 it comprised the four states of Montana, Idaho, Oregon and Washington, now under a legally constituted authority of the Northwest Regional Power Planning Council. At first there were three Columbia hydro plants. Now there are eleven on the Columbia and many, many more on tributaries. With full development by mid-1970s generation reached a plateau.

Era of More Power Ends

Additionally, through a Columbia River Treaty of 1964 between Canada and the United States, three storage dams were built in Canada and one in Montana, to add large increments of beneficial power downstream — to squeeze 2,800,000 kilowatts more prime energy from the Columbia. The Bonneville Power Administration had exhausted the Columbia River's hydro capacity. There were no more big cheap sites left.

To the Bonneville Power Administration the hour of decision had arrived. For forty years the federal government had built huge hydro projects and a vast transmission grid to deliver power at cost to preference customers and to expand sales. Now it could not guarantee power for future growth to anyone. It sent terse termination notices. In 1973 BPA cut investor-owned utilities off from a firm power supply; it informed its direct sales customers (as aluminum plants) that it probably would not renew their contracts when they expired in the 1980s. In 1979 BPA notified its public agencies that it might be unable to meet their future needs.

Consequently, there followed a scramble by over 100 utilities in the Northwest to secure energy sources in an economy of rising inflation and high interest rates.

The private utilities spent enormous funds to build coal-fired and nuclear projects; nor could they keep electric rates low by melding their high-cost energy with low-cost federal hydro power. The public agencies formed a consortium, The Washington Public Power Supply System (WPPSS), and took on the ambitious task of building five nuclear power projects—only one was completed, the other four went into default. And the aluminum plants were shutting down.

Alarmed, congressmen of the western states, their governors, and the utility leaders, saw that new enabling legislation was needed to set priorities straight; and with shared resources avoid rate jolts. They went to Congress.

Northwest Regional Power Planning Council

After four years of congressional debate, on December 5, 1980, President Carter signed the Pacific Northwest Regional Power Bill, which was consumer oriented that created an 8-member Power Planning Council, of two members each from the states of Montana, Idaho, Oregon and Washington, appointed by their respective governors. This gave home rule to energy resources. The Council was also mandated to sort out and plan the energy future of the Northwest Region.

Led by the former Washington governor, Dan Evans, a 20-year energy plan was drafted and put into effect April 28, 1983. The plan relied heavily on conservation, on development of small hydro sources, cogeneration with industrial businesses, on combustion turbines for peaking, and on coal-fired plants for future energy needs.

The energy plan was a well meaning document. It was to change the course of future energy demands in the wake of dramatically rising costs. All utilities were to cooperate. The private utilities would have access to BPA power, and with BPA guaranteeing to purchase the output from new generation, utilities would have a means for financing new construction, and Bonneville legally prohibited from building its own generation, would have the future resources to satisfy its customers.

Part Sixteen

ACTION PACKED FORTIES

The decade of the Forties was action packed and harrowing. The decade began with a global war of many battles and its related political, diplomatic and economic struggles. Many men and women employed in war industries were all subjected to sacrifices, including meat rationing, gas rationing, sugar and butter curtailment, blackouts and guarded areas.

In the middle of the decade the war ended, with V–E Day declared in Europe when Germany surrendered on May 7–8, 1945, and V–J Day in the Orient with the surrender of Japan on September 2, 1945. Then came the assimilating of homesick G.I.s back into a peacetime world.

The State of Washington made two unique contributions to World War II. One was the superb Boeing-built Flying Fortress, and the other the Hanford Engineering Works, where an army of 50,000 workers and their families had moved into the hastily built tar paper city of Hanford and under rigid security began the production of plutonium in sufficient quanitity to create atomic bombs. It was a Flying Fortress that dropped an atomic bomb on Hiroshima on August 6, 1945, and three days later Nagasaki was the target of a second bomb.

The electric power companies had referred to Hanford as " The Mystery Load." George Quinan, chief engineer of Puget Power, a voracious reader of scientific papers, later admitted that he had surmised the nature of the Hanford effort but had kept his opinions to himself.

When peace came he commented that he had noticed at the outbreak of the war that published works on radium by Madame Curie, a Nobel Prize Winner, had been quickly withdrawn from libraries, and also he heard echoes that "heavy water" was in big production at Hanford. Heavy water is deuterium oxide produced by electrolysis of water. These clues led Quinan to suspect the production of plutonium.

Splitting the atom had already been conjectured in the Thirties by two Nobel Prize winning physicists, Ernest O. Lawrence, developer of the cyclotron, and Robert A. Millikan, known for his work of measuring the charge of an electron. Ironically, it was the war effort that gave us atomic power.

Achieved Three Critical Goals

While shafts were thrown at Puget Power with growing intensity, it was able to achieve three critical goals of its own, and the year 1943 was to be a milestone in the history of the Company's progress. It refinanced its debt, it recapitalized its stocks, and it met the federal order of divorcing itself from its holding company, the Engineers Public Service Company. Business conditions had reached a new high, and peak demands for electricity set new records. To this business stimulation, Puget Power's

management was very sensitive and forthwith achieved these goals. From them, too, Puget Power drew new spirit and vitality.

Puget Power refinanced its outstanding bonds in April 1943, by the sale of $52,000,000 of 4¼% First Mortgage Bonds due in 1972, and by placing bank loans of $6,000,000 bearing 3⅛% interest and maturing serially over a five year period. The bank loans were placed with one Eastern, one Midwestern and nine State of Washington banks. Proceeds from the bonds and the bank loans were used to redeem existing mortgage bonds maturing in 1949 and 1950. This refinancing was highly advantageous in view of the uncertainty as to the future of Puget Power, and $873,000 were saved annually in interest and other charges.

It recapitalized its stocks with a formula for each class of stock of providing additional shares and some cash in settlement of all accumulated and unpaid dividends.

Finally, on September 13, 1943, Puget Power divorced itself from the Engineers Public Service Company to comply with the Public Utility Holding Company Act of 1935. Puget Power had been registered as a subsidiary of Engineers under the federal Holding Company Act, and in 1940 the Securities and Exchange Commission required Engineers to dispose of its interest in Puget Power. In the 1920s and the 1930s much help had been given to Puget Power by Engineers. It was through Engineers that funds were obtained for construction of the Shuffleton Steam Plant and later the Rock Island Dam. Engineers lost heavily in this compliance with the federal government.

This overall perceptive reordering was done by the company so it could deal from a position of strength in the agonizing crucial days ahead. All indications were that the various public agencies would separately and in consort press mightily to dismember the company.

To Puget Power the goals achieved were golden. Through the refinancing and recapitalization, its earned surplus would be lifted from zero in 1943 to millions within the next ten years. Also, the average annual return on its property would stand at 6 percent, notwithstanding doubling of wage rates, material costs and taxes. Furthermore, being no longer a subsidiary of Engineers, a registered holding company, Puget Power was not subject now to the jurisdiction of the Securities and Exchange Commission.

Observes Sixtieth Year

The year 1945 marked sixty years of history of Puget Power. In 1885 a predecessor had formed to provide electricity for the first time in Seattle, and now Puget Power paused a moment to celebrate.

With professional players and actors from its Radio Show, the Company presented a 45-minute dramatization of its beginning and the highlights of sixty years of growth. It took place before a packed luncheon meeting of the Seattle Chamber of Commerce.

At the start of the show, lights were dimmed in the banquet room, and actors strolled on-stage, then at the signal of a trumpet fanfare, a Town Crier in an excited voice declared: "Ladies, and Gentlemen, we are about to witness a marvelous spectacle! You will see the beginning of a new and luminous science — here and now — EEEE-LEC-TRICITY!" He continued, "Before us, in this little power-house, when the dynamo is started, instantly, this room will be brilliant with a clear white light!"

Then, with appropriate "oh's" and "ah's" the strolling actors onstage viewed a string of eleven luminous 16-candlepower lamps that festooned the room and one 30-candlepower lamp at the doorway. That was how this electric industry began in the dim past of sixty years ago. The show continued.

The finale was truly a high point. Now with a powerful fanfare, this time with all the brass in the orchestra sounding forth double forte, the Town Crier came forward again and with a voice pitched higher repeated: "EEEE-LEC-TRICITY!" Then on cue the whole banquet room was bathed in a dazzling white light. Everywhere along the perimeter of the four walls 1000-watt floodlights placed there before the show now flashed their brilliance on walls and ceiling, energized from a veritable powerhouse placed in the alley outside.

The audience left, infused with the force of the story, though it knew that the script had not mentioned how Puget Power was being choked in a web woven by zealots, placing it in the throes of the most turbulent and tormented time of its history.

Multiple Political Onslaughts

On the following pages are detailed the predatory actions taken by public agencies, intent on putting Puget Power out of business. These were certain cities, the Federal Government, the State and various county Public Utilities Districts. Together they were creating a maze of political uncertainty. These intensely ambitious public agencies, each jealously guarding its prerogatives, were jockeying to top position in the conquest. Their multiple actions resulted in a situation which was complex, fluid and volatile. Puget Power was sitting on a powder key, as it were.

This siege on private power was both local and national. Locally it seriously began in the Deep Depression with the sanction of county-wide public utility districts in the Washington State legislature of 1930. To villify the power company was a ready political forum. On the national level, to promise full development of the Columbia River by the people was a popular appeal to voters, made by the newly elected president, Franklin D. Roosevelt, who, first elected in 1932, remained in office for a fourth term, until exhausted by wartime duties, collapsed and died. Harry S. Truman became president on April 21, 1945. He, too, applied the public ownership pressures as under Roosevelt. The siege of Puget Power was to continue for the amazing period of more than twenty years.

Regarding the onslaughts on his Company, and pleading that a constructive solution was urgent, Frank McLaughlin, of Puget Power, told his stockholders in 1949:

Puget is afflicted with a sort of perpetual uncer-

tainly which has a paralyzing effect. This Company is in no sense master of its destiny. The solutions of Puget's problems do not lie within the province and control of management. It cannot plan intelligently nor function effectively. Instead of able statesmanship dedicated to bring order out of chaos, in some cases the moral aspects are quite shocking. It is tragic that there is sabotage of constructive effort. Puget does not know where the axe will fall next. The woods seem full of 'obstructionists' who would 'tear down' what they cannot 'build.'

Bare Bone Facts

Though the nation was engulfed in war, political proponents of public power were hacking away on the home front. Their tactics wrenched at the soul of Puget Power. The Company had mobilized for the war effort, yet it was being overwhelmed by a dozen condemnation cases at home.

When the United States entered the war after the bombing of Pearl Harbor, out of loyalty the Company mobilized for all-out victory, making supreme efforts. Three thousand employees were on the home front backing up their 500 associates on the fighting front, and electricity remained unrationed.

Meanwhile by 1944 the costs of living had risen 32% in the past ten years, yet Puget Power declared a rate reduction in 1941 and again in 1944, attaining for the same ten years a 42% reduction in the cost of electricity. Moreover, by 1945 the Company's taxes soared to 26% of revenue. All this was understandable. The cost of electricity was not a factor in the power battle. So to be assaulted from within at a time of war was sickening.

The very leaders of government, to whom all respect and loyalty were due, were driving relentlessly to gain political aims — to dismember and to take over all private power companies in the State.

Unmindful of war stresses, condemnation suits were carried to the Courts. Awards affecting Puget Power were declared as follows: Whatcom County, August 7, 1940, $5,000,000; Thurston County, May 10, 1942, $4,400,000; Lewis County, May 10, 1942, $2,100,000; Cowlitz County, May 10, 1942, $1,100,000; Snohomish County, March 19, 1943, $9,500,000; and Clallam County, July 5, 1944, $600,000. Cases in Chelan, Douglas, Jefferson and Kitsap Counties were dismissed in 1944 for want of prosecution. Values set by the Courts were approximately twice what the Districts said the properties were worth.

Only Clallam County went all the way and took over the property. Piecemeal condemnation was not an idle threat. However, PUDs did not like the high costs.

Seattle Says, "No Franchise Renewal"

On November 29, 1943, the Seattle City Council passed a resolution to the effect that it was the intention of the City to expand its facilities so as to take care of the entire electric power and light load within the City when Puget Power's fifty year franchise expired in 1952. From 1905, when the City took over its street lighting, it had built a competing electric system. With some second thoughts, in

February 1944, the City Council appointed the Bonneville Administrator to act as agent in negotiating a purchase of the Company's properties within the city.

Said Frank McLaughlin of Puget Power:

> By declaring the Company out of business in 1952 the City had hogtied, hamstrung and prevented the effective functioning of the Company. As far as capital improvements and betterments to its Seattle system, the City in reality has declared the Company out of business now.
>
> If the City were not growing and the electric business were a static one there would be no immediate crisis. It was most unrealistic for the City to declare the Company out of business and then expect it to obtain reasonable assurance that those who put up the money will get it back. What is happening in Seattle is proof of the pudding that the only way to preserve private enterprise is to keep government out of business. The situation is an impossible one where a government which has the say as to whether or not you can live, is also your business competitor.

Years later, towards the end of 1947, the Seattle City officials took initial steps that led to the City's purchase of the Company's properties at a fair price, by employing the engineering firms of Ford, Bacon & Davis of New York and the Carl D. Pollock Company of Seattle to evaluate the advantages to the City of such an acquisition.

BPA Administrator Makes Offer

The Bonneville Administrator, on March 18, 1944, wrote letters to the Directors of Puget Power stating they desired to acquire all the Company's electric properties for a price of $90,000,000 as of December 31, 1943. This was a bid by the federal government. On April 13, the Board of Directors replied in substance that a bonafide purchase proposal had not been made, and that they had not hung a "For Sale" sign on the Company's property.

Referendum No. 25

Shortly after this notice came the heaviest threat and challenge to the private electric companies. A State Referendum No. 25 was to be voted upon at the November 1944 election. It was a so-called political power bill, with its immediate objective the elimination, by condemnation or otherwise on a statewide basis, of all private electric utilities. It revealed clearly the federal government's hand to reach in and dominate the power field in the Northwest.

Referendum No. 25 was a red hot political issue. It was a regular bombshell. Of it Dave Beck, the vice president of the powerful Teamsters Union, said:

> The worst feature of Referendum 25 is that it would set up a soviet to manage all of our electric power industry in the state. Get this straight — sovietism and socialism have no place in the scheme of things for free labor unions . . . American Labor does not want socialism. We know we will fare better as free men and free Unions, dealing

with free industry.

The referendum was decisively defeated. The people of the state wanted home rule of their power resources.

Guy C. Myers Proposes

On January 16, 1945, Guy C. Myers of New York City, who had actively promoted the sale of utility properties to public power agencies in Nebraska and elsewhere, and who for ten years had been working with public power groups on plans for the acquisition of the Company's electric properties, wrote a letter to Puget Power, stating he had a banking group interested in financing the purchase of the electric properties of the Puget Sound Power & Light Company for the purpose of transferring such properties to various Public Utility Districts and cities. He would be the sole negotiator. To this the Company replied that it would make available the requested information. Mr. Myers failed to supply a fair proposal backed by evidence of ability to perform.

Valley Authorities

During the early part of 1945 two bills were introduced in Congress for the formation of a Columbia Valley Authority, embracing the States of Washington, Oregon and Idaho, as well as parts of Montana, Wyoming, Utah and Nevada. Always in the background was the concern as to what might be done on a national level affecting electric users in the State of Washington. The national government had already pre-empted development of the Columbia River; in fact, by the Forties it was the major producer of electric energy in the Northwest.

The creation of a Columbia Valley Authority would give control of the economic life of the Northwest to the New Dealers, which they had long cherished under President Roosevelt, and now under Truman it was again revived.

The objectives of these bills were the same as those of the Tennessee Valley Authority. They stirred up much controversy because they were in essence "planned economy" measures and would circumvent state rights. Men of the West still had strong instincts to manage their own affairs. Governors Langlie of Washington, McKay of Oregon, and Robins of Idaho appeared before hearings in Washington, D.C., to oppose the CVA legislation.

The two bills died with the expiration of the 79th Congress. The 80th Congress was also unable to do more. But pressures continued. On January 24, 1949, President Truman directed a number of government departments and agencies to begin work immediately on legislation setting up a Columbia Valley Authority. Nothing new was consummated in either 1949 or 1950. Locally, government spokesmen campaigned vigorously and intensively during both years to gain acceptance of a CVA. Efforts continued for twenty years. There was to be no CVA.

Why should there be a CVA? The Bonneville Power Administration had been set up under a Federal Act and J. D. Ross, superintendent of Seattle City Light, on October 9, 1937, was its first administrator. There were no real shortcomings in the Act. Under it and subsequent directives, federal electric power was sold at cost delivered through its transmission grid, with preference or first call given to municipals, PUDs and cooperatives. Industries and private utilities would get what remained. The Bonneville Act was most liberally administered.

Pro-Public Power Policies

The administrator of BPA got his directives and support from the Secretary of the Interior, Harold L. Ickes, of Washington, D.C., who was direct and adroit in expanding the government's electric power network at the expense of privately owned companies. Below is an excerpt from a memorandum on Power Policy, dated January 3, 1946, sent to all staffs and departmetns, titled "Operations and Sales."

a. Active assistance, from the very beginning of the planning authorization of a project, shall be given to the organization of public agencies and cooperatives for the distribution of power in each project area. The statutory objectives are not attained by merely waiting for a preferred customer to come forward and offer to purchase the power . . .

f. No contracts shall be made that operate to foreclose public agencies and cooperatives from obtaining power from Government projects. Contracts with these organizations shall recognize their preferential character and assure them full opportunity to secure the benefits of Federal power. Contracts with privately owned companies shall be limited in time and shall contain provisions for the cancellation or modification by the Government as necessary to ensure preference to public agencies and cooperatives . . .

i. Public agencies and cooperatives which are existing or potential customers of the Federal project shall be given every assistance in promoting sound programs and operations.

The Bonneville Power Administration exhibited much zeal and fervor when it came to expanding the Interior Department's power policy.

Peacetime Power Shortages

Peacetime demands started a resurgence of growth. The year 1946 was bigger and busier than any previous year in the state of Washington's peacetime history. Unexpectedly there was an electric power shortage.

The population had increased about 25% since 1940, and war workers were not leaving. Demands for lumber in 1946 were in excess of supply, the fishing industry enjoyed a good year, the 1946 tonnage of food production was the greatest in the state's history, and the Boeing Plant in Seattle had a large backlog of orders, including 198 planes for both military and commercial use and several experimental projects. Business was booming.

Just after VJ Day, Paul Raver, of the Bonneville Administration, said, "Though cutbacks in war loads left us with a power surplus of about 500,000 kilowatts, our market studies indicate that prime loads far in excess of our immediate losses can be developed."

This was far off the mark. It turned out that the aluminum loads started picking up tremendous chunks of power,

taking about half of the BPA firm power generation, and otherwise demands for power by small industries provided another strong push in power use.

Within one year after VJ Day the Bonneville Power Administration admitted that a power emergency existed in the Pacific Northwest. Its hydro power was not sufficient to meet the demand, so it became necessary to operate the steam plants of the Northwest Power Pool in the winter of 1946 as well as for several years later. Immediate action was needed. There was a serious energy crisis.

On November 8, 1946, the Bureau of Reclamation announced that contracts had been awarded for three additional 108,000 kilowatt generators to be installed in the right powerhouse at Coulee, with all to be operating by October 1949.

Joint Statement of Power Policy

In the meantime the utilities in the Pacific Northwest were alarmed. They prepared a joint statement of policy addressed to the Corps of Engineers and the Bureau of Reclamation, stating in essence that the future economy of the Pacific Northwest depended upon construction of multiple purpose projects on the Columbia River and its tributaries, that the Federal Government, by numerous Acts of Congress, had assumed responsibility for the construction of these projects, that the assumption of this responsibility had caused investors and management of both publicly and privately owned distribution enterprises to plan their projects and programs on the basis that Federal policy would continue, and that the maintenance of an adequate power supply was of extreme importance.

Conferring with Federal agencies concerned, these spokesmen had given careful consideration, first, to power requirements by the years through 1953, and second, to the need for backbone transmission circuits to bring power to the region's load centers, and as a result, they had determined and agreed that new Federal generating capacity in the amounts of 1,063,000 kilowatts were required by November 1, 1949, and another 1,565,000 kilowatts were required by November 1, 1953.

This statement of policy for future power supply was made by the Northwestern Electric Company, the Pacific Power & Light Company, the Washington Water Power Company, the Portland General Electric Company, the Puget Sound Power & Light Company, and the Seattle and Tacoma municipal plants. They pressed their appeals before Congressional Appropriations Committees, and many other organizations also presented similar testimony.

The limited supply of electric power from the Federal projects again worked to discriminate against private power companies. BPA would first take care of its public agencies in accordance with preferences given in the Bonneville Act; it would take care of private utility company loads above and beyond those which the private companies could handle themselves; that is, the private companies had to bear the expense of operating steam plants, while public agencies obtained their increased needs from BPA, and BPA would take care of its existing industrial customers. Especially during the power shortage BPA operated to shut out private power companies.

Learning from this grim lesson, the private power companies would in time build their own plants in order to never again be solely dependent upon Government Power.

BPA Sets Goals

From its inception under the Federal Act of 1937, the Bonneville Power Administration was given sweeping programs for building hydroelectric facilities both in power plants and in transmission lines. Congress had been liberal with funds. Through the Federal Power Commission, which has authority for granting site permits, the BPA pre-empted all sites on the Columbia River, and in later years the Commission gave preference to Public Utility Districts to the exclusion of private power companies.

Furthermore, BPA was able to pare down apparent costs by bookkeeping methods by assigning large expenses to flood control, irrigation and navigation. Its power rates were thus subsidized. Private power companies are not given credits for flood control and environmental requirements at all.

So encouraged, BPA's larger goals were set forth on November 8, 1948, when the U.S. Army Engineers issued a public notice and held hearings of a comprehensive program for the development of the Columbia River and its tributaries.

This "308 Report" called for expenditures during the next ten to twenty years of more than three billion dollars for recommended projects, which would provide 6,000,000 kilowatts in addition to projects already authorized. Those already authorized were Grand Coulee, Bonneville, Hungry Horse in western Montana, McNary in Oregon, Detroit in Oregon and Chief Joseph in Washington. These six projects had a capacity of 5,000,000 kilowatts, so with the new proposed projects, the total goal of BPA would be 11,000,000 kilowatts.

PUDs Make Joint Purchase Offer

The next form of concerted action aimed at Puget Power was a proposal for purchase of all the Puget Power's properties and assets and payment of all its obligations and liabilities, made on August 14, 1945, by the public utility districts in the Company's territory.

They proposed to issue around $135,000,000 of public utility revenue bonds. The proposal also spelled out that the alternative to the acceptance of their offer was their acquisition of the Company's property and business by other means, viz., condemnation, duplication and destructive competition. The Company was given ninety days to call a special stockholders' meeting to act upon the proposal.

No meeting was called. The Company felt there was a lack of reasonable assurance of the districts' ability to perform; furthermore, there was a real question of their legal right to join in a purchase.

A test suit to determine the validity of the proposal was tried in the Superior Court, and the Court ruled in favor of the districts. The case was appealed to the State Supreme Court. On June 16, 1947, this Court handed down a 5 to 4 decision holding invalid the public utility districts' purchase proposal. So, from this point on, Puget Power sat on a powder keg of explosive condemnation suits intended to dismantle this close-knit electric company.

Sale of "Fringe Properties"

Though the first property of the Company to be condemned and sold was that in Clallam County, taken over by the PUD in 1944, which produced only about 1% of the total annual electric revenue, now in 1948 upon receiving what was considered fair offers, Puget Power sold its electrical properties (excluding power plants) in Cowlitz, Mason, Chelan, Douglas, Grant, Lewis, Pacific and Grays Harbor counties. The aggregate price was about $14,000,000. They constituted about 6% of the total book value of the Company's electric utility plant. Revenues and number of customers involved were both about 10% of the total for the Company. They were fringe operations. The remaining property comprised the heart of Puget's system.

Sales of Subsidiary Properties

On September 20, 1945, the Company sold its gas properties in Bellingham and in Wenatchee, and on December 22, 1945, sold its telephone properties on Vashon Island. These were minor properties obtained years ago along with predecessor electric systems. On October 22, 1947, the North Coast Transportation Company, also a subsidiary, was sold to the Greyhound Corporation in excess of $3,000,000. These were belt tightening sales.

Snohomish PUD Goes into Business

On August 27, 1948, the Snohomish County Public Utility District filed its second condemnation suit. It would entail about 12% of the revenue and 15% of the electric customers of Puget Power. At a previous award a jury had placed the value at $9,500,000 as of March 19, 1943. This had been rejected by the PUD as too high.

Now under the gun of a second suit set for trial in the U.S. District Court for August 16, 1949, the Company, on September 1, 1949, sold its electric distribution properties in Snohomish County and on Camano Island to the Snohomish PUD. The price paid was approximately $16,500,000 plus accounts receivable and was considered fair.

Guy C. Myers Was Key Man

In various suits Puget Power had staved off major sales to PUDs up to 1945. Then when a new series of suits were brought against Puget Power, its resistance seemed to cave in and suits tumbled towards sales. Now in 1948 PUDs in the counties of Cowlitz, Mason, Chelan, Douglas, Grant, Lewis, Pacific and Grays Harbor brought condemnation suits and secured Puget's fringe properties for an aggregate value of $14,000,000. Why now?

In these sales the key man had been Guy C. Myers. He was a personable financial operator from Nebraska and New York, now advisor to the PUDs. He was regarded favorably by both the PUDs and Frank McLaughlin of Puget Power. Being on a commission he was inclined and able to raise the price. Myers was able to produce high purchase awards. Myers achieved a shrewd point through the sale of the Snohomish County properties. This was a large body of Puget Power. Now he could hope to force Puget Power into an overall sale of its remaining system.

The floodgates were now opened and cities and others were also eyeing Puget Power. Shortly Puget Power's hydro plants too were layered with condemnation suits.

Tacoma Condemnation Proceeding

On April 6, 1949, the City of Tacoma filed a condemnation proceeding against the Company for acquisition of its White River and Electron hydro plants, together with certain transmission and distribution lines. The Thurston and Kitsap County PUDs were named as additional defendants in the Tacoma action, having previously filed condemnation actions involving the same hydro plants. These proceedings were striking at the heart of Puget Power's operations.

Expansion of Rock Island Project

In an attempt to forestall and prevent immediate federal seizure and the possible confiscation of Puget's Rock Island hydroelectric project on the Columbia River, the Company and the Chelan County PUD, on December 19, 1950, agreed upon the basic elements of a plan for joint expansion of this plant. Under the cloak of a national emergency (Korean War) the Federal Government under President Truman had planned to take over Rock Island.

The Rock Island project had been built by Puget Power in 1930–1933, including the dam and four generators, with provisions for the ultimate capacity of ten generators. Now Puget Power and the Chelan PUD entered into a 50-year lease and operating agreement for the expenditure of $25,000,000, to be obtained through revenue bonds for adding new gates on the dam and to enlarge the plant in progressive stages from its initial 80,000 kilowatts to 245,000 kilowatts, by June 1, 1953.

Viewed in retrospect, this was the first ray of hope for a solution of the chaotic battle between public versus private power, with a view of letting both live. This was the beginning of a partnership concept, of private companies and public utility districts building hydro plants together, with costs shared in the proportion of plant capacity each would want to finance. To private power companies it pro-vided the access to Columbia River hydro power. And, at long last, to each the cost of wholesale power was the same, a new competitive fact of life.

Box Score at End of 1950

Though doing business in a topsy-turvy situation of unbelievable uncertainty, even so, Puget Power's finances and earnings looked surprisingly good by the end of 1950. Its gross revenue had risen from $14,915,000 in 1940 to $26,636,000 in 1950; net earnings in 1940 were $1,659,493 and in 1950 stood at $4,270,558. This was obtained though Puget Power had lost fringe properties of its system to PUDs and one solid core area, the Snohomish County operation, and it had sold its gas, telephone and bus subsidiaries.

Puget Power's management was ever alert. In recognition of its obligation to stockholders and at the same time to retain financial flexibility in the event of further dismemberment, on May 31, 1950, it redeemed 137,500 shares of $5 dividend Prior Preference Stock at $110 per share and accumulated dividends. Funds for this were secured principally through a ten-year note of $15,000,000 bearing 3% interest from the Metropolitian Life Insurance Company. The annual savings of this refinancing amounted to about $300,000.

At this time there was no private utility in the country which was as maligned by public power as was Puget Power. In his annual report to stockholders Frank McLaughlin wrote:

Due to condemnation suits Puget's position has become unbelievably complicated. It is the grip of a demoralizing uncertainty with a dozen axes ready to chop its system to pieces. It is the height of absurdity for anyone to think that Puget can have continuity in business under such conditions . . . these condemnation acts impose a death sentence . . . there is no other private utility in the country which is victimized as is Puget.

Consequently, considerable time and patience are required to keep the record straight and to make progress in such a topsy-turvy situation.

PART SEVENTEEN

EMPLOYEE INSIGHTS

Significantly, in the 1930s and even more so in the 1940s all Puget Power employees showed a real concern for their jobs. The bombardment by public power advocates made them feel like they were working in a shooting gallery. Employees had the disquieting feeling that their jobs were in jeopardy when fragments of property were involved in condemnation suits by PUDs

Supervisors See Need to Organize

So in 1935 the supervised workmen, to secure collective bargaining under new favorable national social legislation, joined the International Brotherhood of Electrical Workers, Local 77.

Supervisors, on the other hand, also a sizeable group, did not want to join a labor union, for they believed they were part of the management team. Witnessing in the 1940s condemnation suits sweep from courtroom to courtroom, these craggy and toughened leaders did organize in 1947 for mutual unity and protection — not as a union — but as a supervisors' association.

For their self-interest they needed to be able to speak with the force of an organized group, especially when their jobs were also threatened through impending sales of Puget Power property. So they achieved group action by forming the Puget Power Association of Supervisors.

They assessed dues to build a war-chest should legal action be needed, and through the years have become a vital and valued influence in the operation of Puget Power.

They made immediate impact. When actual dismemberment of Company property took place, in 1948, 1949 and 1951, their demands for severance pay for those losing their jobs were honored. Severance pay amounted to as much as a full year's salary depending upon years of service.

Moreover, one of the stated purposes of the association was to promote the well-being of Puget Power. So through the years many ideas have been reviewed and agreeably implemented by the management. Such items include: Better communications, empathy and sympathy between departments by a planned program of joint functional meetings, supervisors' handbook on policy and information, handbook on interpretations of union contracts, group term insurance through payroll deductions, retirement program and pension plan, modification of pensions for early retirements with only minor penalties, job and salary evaluation for better balance of responsibilities and pay, reimbursement for home relocation when moving to a new job, investment program by payroll deduction and professional management of these funds, a weekly news sheet, "Puget Briefs," for prompt release of information to supervisors and all employees before given to the news media, and a sustained liaison between the Association and the president of Puget Power. These were not done all at once, of course, but the effort is a continuing one.

The Supervisors are a group of men of exceptional skills, for they are able leaders. In general they are leaders in their community, active in Rotary, Chambers of Commerce, Elks, Masons, Lions, Kiwanis, PTAs, churches, Boy Scouts, United Way, fairs, hospitals, Red Cross and also in trade and business associations.

So, when it comes to running their own association, the supervisors do it with flair, deftness and cordiality. Though the subjects discussed may be knotty problems, their business meetings appear as casual social meetings.

For more than a quarter century now they have been a vigorous group and have been able to attract new recruits.

Poking Into Research

Every office and division was a segment of the whole of Puget Power, and no employee anywhere was ever free from the slicing and oblique attack of public power advocates. I felt it in sales, general offices, power plants and now in 1946, as director of Puget's Experimental Laboratory. Even so, the few years I spent there were happy ones, and the story of the Laboratory is a vital one in the history of Puget Power.

In the early part of 1945 when World War II was expected to conclude I received a friendly call from Charles Wildebour to join him for lunch. Charlie, a former division sales manager and now director of the Experimental Laboratory, was an inventor. Among other things he had devised an electric soil sterilizer for greenhouses and for specialty gardeners. His latest idea was a scheme for a gas hose valve (now standard for gasoline station pumps) which would shut off unattended when a car's tank was full. Charlie wanted my ideas on his shop's future.

We had a stimulating discussion, and at his suggestion I wrote down ideas, a half dozen for each of Puget's sales areas, commercial, industrial, farm and home service. Some were serious; others were facetious. Here are a few:

Control the static on printing presses — a printer's bugaboo — by first giving a positive charge to the moving sheets, then by electro-static controls balance this with a negative charge and that way wipe off any charge.

For the farmer, go all out in devising electronic devices such as electric eye systems for counting apples, bulbs, seedling plants, bunches of carrots, or seedling nursery stock. Also, redesign hay driers to replace the crude wooden air ducts with streamlined ducts to hopefully double their efficiency.

For social betterment, to ease the disturbances to sleepers in small towns awakened by train whistles, it was suggested to design a parabolic reflector for the train's air blast so that the sound was projected straight ahead down the track giving warnings to those at crossings; there would be no stray sound to distract those asleep in homes.

With tongue in cheek the following ideas were detailed: Develop a siren for the farm, which would begin in the audible range and rev up to the ultra high sound above audible range. When started, the siren would alert the cows to come to the barn for milking. At the ultra high range it would pain the robins and bluejays in the blueberry bushes and cherry trees and drive them away; furthermore, as the cows brushed past the barn door, this high pitched sound wave would kill flies and break wings off mosquitoes. For stock investors, interested in new ventures, we suggested that a new kind of public utility company be formed. It would invest in a central station tobacco burner, located in the heart of a city, for piping tobacco smoke to office buildings. At his desk the cigarette smoker would have a choice of Old Gold, Lucky Strike, Viceroy or Chesterfield for a clean, cool smoke from a selection of tubes to which he could clip his cigarette holder. Nicotine would be extracted at the central station incinerator as a by-product and sold for orchard spray as Black Leaf Forty.

The report was sent to Charlie Wildebour. His interest did not stop there. He next asked for my thoughts on the operation of the Laboratory. Seriously the advantages and disadvantages of its present location in Puyallup situated near the Experiment Station of the State College were detailed, and also those as they pertained to a location in Seattle near industry and the University of Washington laboratories and its libraries. Also, it was stated that the director should not report to the general sales manager, but to top management, presumably to a vice president.

The point to all this was that the Company's personnel manager advised me that Wildebour was leaving to work for the Pacific Car & Foundry and that I was to succeed him. So on June 1, 1945, I began a new venture, as director of Puget's Experimental Laboratory, on the terms I had spelled out, reporting to Pat Johnson, vice president.

The Company's Laboratory was started by John C. Scott, when he was hired as Puget Power's first agricultural engineer in 1926. At the time electrical devices for farm use were unthought of, so through research labor saving devices were developed, and in helping the farmers become more prosperous by providing new methods to save labor, the Company too would profit. Regarding the history of the Laboratory, George W. Kable, while editor of the magazine Electricity On the Farm, said:

> No other institution in the United States has put out so many original ideas for the use of electricity on the farm as has the Puget Sound Power & Light Company alone and in cooperation with the Western Washington Experiment Station of the State College. I am constantly running into these in operation in different parts of the United States.

Glen Cushing, working under Scott's direction was first to experiment. Cushing had an insatiable interest in hobbies, was a trained machinist, and also was an experienced electric power salesman. He started making devices in his home shop.

The first electric hotbed used in the United States was built by Glen Cushing at his home in Puyallup and tested by him in 1924. Its development was a dramatic story. Soon American-made heating wire and cable were being sold in many parts of the world for many uses, including electric panel heating of homes. Other devices created in the Laboratory make an imposing list, most of them having been designed for poultrymen, orchardists, holly growers, bulb farmers, pelt growers, dairymen, greenhouse operators and horticulturists.

Thinking back, as many another experimenter and research worker discovered, I found this new work to be most satisfying; and recall telling my boss that with our ideas and other people's money we should have fun.

I was at the Laboratory only a few very eventful years. Now in the post-war period the promise for new developments was very bright. It was the time of robot guided trans-Atlantic airplanes, jet-propelled missiles, excitement over orbital flights, atomic power for peacetime uses, flying saucers and many push-botton appliances.

But with the imminent dismemberment of Puget Power by public power advocates, the Laboratory was closed, and on June 16, 1948, I was off to another assignment, that of assistant superintendent of the Lower Baker Power Plant. Again I was in familiar surroundings.

The impact of the heavy hand of public power men had not been lost on me. Management had given me extra work to do at the Laboratory, very much apart from pure research. For some months it was to examine the minutes of exhausting meetings between Bonneville Power Administration and Puget Power regarding Northwest Power Pool "wheeling charges," the cost of transmitting purchased power over B.P.A. transmission lines. Negotiators were repeatedly at a stalemate. B.P.A. men made inflexible demands. Their minds were fixed as granite. It was obvious that they were only interested in wearing out, tiring, and demoralizing Puget's men. My assignment was to brief and document evidence for the possibility of the Company presenting it at a Congressional Hearing. The hearing, as it turned out, never was held. Under President Eisenhower the political atmosphere changed, and Puget Power again breathed freely.

Changes and Innovations

At the Baker River Hydro Plant, situated in the foothills of Mount Baker, Mount Shuksan and the snow-capped peaks of the Cascade Range, we were in an area of extreme winters. Puget Power maintained a weather station at the plant, and for two of the three winters I stayed at Baker River the annual snowfall measured 104 inches. Snow plows cleared single lanes on downtown streets of Concrete, leaving a center strip four feet high, so that driving there was like driving through snow tunnels. Some winters were marked by heavy rains too.

This was at the time of peacetime power shortages in Washington State (1947 - 1952) when the Bonneville Power Administration had pre-empted all developments on the Columbia River but had failed to pace its growth with power demands. So, here again, the impact and rigidity of public power was very evident. BPA's discriminatory allocation of power to its preferred customers was forcing private power to run their expensive standby steam plants and to make stringent economies. For example, all employee cottages at the hydro development were converted from electric heat to oil heat — to save electricity.

Also, a very prudent move was to rewire generators at the

various hydro plants, using a new concept in coils for upping generator output of 20% to 30%. The new coils had mica insulation which permitted more copper and higher temperatures; moreover, the coils were placed in the slots with "Raebel" transpositions which overcame eddy current heating. These were innovative and inventive measures.

Power plant work was interesting and invigorating; however, early in 1951 I was called back to Seattle, to take over the position of advertising director and editor of the monthly magazine, *Puget Power News.* I was reluctant to leave the area of rugged outdoors where also I learned to appreciate the honesty and directness of workmen, some who liked to make things go with brute force, horsepower and profanity.

In my new work I worked with men of subtlety and suave manners and was thrust directly into a swirl of events of the most trying times of Puget Power.

The sale of Puget Power's Seattle properties was under way, so in closing down our local operations we had to say "no" to many people, while the ideological fervor of the public power people was at its highest pitch. Also heavy court battles and actions reached feverish level. In the heat of the battles I remember telling my boss, Pat Johnson, that all I would have to do to meet the exigencies of my public relations work was to change the masthead of *Puget Power News* to *PUDget Power News.* This was a time of torment, peril and relief.

PART EIGHTEEN

HOT TENSIONS DISSOLVE

There was a hot war in Korea (1950–1953) and a cold war in Berlin, and to Puget Power the years 1951, 1952 and 1953 were also weird with confusion and paralyzing with uncertainty. In his report to stockholders in 1951, speaking in a context of the world situation and of a man living in his home, Frank McLaughlin wrote:

It continues to be about as difficult to constructively resolve the critical power problem in Puget's service area as it is to bring about world peace. Just as the world is gripped by 'hot' and 'cold' war crises, tensions, frustrations, uncertainty, perplexity and insecurity, so is Puget. With the world it is the 'Hammer and Sickle.' With Puget, it is the 'Condemnation Axe.' He continued, Perhaps the best way for you to get the feel of the situation is to imagine you are living in a house while a gang of workmen are busy demolishting it.

Fight Builds to Crescendo

Within the span of these three years, Puget Power's fate hung in the balance as the battle for survival swirled with mounting intensity across courtroom and boardroom. In rapid actions it divested itself of its Seattle properties, entered into discussions and an over-all sale to the PUDs which fired up violent moves, and also fended off a red-hot controversy over a merger with the Washington Water Power Company. By now, with its cash reserve of millions, Puget Power was an attractive financial plum, and in an over-all sale or a merger it was adamant in demanding cash on the barrelhead. At last, in a most dramatic way, Puget Power remained in business.

Sale of Seattle Properties in 1951

The Company sold its electric properties in the Seattle competitive area to the City of Seattle on March 5, 1951, for a price of approximately $27,000,000. It represented about 25% of Puget Power's total plant and 40% of its 1950 revenues. This was a loss to Puget Power of 80,230 customers.

The plan began to perk in the minds of the City officials in 1943, when the City declared to do all the light and power business in Seattle when Puget Power's franchise expired in March 1952. The City was in the driver's seat from every viewpoint, so the Company took the alternative to negotiate a sale. It was felt that the solution of the dynamite-laden Seattle power problem, under the circumstances, was fair to all concerned. John M. Nelson, the superintendent of the City Lighting Department, negotiated with sincerity.

As a condition of the sale, Puget Power agreed to supply the City with 83,500 kilowatts of firm power until February 28, 1953, when the City would have new generation from its Ross project. The price was 4 mills per KWH. Puget Power's average revenue per kilowatt-hour was around 13 mills, so the replacement of the 4-mill electricity upon expiration of the contract would materially improve its earnings.

The fact that the Seattle Lighting Department was able to pay cash for the Puget Power property was most revealing of its earning power. The war years had been profitable, and the City also held an enormous advantage over its private competitor in that it paid no federal or local taxes, even though the electric rates of the two utilities were the same and the business was about equally divided between them.

To illustrate: Puget Power's taxes paid in the 10-year period prior to the sale, 1941–1950, were $57,400,000. Segregated for the Seattle operations of Puget's for the same term the totals were $18,200,000 — $8,400,000 federal income taxes, $2,000,000 federal taxes on sale of electricity and $7,800,000 state and local taxes. Operating under the same rates for sale of electricity, the tax subsidy to the City produced a tidy amount of earned surplus for it, with which it bought out its competitor, the private power company.

Sale of Steam Heat System

On October 24, 1951, the Company entered into an agreement of sale with the Seattle Steam Corporation, which was incorporated by steam heat users to conduct a steam heat business and to acquire Puget Power's central heating property. The price was $417,000. The purchasers were a group of large downtown property owners who bought the system in the case of self-protection. It has since become a very successful operation.

Battle for Over-All Acquisition

Now in rapid-fire actions like bullets on a target, events and decisions impinged upon Puget Power's management in a battle that became a triangle. The PUDs were pressing for an over-all purchase of its facilities and power plants, the Washington Water Power Company was countering with a merger proposal, and Puget Power was caught in a new cross-fire and was fighting for self-determination.

The PUDs now had a clear legal right to go on the offensive. The State Supreme Court, on February 23, 1951, had affirmed the constitutionality of the 1949 State Law enabling county-wide Public Utility Districts to jointly acquire Puget Power by an over-all purchase plan. They began to move decisively. The Washington Water Power Company, serving portions of eastern Washington and northern Idaho, in a red-hot divestment issue had wrested dependence from the American Power & Light Company. It now sought a merger with Puget Power to head off the over-all sale to PUDs and to keep the Puget Sound Power

& Light Company in the ranks of private enterprise. The third party to the contention was, of course, Puget Power, and its president, Frank McLaughlin, was playing his cards close to his vest, facing querulous men on all sides of the negotiation table, including at one point a challenge by a minority stockholder suit. The events and actions can best be explained in chronological sequence.

In November 1951, R. W. Beck & Associates prepared a report for his clients, a group of Public Utility Districts, outlining performance and financial results of PUD operation of Puget Power's electric system on the basis of an assumed purchase price of $93,000,000. This report was the first of many steps to be taken. There were seven interested PUDs — Chelan, Jefferson, Kitsap, Skagit, Snohomish, Thurston and Whatcom.

On January 3, 1952, the Western Investment Banking Voluntary Credit Restraint Committee of San Francisco, set up during the Korean War, declined to approve the application of the PUDs for the issuance of $115,000,000 of revenue bonds, approximately $96,000,000 of which were proposed to be used to finance the purchase of the electric properties and certain current assets of Puget Power. Their reason for the turndown was that the National Voluntary restraint Committee requested postponement during the period of the War Emergency purchases of privately-owned utilities by municipalities which involved borrowing to replace equity capital.

So the purchase proposal made in 1951 remained unresolved. By its sheer complexity of conflicting interests, all seven PUDs had not yet accepted the terms of the proposal.

On September 10, 1952, now six PUDs (Whatcom had dropped out) presented an offer to purchase all the utility properties of the Company, except certain parts used in serving Whatcom County. Whatcom was adamant and stayed out. The proposal was a firm offer, and the Company was faced with the very real threat contained in a letter dated September 11, 1952, from the six PUDs that stated if the stockholders did not accept their offer they would immediately proceed with piecemeal condemnations. A special meeting of stockholders was called for October 21, 1952.

Another campaign surfaced. A letter dated October 9, 1952, sent by the Washington Water Power Company to Puget Power, proposed negotiations to work out a merger between that company and Puget Power. Furthermore, knowing of the October 27 call for a stockholders' meeting, the WWP conducted a letter writing and newspaper advertising campaign to induce Puget Power shareholders to vote "No" on the PUD purchase proposal or to revoke their proxies if already given in favor of the sale. Kimsey Robinson, president of WWP, was vigorously trying to squelch attempts of the PUDs to seize Puget Power.

All factions were on hand on October 26 at Boston, the day before the special stockholders' meeting, pursuing intense bargaining behind closed doors all day and well into the night. Frank McLaughlin, Puget Power's president, was the chief target. With him were Lowell Mickelwait, his attorney, and Jack Clawson, his treasurer. No matter how decisions and bargains were struck that day, McLaughlin had in his pocket proxies of over 80% of the shareholders' votes. The PUD negotiators were camped there, as were representatives of the Washington Water Power Company,

and some minority stockholders. It was a tense day.

The minority stockholders were knowledgeable men who were edgy because they knew that large chunks of Puget Power's property had been sold piecemeal to the PUDs, leaving power plants most of which were of old vintage in the hands of the Company. They favored a merger with WWP. The PUDs felt confident that they could deliver on a purchase plan, and with cash they would buy shareholders' stocks above market value. Still, at the close of the day the private power men had won their point on merger with WWP; they had argued persuasively that at this time nowhere was a private power company going to public ownership except in the Puget Power area.

By the end of the day, word reached the PUD camp that Frank McLaughlin would recommend a merger with WWP the next day. Now the PUD negotiators were incensed. That night they bore down on McLaughlin. They had invested heavily in the purchase plan. They had already threatened by letter that if denied they would immediately start condemnation suits, cutting up Puget's property even while it would be busy getting approvals for a merger from the regulatory commissions. They could totally stop such a merger. They would release the forces of public power, the State Grange, the State Federation of Labor (A.F. of L.) and other powerful interests. They would vigorously oppose a merger with WWP while also cutting up the Company by condemnation suits.

By next morning McLaughlin had made his decision. Then at the special stockholders' meeting called to vote on the PUD proposal for an overall purchase of Puget Power's property, the vote was taken. Its results, however, could not be revealed then due to a temporary restraining order.

On November 6, 1952, after the Boston Court had vacated its temporary restraining order in the minority stockholder suit, Puget Power executed the Purchase Agreement with the six PUDs. The vote at the October 27 meeting had been 84% favorable. That stirred up other action.

On November 7, 1952, a C.E. Ferguson, having been newly elected as a commissioner of the Kitsap PUD, filed a suit against the Kitsap PUD and obtained a temporary restraining order enjoining the Kitsap PUD from taking any further steps to consummate the six-District purchase.

On November 19, 1952, the majority commissioners of Kitsap District adopted a resolution assigning to the other five Districts jointly the rights of Kitsap PUD under the Purchase Agreement with Puget Power and consented to the acquisition by the other five Districts of Puget's properties located in Kitsap County. This the other five PUDs accepted the same day.

On November 20, 1952, the plaintiff Ferguson, without any notice to the other parties in the action, obtained an amended temporary restraining order which restrained the Kitsap PUD from continuing to consent to the acquisition.

On November 25, 1952, Puget Power joined with the six districts and made an application to the Supreme Court of the State of Washington for a Writ of Prohibition to restrain the Kitsap County Superior Court from enforcing its order of November 20.

On December 1, 1952, the plaintiff, C. E. Ferguson, took office as a commissioner of the Kitsap PUD, and the majority which had previously favored participation in the purchase was thereupon reversed. He and J. W. Bryan that day held a meeting at which they adopted a resolution purporting to revoke and rescind the consent given on November 19 by the Kitsap PUD.

On December 2, 1952, visiting Judge Max Church presided over the hearing in the Kitsap County Superior Court, at which a supplemental complaint was filed, which added another plaintiff, George C. Lewis, and alleged that the consent of the Kitsap PUD was invalid. Judge Church continued the entire matter over until January 20, 1953, and the two restraining orders were continued in effect until that time.

On December 9, 1952, Puget Power commenced action against the Washington Water Power Company in the Chelan County Superior Court against the Boston minority stockholders and J. W. Bryan and C. E. Ferguson alleging that if the sale were prevented by the activities of the defendants, Puget Power would be damaged thereby "to the extent of millions of dollars," and asking a judgment for whatever damages are sustained.

Late in the afternoon of December 31, 1952, a suit was filed in the Thurston County Superior Court for the purpose of restraining Thurston PUD from participating in the joint PUD purchase of Puget Power's property. The plaintiffs in this action were Kitsap County PUD and two of its commissioners. No temporary restraining order was obtained. And so the fate of Puget Power was precariously delayed at the end of 1952.

On January 12, 1953, the Thurston District filed its answer and requested an early trial date. February 16, 1953, was fixed as the trial date.

On January 10, 1953, Puget Power received from the Washington Water Power Company a preliminary draft of material having to do with a merger. On January 16, after full consideration by its Board of Directors, Puget Power forwarded to WWP its comments, set forth its position on basic matters and raised specific questions to which answers were desired.

On January 21, 1953, Puget Power received a letter from the president of WWP, Kimsey Robinson, enclosing a copy of a resolution by its board. This time the conditions were much more attractive; however, it stated that, "If the termination date is to be extended beyond February 27, 1953, of the PUD Purchase Agreement, the Washington Water Power Company may be forced to discontinue negotiations with respect to the merger."

By letter, on January 27, 1953, Puget Power informed the Washington Power Company that at this time it was unwilling to commit itself not to extend the closing date of the District Purchase Agreement. Said president Frank McLaughlin to his stockholders:

> If Washington Water Power had been able to come up with a cash-on-the-barrelhead type of proposal, it would have eliminated the risks to Puget and its stockholders inherent in a merger, and would have presented an entirely different sort of situation.

Puget Power's battle to survive had now been fought tooth and toenail for more than twenty years. Frank McLaughlin had become a master strategist. Just what was in his mind now? Was he still buying time? Was his acquiescence to the overall PUD purchase plan only an action to hold condemnation suits in suspense? Now with his back against the wall, was this a delaying action to give time for a new national administration to take office in March 1953 and finally end the New Deal? Was the dilemma of a merger with WWP a case of bad timing, a bad bargain between his company nearly debt-free being sought by the WWP to improve its equity? The events of the future turned out well for the Puget Sound Power & Light Company.

Descent into a Maelstrom

Puget Power, like a ship that had weathered the lightning flashes and buffeting of twenty years of stormy socialistic winds gusting from all sides, now was inextricably caught in a descent into a maelstrom. It went circling and scudding down into the vortex. The ship, with quickening speed, was carried faster and steeper, racing down the glistening slope of a gigantic whirlpool headed for destruction.

In the meantime, its skipper, Frank McLaughlin, was in the pilot house smoking his pipe, preoccupied with a masterly chess game and playing for keeps. In the chess game, the "Pawns" had been separate sales of fringe properties. Through such condemnation sales over a period of years he had sacrificed ten of the original operations of nineteen counties.

"Knights" and "Bishops" were used with finesse to distract, defend and diffuse the siege. These were refinancing, rate reductions, recapitalization, sales of subsidiary properties including telephone lines, gas companies and bus lines; also the preoccupation with an overall sale to the PUDs.

Even his "Queen," the Seattle service area, was sacrificed through sale to the City of Seattle in 1951. But his "King," the backbone system of power lines and generating plants, was continually protected.

The crucial move in the long, drawn-out chess game was the over-all purchase agreement by PUDs, or on balance, a merger with the Washington Water Power Company. These actions became a national debate. Finally, disposition of Puget Power was averted through the election of a Republican president, Dwight D. Eisenhower, who believed in match-making with industry rather than a government take-over.

Thus, incredibly, in 1953 the ship's doom was averted, making all the more fantastic the reading of the decade of the Fifties. Frank McLaughlin, like many another skipper, had kept his composure, for he believed in Divine guidance. Long after his retirement, in a letter to me written only a few months before his death, which took place May 28, 1972, at the age of 77, he wrote: "I have always considered that God was very good to me, otherwise we would never had survived the ordeal of fire and brimstone which battered us for many years."

The Press Came to Life

At this time, when Puget Power was precariously hanging on for an honorable solution to its existence, backed to the wall by an over-all acquisiton threat by PUDs, as well as entangled by twelve condemnation suits by towns and small cities that did not want PUDs to serve them, the press across the country sensed a new mood and also a responsibility.

Editors became articulate about the herculean battle.

Their interest and concern was that the choice was rapidly narrowing not so much between private and public power locally, but from that of a graver threat, federally controlled power undisguised. They began speaking of the "Perils of Puget" and the menace of Federal control of electric power—at the time of dim-out and power shortage in the Pacific Northwest where Federal power produced 75% of the electric energy. So, at long last — if not too late — national, regional and local publications became an ally of Puget Power.

Hard-hitting editorials headlined papers and magazines from the mightiest centers to the small towns. Here is a random list of such publications: *The New York Times, Forbes, Financial World, Investors League Bulletin, Barron's, Utility Spotlight, Public Utilities Fortnightly, Public Service Magazine, Christian Science Monitor, Electrical World, East Side Journal, Daily Olympian, Bellingham Herald, Seattle Municipal News, Kent News-Journal, Seattle Argus, The Seattle Times, Seattle Post Intelligencer, Mount Vernon Argus, Mount Vernon Herald, Bremerton News Journal* and *Sumas News*.

It was the *Seattle Post Intelligencer* that voiced the most perceptive editorial, expertly timed, entitled "A Lively Corpse." Somehow it was so apt it was flashed across the State. It said that the people needed and wanted Puget Power. This timely editorial also copped the top prize in the Washington State Press Club's 1953 Best Editorial Awards Contest.

The Sun Came over the Mountain

The tensing drama of 1951 to 1953, a fight between the ideologies of socialism versus private enterprise that had eddied with mounting intensity across courtrooms, board-rooms, and financial centers, ebbed to a standstill in the early months of 1953.

A Republican president, Dwight D. Eisenhower, had been elected in November 1952; now he took charge, and there was a crispness in the air indicating change. When the new president replaced the public-power minded Secretary of Interior, and in turn appointed a new Bonneville Power Administrator, it was a signal to Public Utility Districts that the battle was over.

Then, strangely and beautifully, like the glow of the morning sunshine bursting fresh from behind Mount Rainier, came the warmth of appreciation and the promise of a bright future ahead. After nearly a quarter century of oppression and siege by public power zealots, now again the sun came over the mountain for the Puget Sound Power & Light Company.

Decade of Dynamic Plans

The Fifties marked the United States as the most powerful country in the world, and, following peace in Korea in 1954, the nation embarked upon an era of growth, prosperity, full employment, and also, inevitably, started on a path of inflation. And on the local level, what was truly amazing, the issue of private versus public power died. Puget Power became unfettered and in a new spirit showed tremendous life.

These fantastic Fifties with their sweeping and swift changes had begun with a grim prediction of Puget Power's demise followed by an about-face in 1953 with a promise of a rosy future and a new day in the sun for the Company; and startlingly, by 1955 the Company could speak of optimism and well-being as it had the best year on record when electric revenues reached an all-time high. Out of its past struggles evolved a strong and dynamic Puget Power.

With new and widespread endorsement and expressions of confidence, Puget Power moved at full speed ahead with dynamic forward-looking programs, and in 1955 it spoke jubilantly of "Life Begins at 70!" (In 1885 its earliest predecessor entered the electric utility business in this mostly wilderness frontier territory.)

Immediately in 1953 it set about to wipe its slate clean of condemnation suits, to obtain new franchises in various cities and towns, to develop new power plants of its own and to form a unique partnership with former foes to greatly enlarge the power supply potential in the Northwest.

Lifts Condemnation Suits

Now with the vote of confidence highly evident, within a little over one year ten condemnation suits held against Puget's properties were dismissed. They were as follows: Two actions brought by the Kitsap County PUD were dismissed by motion of the PUD in 1954. In rapid succession the cities of Enumclaw, Kent, Renton, Sedro-Woolley and Sumner terminated their suits in April 1955, and granted new franchises. The Skagit County PUD's suit was dismissed on October 24, 1955. The Douglas County and the Chelan County PUDs dismissed their suits against the Rock Island Dam on January 6, 1956. The City of Tacoma terminated its suit and agreed on a service area boundary in 1957.

The only remaining suit unresolved was that of the Thurston County PUD. It stayed as a thorn in the side of the power company until final dismissal in 1972, when it was necessary to terminate the suit to clear title in a trade of substation sites with the State to accommodate its enlarged Capitol Campus in Olympia.

Dismissal of condemnation suits was the first requisite to borrowing money for plant investments.

Puget Sound Utilities Council

A most promising and far-reaching development power-wise took place in 1954 with the setting up of a Puget Sound Utilities Council. It was unique in concept and in makeup. It was a marriage of former foes. The Council's members were the private and public utilities of the Puget Sound - Cascade area. They were the Puget Sound Power & Light Company, the Seattle and Tacoma municipal systems and the Snohomish and the Chelan County PUDs. Former contenders now were planning and building new power projects in harmony for the critical needs of their service area.

Partnership Projects Started

Pursuing the new pattern of partnership with public utility districts, Puget Power was successful in securing long term contracts on "service-at-cost" basis of large blocks of power with the Chelan, the Grant and the Douglas County PUDs. These embraced the projects on the Columbia River of Rock Island, Priest Rapids, Rocky Reach, Wanapum and Wells. The contracts were advantageous to both parties.

Puget Power would share in the responsibility of sale of the power, making possible financing through revenue bonds, and also Puget Power would enjoy advantages as though it itself had installed the facilities.

Puget Power's urge was irrepressible. Its experience of former days of political harassment, when it was held in a straight-jacket, had taught it the grim lesson that to be free of federal power reliance was the only way for self-determination. Puget Power's highest priority in the Fifties was to secure electric power resources for years ahead. It acted upon this resolve.

Contracts for partnership developments were as follows: On January 6, 1956, Puget Power sold its portion of the Rock Island Project to the Chelan PUD, for which it received $28,276,200; and in the deal Puget Power contracted for 50% of the total enlarged output of Rock Island, assuring 124,500 kilowatts of power for a period of the next 48 years. Also, on the same day a second contract was signed with the Chelan PUD for Puget Power to receive 50% of the Rocky Reach power for a term of 50 years with an initial capability of 710,000 kilowatts and an ultimate of 1,000,000 kilowatts. Puget Power's initial share of the proposed Rocky Reach project would be available in 1962. The Priest Rapids and the Wanapum Developments were undertaken by the Grant County PUD. In 1956 a long term contract was entered into with Puget Power for more than 100,000 kilowatts from the Priest Rapids Project, to be in operation in 1959, and another 123,000 kilowatts from Grant County's Wanapum Project, to be completed by 1965.

Under another agreement, this with Douglas County PUD, Puget Power contracted for one-third of the Wells Project for a term of 50 years for 133,000 kilowatts of similar cost-of-service terms.

By these long term contracts through partnerships with the PUDs of Chelan, Grant and Douglas Counties, the Company had assured itself 1,000,000 kilowatts of new Columbia River generation.

Puget Power Builds New Plants

Utilizing its own sites, in 1955 Puget Power launched plans for installing an additional 64,000 kilowatt generator at its Lower Baker Plant and also began building a new project on the Upper Baker River site — a 94,000 kilowatt project which would impound waters of a nine-mile lake, making possible the added generator at Lower Baker. Upper Baker was in operation by the end of 1959, and Lower Baker's new generator began spinning in 1960. Also started in 1955 was the addition of a 22,000 kilowatt unit at the Snoqualmie Plant. It was finished in July 1957.

Atomic Power Research

This was now the atomic age. So in 1958 Puget Power joined more than 50 utility companies in America in the formation of a non-profit corporation called the High Temperature Reactor Development Association, Inc., with a proposal to the Atomic Energy Commission to develop and build an advanced prototype atomic power plant. Approval was granted in August 1959 for the construction of a 40,000 kilowatt plant, the world's first high performance, gas cooled, nuclear power plant. It was built on the system of the Philadelphia Electric Company.

Other New Structures

In 1956 the personnel and functions, formerly located in the Electric Building in Seattle, were moved to new, attractive buildings built during the year in Bellevue, Renton, and Kirkland, so that they again were closely identified with the territory Puget Power served. And new centers were popping up in its outlying areas too.

Finances in Excellent Shape

Puget Power had weathered its long siege of dismemberment in an exceedingly strong financial position. Its capitalization ratio was 40% debt and 60% stock equity, and it moved still forward to open a wider line of credit. Its stockholders authorized the modernization of its mortgage with the favorable provision to issue an additional $25,000,000 of bonds against property, which could not have been done under provisions of the old mortgage. Also a very favorable 3-year Bank Credit Agreement was entered into on August 1, 1955, under which Puget Power could borrow up to $20,000,000 at an interest rate of 3%. Another optimistic move was to split stocks. On November 23, 1955, stockholders received an additional share of Common Stock for each two shares held.

The Company planned to spend $87,000,000 for new construction between 1956 and 1959.

Acquires New Systems

During October 1956, voters of Pacific City and South Cle Elum overwhelmingly approved the sale of their towns' electric systems to the Puget Sound Power & Light Company.

The Old Warrior Retires

The head of Puget Power, Frank McLaughlin, was reaching retirement age by 1960. He was the man who took over the leadership of the Company in 1931 during the demoralizing time following the stock market crash and the trauma of the Great Depression at the time when Puget Power was depicted by its distractors as a giant corporate octopus far removed from the people it served.

In the ensuing fight he had kept his feet solidly on the ground and his eyes straight upon one objective: To wipe the slate clean and to win public confidence. It was a man-killing battle. He won. He had tested his credo in tense times and then was able to retire in the climactic excitement of public confidence and personal success.

On September 18, 1959, Frank McLaughlin, president and director, was elected chairman of the board of directors, and Jack Clawson, treasurer and senior vice president, was elected president and director of Puget Power. This was an interim shift of leadership. In May 1960, Frank McLaughlin retired. He was 65.

Part Nineteen

THE SOARING SIXTIES

In the decade of the 1960s the tempo of life in America seemed to pick up and spread in all directions, even to space-age flyby of planets and placing men on the moon. This decade followed many years of sustained prosperity, and by now there was an elevated edge of inflation as the country took a big leap forward towards the good life.

It was a time of high living standards in homes, of more working women and of a zooming population growth. Science and technology had given us color television, electronic ovens, air-conditioning, microwave radar, jet rockets, the laser beam and the transistorized computer.

On the one hand we were racing ahead; on the other, there was a terrible tearing between the old and new styles and a drain of manpower and emotions as the world underwent its worst war crisis in history.

Then, as the decade came to a close, marked by a dip in the economy in 1968 and a relaxing of war tensions, we took a turn to more sobering years, and the world too could breathe easier again.

War Crisis

At the beginning of the Sixties Premier Khrushchev of Russia had shouted, "We will bury you!" Forthwith the Communist Block created incidents in Cambodia halfway around the world and in Cuba offshore from the United States.

The newly elected president, John F. Kennedy, was drawn into a global conflict in those troubled times. In 1961 he sent 15,000 advisors to South Vietnam to save a fast deteriorating defense against a Communist takeover, and in 1962 the United States and Soviet Russia moved toward a nuclear showdown over the establishment of Soviet missile bases in Cuba. The Russians had planted offensive missiles in Cuba.

President Kennedy gave a somber television announcement that Russian ships bound for Cuba with offensive weapons would be intercepted and turned back; moreover, any missiles launched from Cuba would be regarded "as an attack by the Soviet Union on the United States, requiring a full retaliatory response."

The Cuban crisis ended six days later when Moscow accepted Kennedy's assurance that Cuba would not be invaded and announced that Russia would withdraw its missiles. The Cuban missile incident had brought to a boiling point American-Russian tensions, already severely strained by the erection of the Berlin Wall a year earlier.

The Vietnam War was to grow and drain both men and their minds for the next ten years. Kennedy was assassinated November 22, 1963, and Lynden B. Johnson became president. Under him the forces of Americans in Vietnam grew to 550,000 men. Only when Richard A. Nixon was elected president in 1968 did our country begin to defuse this war with the withdrawal of American ground forces and with bids for an honorable peace. By now it was felt that the 2,000,000 man army of South Vietnam was able to defend its country.

Troubled Youth

On the home front during these troubled times there was a great surge of young people dissatisfied with time-honored values. They fomented Peace riots, created crises in schools, picketed and burned campus buildings and joined anarchists in riots to vent anger and dissatisfaction with institutions and the government. Teenagers and young adults took to pill-popping, narcotics, rock music, long hair, sloppy dress, free sex and free living. As opposed to youth, there was a bulge of older people who distrusted changes and shuddered at the speed of these changes.

Sobering Years

Through management of social changes, the defusing of the Vietnam War, establishing entente with both China and Russia for trade and social exchanges, controlling price and inflation, from war and fear there again came accord. By the close of the 1960s the country would remain as always vital, alive, ever-changing, alert to the problems and moving vigorously to solve them.

Changes and Growth

Business leaders, too, were concerned in this decade of the Soaring Sixties. Though there was a great growth in the national product, there also was a loss through lawlessness, a growing rate of inflation and heavier taxes. Puget Power, as a member of the business community, shared in the prosperity and the anxiety.

A President of Solid Values

Jack Clawson succeeded Frank McLaughlin as president of Puget Power in 1959. Clawson was sixty and the most experienced member of the management team, a person of solid values. He had been originally employed in 1923 as an auditor, became assistant treasurer in 1936, controller in 1946, treasurer in 1947, vice president in 1958 and now president in 1959. He was very comfortable with all his fellow employees. He held deep inner values and a solid belief in the future of his Company.

One of his first actions as president of Puget Power was to reorganize the Company as a Washington corporation. It had been a Massachusetts company since its beginning as the Puget Sound Traction, Light & Power Company in

1912. Distinct tax and regulatory advantages resulted in this move, but, fully as important, was management's pride and faith in the State of Washington and in the area it served.

JACK CLAWSON

Inflation Pricks Costs and Rates

The new 94,000 kilowatt Upper Baker Development was completed late in 1959, and an additional generator of 76,000 kilowatts of new power was added at the Lower Baker Plant in October 1960, for a total of 170,000 kilowatts of new investment. Both projects had been economically conceived; however, they were built later in times of rising inflation.

So, for the first time in its history, Puget Power filed with the Washington State Public Service Commission a request for a general rate increase. The forces of inflation and the costs of doing business, which had spiraled greatly for years, finally outran technological advancements.

In its testimony it showed that since 1929 to 1959 the cost of living index increased 80%, State taxes rose 360%, and annual wages, including fringe benefits, had grown 425%; for the same period the average price of electricity had been reduced 70%. After a study of the testimony and a hearing, a 10% general rate increase was granted, effective in January 1960.

With continuing inflation the electric rates were notched up still further in 1963 to help meet the impact of more than $8,000,000 additional annual power costs to the power company. The economy continued to be fired till 1969, then there was a leveling in growth, and only in 1972 — nine years after the last rate increase — did Puget Power again request permission for a further increase in electric rates to its customers. An 11½% increase was granted. Inflation in the future would bring more rate increases.

Leadership Change

Jack Clawson become president of Puget Power in 1959 at the age of 60. In another five years he would retire at the mandatory age of sixty-five. So to give training to a successor Clawson was elected chairman of the board and chief executive officer in June of 1962, and Ralph Davis,

Puget Power's secretary and vice president, elected president.

Davis, forty-three, fitted in well with Puget Power's image of being a Washington corporation. He was a graduate of the University of Washington. He had entered private law practice in Bellingham in 1948, was named assistant attorney general of the State in 1952, and later served as chairman of the Washington Public Service Commission, which regulates private utilities. Ralph Davis joined Puget Power's management team as its secretary in 1957.

With the selection of Davis as president, the Company now had the image of being wholly oriented to the area it served. It had adopted Washington as its legal home and now it selected a native as president.

RALPH DAVIS

Political Threats

One would have thought that the public-versus-private power battle had been settled in the 1950s when public and private power partnerships began building a half-dozen hydro-plants together on the Columbia River.

Yet, some of the zealots of the New Deal era still carried a political clout. So on the debit side, in 1960, against the wishes of the great majority of people living in the area, the Thurston County Public Utility District instituted condemnation proceedings against Puget Power's properties in that county.

Puget Power countered by its employees doorbelling for the election of friendly PUD commissioners. Such voters' efforts were needed every two years, and by this political vigilance the PUD continued to operate a water system only. Final lifting of this condemnation suit was accomplished by Court action in 1972, to quiet title to a substation site which the State Capitol Campus Committee wanted for campus expansion and was willing to trade sites.

Also in 1960 the City of Seattle sought to extend its lines into Puget Power's franchised area in the Town of Tukwila. Because Tukwila depended upon the City for its water supply, Seattle demanded a franchise to also serve Tukwila with electricity. Puget Power effectively stopped this by calmly buying a 325-acre development in Tukwila, the greater part of the town, and making it an outstanding industrial park, which it named Andover Industrial Park.

By legislative action in 1969 some of the teeth were pulled of the punitive 1931 Power Bill which had given the right of willful PUD commissioners to go into the electric power business without a vote of the people. The 1969 Washington State Legislature passed two long-sought laws. One required any existing PUD not engaged in the sale or distribution of electricity to first secure voter approval before beginning any condemnation proceedings against a privately owned company. The other law gave legislative recognition to the need of preventing duplication of electric facilities by an act for setting up agreements for service area boundaries. Once such an agreement is signed it becomes legally enforceable.

Treaty for Storing Columbia River Power

Before entering Washington State the Columbia River flows 480 miles in Canada, through a steep stretch in a wilderness area suitable for storage reservoirs. There three high dams would add about 2,800,000 kilowatts of prime power downstream to the eleven existing dams in Washington. After five years of negotiations, in 1964, a treaty was ratified by Canada and the United States for cooperative

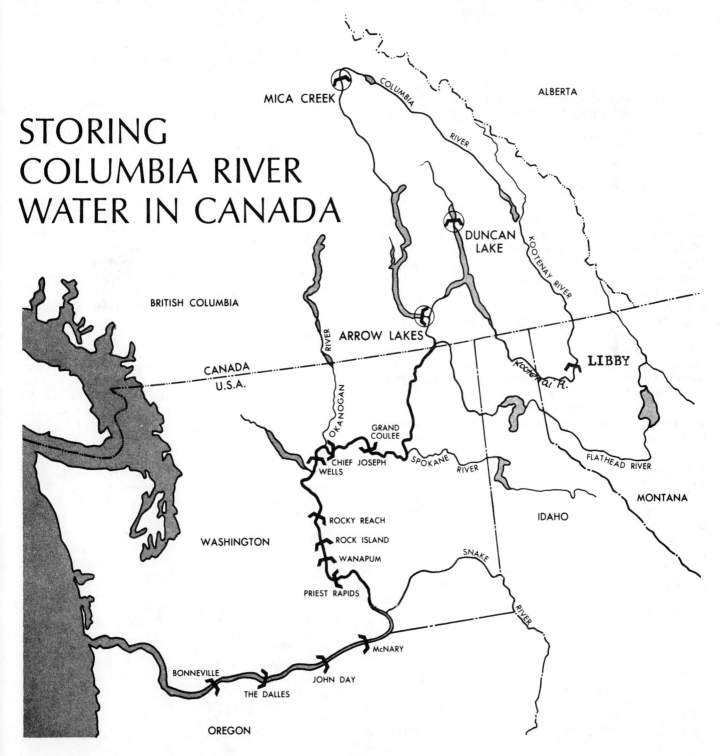

STORING
COLUMBIA RIVER
WATER IN CANADA

development of water resources of the Columbia Basin.

It was a landmark pact with political overtones. Congressmen of the Northwest teamed up with their conterparts from Tennessee, Mississippi, Colorado and California and with utility men from the Northwest and the Pacific Southwest. Two of Puget Power's best minds, John Ellis, an attorney, and David Knight, an engineer with a near-photographic memory of Northwest Power Pool dams and power lines, contributed much to bring about congressional consent.

The pact called for construction of three storage dams in Canada and one, Libby Dam, in the U.S. The Duncan dam was built in 1967, Arrow in 1969, Mica in 1973, and Libby in 1975. Libby, in Montana, was on the Kootenai River, which begins in Canada, loops south into Montana, and then turns north back into Canada. Its reservoir was named Koocanusa, a contraction of Kootenai, Canada and USA.

Under the treaty half of the new firm power belonged to Canada. Since Canada did not need the power U.S. utilities contracted to buy it for $254 million, money which Canada used to build the three dams. Canada's hydro power is one of its greatest assets, a dazzlingly attractive renewable resource.

The treaty had something for everybody. It gave Northwest utilities preference on prime power, Canada attained a market for hydro power to both the Northwest and to California, the Bonneville Power Administration now could extend its grid to California, and all dams would be operated as though owned by one utility.

Built in segments by six power entities, two 500,000 volt AC lines extend to the Mexican border, and a 800,000 volt DC line extends from The Dalles to Los Angeles — upgraded in 1985 to 1,000,000 volt. Because of the pact, utilities of 11 western states can share in power exchanges.

Total Underground

Early in 1963 the Company took the bold step of planning total underground wiring for residential plats. Costs per home owner would be much higher than with pole lines. Installations needed to be buried for the whole development at the beginning. This meant a risk, making a large investment of buried copper, conduits, vaults, transformers and switchgear to serve many homes even before a single house was built. "To bring the poles down" was the challenging thought.

So, in planning a comprehensive underground system, Puget Power joined forces with the Pacific Northwest Telephone Company and equipment manufacturers to make such wiring feasible for new homes. Study was given to the results of extensive interviews with 1,300 home buyers in four Western States and careful market research with the construction industry. The word was "Go!"

Puget Power led off by forming a subsidiary, Puget Properties, Inc., in 1963, for the purpose of converting 515 acres of non-operating land, an old coal field, into residential plats. Here, late in 1964, Puget Power installed the first Total Underground residential wiring system, the first of its kind in the nation. All utilities were buried.

Initially the costs per lot were nearly $400, but cost reduction efforts based on experience sliced down the expense. In a few years the cost per lot for new plats came down to $160. At first State Safety Rules required that the wires be layered in sand with wooden planks used as separators. This was unrealistic, as any wire fault would be grounded right where it lay, so by simply bundling conductors in one trench the price was reduced greatly. Moreover, manufacturers were able to build immersible auxiliaries, reducing costs of vaults.

For its outstanding success in developing the Total Underground System, Puget Power was selected by the American Marketing Association as the Marketing Company of the Year in 1966. In Bellevue, Washington, as a symbol of its appeal, when the last pole came down the townspeople held a celebration and burned it in the town square.

The 60s were good years. The Western Washington economy was stimulated in 1962 by the highly successful Seattle World's Fair, which attracted 10 million visitors and resulted in a total spending of $250 million. Business and employment gains in 1966 were the best in twenty years; 90,000 new jobs were added in the state and 14,716 new customers were welcomed by Puget Power. An additional 23,709 new customers were added in 1968. By 1969, there was a leveling off, and the decade ended with a subdued economy.

Part Twenty

THE SOBERING SEVENTIES

The 1970s held the promise of a sobering and a reflective future for Americans. This decade began with a depressed economy, in some ways a relief from the soaring, chaotic, and explosive 1960s. There was a consciousness of the need for protection of our environment, of the population explosion, energy depletion, detente with our adversaries, and the use of our great influence for the peace in the world.

Hearings were held in Congress on the development of low-emission and enhanced safety features for automobiles. The Clean Air Act with strict standards in it was passed in 1970. Senator Domenici of New Mexico encapsuled the situation when he said: "With all of Detroit's faults, I'd sooner drive one of its cars than one designed by one hundred senators."

For 1972, the birth rate in the United States dropped to 2.03, its lowest in history, below the replacement level of the country's population.

President Richard Nixon visited both China and Russia to establish entente for peace. On March 2, 1973, the Vietnam peace settlement was officially approved by twelve governments. The nine-point declaration provided for outsiders to stop meddling in Indochina and for a system to deal with truce violations. The United States was pleased that both the Soviet Union and China signed the declaration. Prisoners of war now would be sent home, although this treaty the Viet Cong quietly violated.

They pressed on, in an ironic twist, after 25 years of war; by 1975 the Vietnamese lost the will to save themselves. Then, with a shocking suddenness, the Viet Cong easily overran their country; on April 30, 1975, they occupied Saigon and a truce was declared. This was a Communist takeover with Russian-made tanks. Some 100,000 Vietnamese refugees were brought to America, leaving by jet airplanes, helicopters, and ships, fugitives from Communism and possible death.

The Chaotic Middle Years

On the other side of the world, war flared up in the Middle East between Israel and the Arab States. The Suez Canal was plugged with sunken ships. There was serious potential for another world war so major nations stepped in to attempt to settle it. In 1973, the Arabs in possession of valuable resources, used their clout by imposing an oil embargo. They formed a cartel which was to boost oil prices around the world by nearly 400 percent, creating a world-wide energy crisis.

On peace-making efforts President Nixon and his secretary of state, Henry Kissinger, toured Arab nations, Israel, European capitals, and Moscow. In July 1974, civil war flared up on the little island of Cypress. Again our government acting through the United Nations was able to start peace negotiations.

At home, in 1973 and 1974, scandals broke close to the president. It was known as "Watergate," because of a bizarre break-in and wiretap of the Democratic convention at the Watergate Hotel. One by one, Nixon's aides were forced to resign; even Vice President Spiro Agnew was indicted and resigned. Gerald R. Ford, Republican Speaker of the House, was appointed to replace Agnew. Nixon's position as President became untenable when the House voted on three articles for impeachment. He resigned on August 9, 1974. Gerald Ford was sworn in as President. The nation had been badly shaken, but found its constitution was sound and working. Ford moved fast to heal the wounds.

At the next general election in 1976 Ford lost to James Carter for the presidency. Overwhelmed by problems of inflation and zooming interest rates, Carter was succeeded in 1980 by Ronald Reagan as president. Reagan believed in lower taxes, conservative economics, and a reduction of the role of the government.

The energy crisis had triggered a business recession in the United States with unemployment reaching 9.2 percent. Early in 1975, income taxes were reduced and tax refunds given to stimulate business. The recession bottomed out late in 1975. But under Carter's presidency inflation was 13.4 percent and interest rates were at 20 percent by the end of 1979.

Puget Power in the 1970s

For Puget Power, the 1970s opened with an economic slowdown — a contrast to the super-heated boom of the middle and late 1960s. It was short lived. What began as a sobering era, became a fast-paced scenario of challenges.

Severe water shortages in the winter of 1973-74 brought on regional energy curtailment, followed by the Arab oil embargo and a national energy conservation program. The energy crisis was attended by inflation and soaring interest rates. Also, within the company, though not precipitous, there was a change in leadership.

In 1976, Ralph Davis, president, looking to retirement, moved over to become chairman of the board, and John W. Ellis, executive vice president, became the company's president. At his retirement in 1979, Ralph Davis said, "I have enjoyed an extremely exciting and pleasant career at Puget Power, both in my capacity as a company official and in the opportunities I have had to participate in communtiy affairs." For Eillis, the events of the 1970s became the most hectic of his career.

John Ellis was no stranger to Puget Power. Years before, as its attorney he had had a big part in negotiating a pact signed in 1964 between Canada and the United States for the construction of three large storage dams on the area of the Columbia located in Canada for the benefit of down-stream projects in the United States. Puget Power held contracts for purchase of energy in five downstream projects.

Now, as president in the 1970s, he would be tested with problems and paradoxes never before confronted by his company.

JOHN W. ELLIS

Although nationally the trend for energy use was down, in Washington State it was up. Washington's employment was not responsive to the national trend in the 1970s; it remained well above the national average. The port cities of Puget Sound had their busiest years, because they were the staging area for trans-Alaska oil pipeline construction, and the construction of the Trident submarine base in Kitsap county, which employed 7,000 workmen.

In 1978 alone, more than 100,000 persons had elected to come to the state, adding 31,034 new customers to Puget Power. This was the largest yearly increase in Puget Power's history; it was like serving a new city the size of Bellevue, the fourth largest in the state. During the decade of the 1970s, the company's growth encompassed more than 200,000 new customers.

So in its immediate and long-range planning the company turned to hydro, coal, oil, gas, the atom, and to testing of solar, geothermal and wind power. Puget Power also vigorously promoted conservation of electricity for its customers.

In 1971, a 1,400,000 kilowatt coal-fired plant was completed in Centralia, Washington, by joint ownership. In 1972, a 50-50 partnership between Puget Power and the Montana Power Company began construction of a coal-fired project at Colstrip, Montana, with a capacity of 700,000 kilowatts. In 1975, application for a second Colstrip generation plant was filed by a partnership of five utilities, for a development of 1,400,000 kilowatts. By 1984 and 1986, two more coal-fired plants, Colstrip No. 3 and No. 4, would be completed.

Colstrip No. 1 came on line in November 1975; No. 2 came on line late in 1979 with the added bonus that it offset hydro during another drought. In August of 1979, the last of eight new generators installed at the Rock Island Dam came on line. Also in 1979, construction began on the twin plants of Colstrip No. 3 and No. 4, after four years of delays due to environmental impact hearings. Puget Power invested heavily to meet new energy demands.

To cope with growing winter peak demands, two 89,000 kilowatt combustion turbines (fired by natural gas) near Ferndale, Washington, were scheduled to become operational in May 1981. Additionally, two similar units near Frederickson, Washington, came on line in November 1981.

Davis, Ellis, and other utility executives felt the atom provided the answer to their power needs. But it was not to be; people got in the way, to obstruct rather than construct. Said John Ellis in 1980, speaking before the Society of Professional Journalists:

> Last December (1979) was one of the bleakest months we ever faced. Skagit County residents had voted against two nuclear-power plants Puget Power wanted to build there. The company had invested $190 million and seven years effort in the project. There was no national energy policy. Interest rates on borrowed money were 20 percent.
>
> Now (1980) the reservoirs are filled; the Northwest Regional Power Bill is about to be signed by the President; Puget Power's new-customer load has dropped from about 30,000 a year to 18,000; a residential energy-conservation program has been a success; and the nuclear plants that were stopped in Skagit County now are planned for Hanford.

Strange and Paradoxical

Puget Power had anguished over the enormous costs of new energy sources. Now, paradoxically, it began telling its customers to use less electricity through conservation and asking its stockholders to re-invest stock dividends so the company could hang on to this cash. Both proposals were attractively packaged.

Beginning in 1975, the customers were given incentives to share in energy conservation. Over the next five years, roughly $65 million were committed by the company for weatherized energy audits, and 100 percent financing via interest-free loans. Many homeowners also used wood stoves for heating to cut their electric bills. It became a cost-effective way of stretching power sources.

To give some idea of the magnitude of this commitment, over 130 full-time equivalent individuals at Puget Power were working on various aspects of the conservation program. This corps of employees was advising customers on how to curtail use of electricity. This by a company in the business of selling electricity. It was 1975; but in 1933, during the Great Depression, when the Rock Island Dam had been put on line by Puget Power, the company then worked just as hard to hire 100 salesmen to sell electric ranges, water heaters, and refrigerators — to build load and bring in cash earnings!

Later, in 1985, the conservation program was still valued as a prudent, cost-effective way of stretching generating resources, and was to be continued.

In 1975, the company established a dividend reinvestment

and stock purchase plan. Encouraged by the incentives of a 5 percent discount feature, the absence of commissions or service fees, and the convenience of the plan, about 11,000 or 18 percent of shareholders were enrolled by 1980, for a total of about $20.4 million of new equity capital. With some modification, it continued in effect beyond 1985.

The company continued to grow, although conservation efforts and rising costs of electricity did make a dent in demand. Even so, by 1972, Puget Power attained the status of a big company. It passed the $100,000,000 threshold in annual energy sales and served 365,000 customers.

Amazingly, eight years later, with the fired-up state economy, the energy sales tripled $323,000,000 for 510,000 customers. By 1980 the ten-year growth showed an increase of customers 56 percent, plant 200 percent, revenue 255 percent.

John Ellis, president, was a personable leader, who with intelligence, tact, and managerial skills, had won the warm loyalty of his fellow employees and the respect of the community leaders. He had turned the corner for the company.

PART TWENTY-ONE

PUGET POWER IN THE 1980s

In 1980, a recession settled upon the state of Washington. Nationally, a recession had bottomed out in late 1975, but the state had escaped it with a booming decade in the 1970s. Now, upon entering the 1980s Washington was struck with a three-year recession.

To help cushion an earnings slide, deep budget cuts were made in the areas of personnel and new construction. Painful reductions in staff were made with voluntary early retirement of 140 staff members in 1982. Although the news on the economy was negative, the recession was a much-needed respite from the huge construction burden of the past decade. Puget Power reduced its five-year construction burden by almost $600 million.

With these events came the restructuring of traditional line-and-staff functions. It was handled sympathetically, an experience that brought about a sense of pride and accomplishment in the lean, tough, and "working smarter" environment.

Much credit is due to John Ellis, president of Puget Power, for his sensitive handling of the deep cuts as well as his challenge to his fellow employees for a commitment to excellence.

The Puget Power chief also made deft, effective moves in 1981, as rates rose steeply and ratepayers started to get angry. Ellis inaugurated a program of customer advisor councils. Even the loudest critics were invited to take part and maintained in their discussions a healthy, inquisitive skepticism. By 1985, in its fifth year, the nationally recognized Consumer Program was truly a valuable process. By then, more than 800 customers had served as volunteer advisors and made 650 recommendations to management. Each recommendation was answered in writing and 75% of the suggestions were agreed to in whole or in part and implemented with thanks. Ellis had opened up an innovative and beneficial line of communication.

Nuclear Plants Dropped

The world had viewed the United States as the leader in the development of nuclear energy. So when deprived of cheap oil in the 1970s, other nations turned to America for advice. But they also turned to their own and successfully built hundreds of low-cost, reliable, environmentally impeccable nuclear power plants. In the United States, at the same time, we witnessed the bloom and wilt of nuclear energy. Why?

The scenario that unfolded tested our nation's utilities. They found themselves wandering in a growing wilderness of governmental regulations, were surrounded by scores of siting and licensing tangles devised by activists of imaginative and obstructive skills, whose strategy was to force interminable delays. At the same time, the economy of wild inflation and soaring interest rates forced the utilities into a stranglehold choking off construction funds. With no return on investments, the utilities cancelled new construction of nuclear plants on a monumental scale.

Various nuclear projects of Puget Power were struck down, as were also those of the Washington Public Power Supply System. (In one of their five projects Puget Power had a 5% interest.) Puget Power also shared an interest in an Oregon-based nuclear project, Pebble Springs.

In 1981, the Pebble Springs nuclear project which had been planned for Arlington, Oregon, was formally cancelled by the participants following an Oregon voter initiative which effectively prevented construction of the project.

In 1983, the Skagit-Hanford nuclear project was formally abandoned after the Northwest Regional Power Planning Council said it would not be needed to meet the region's power needs for the next twenty years.

A shocking termination was that of four nuclear plants (five were under construction) by the Washington Public Power Supply System (WPPSS). Only one, Project 2, at Hanford, with a twelve-year construction time, was completed in 1984. In January 1982, Project 4, 25% complete, and Project 5, 15% finished, were scrapped, carrying a default of $2.25 billion that WPPSS had borrowed to build the two now-abandoned plants. The projects were financed through tax-empted revenue bonds. The bonds were secured only by the revenue generated from future electricity sales — sales that would not take place if the plants are never completed.

The remaining two plants were mothballed in 1983. At the time Project 1, at Hanford, was two-thirds completed, and Project 3, at Satsop, was 75% finished.

Puget Power, not a member of WPPSS, held a 5% ownership interest in Project 3, at Satsop, Washington, as did three other investor-owned electric utilities. They felt it was a violation of their contracts to arbitrarily mothball the plant. So in 1984, they filed a suit agains BPA and WPPSS over their action in halting construction.

Wisely, the parties to the suit negotiated for an out-of-court settlement of a multi-million dollar claim. They reached an agreement, signed September 17, 1985, which among other things, gave credit for the existing investment of the private utilities in Project 3, by BPA selling power to them roughly equivalent to what they would have received if the nuclear plant had been finished, at a rate for BPA power as if they were paying the cost of operating and maintaining a nuclear plant. The agreement also would provide, in effect, for BPA to pick up any future costs of the project whether or not completed.

Rate Crises

Repeatedly, as new coal-fired plants were put on line, Puget Power had to go to the state regulatory commission for rate increases. These were granted with reservations and after months of delays. Moreover, painful and dramatic questions were raised on the recovery of funds invested in abandoned nuclear projects. Decisions of the commission were challenged in court.

Said John Ellis, president, in 1985:

> Our objective is to put behind us the remaining uncertainties to our nuclear power plant investments. In 1984, the company did move closer towards resolution of these uncertainties when the Washington Utilities and Transportation Commission authorized recovery of $82 million of the company's $128 million net investment in the Skagit-Hanford nuclear project. With that authorization and the commission's earlier allowance for the Pebble Springs project, we are presently recovering nearly 75 percent of our combined net investment in these two projects.

A group of rate-payers did challenge the commission's decisions. Most of the uncertainties were resolved on December 12, 1985, when the State Supreme Court ruled that the commission had acted within its statutory authority. 1985 was a pivotal year.

Future Growth

During the three-year depression of 1980-83, Puget Power had cut costs and budgets to the bone, and by 1985 it could look to the future with a strong financial base. Growth prospects looked good.

Regardless of economic models or entrepreneural experience, a leader is always wary of forecasting. Consider, for 50 years the growth of electricity in America had been 6 percent annually — a doubling every 10 years. In the 1970s, for Puget Power it continued at almost this rate, 4.8 percent (3.5 nationally). Then during 1980-83, Puget Power's rate dropped to less than 2 percent; and the forecast for 1985-90 was a moderate 3 percent.

Recalling the explosive growth rate of the late 1970s, Puget Power's hard-bitten management team planned to accommodate within existing resources until 1990 but also to keep open several power purchase options, as well as continuing to promote wise, efficient use of electricity.

As we conclude the 100th year of the history of Puget Power, we know the company has the momentum to grow. Yet any historian admits to being uncomfortable when his story bumps against the present. Its hallmark is change. At best he can only give the sense, the direction and aura of the times.

Asked the question, what do you see as the biggest challenge facing your company, Robert Myers, senior vice president of operations, replied:

> The same challenge as always — adapting to change. If you go back in time you would see we have always faced a new environment. Lots of things have changed for us. They'll continue to change. Our biggest challenge is to develop people who have the creativity and capability to react and to solve the problems of a changing environment.

For the serious student of history two chapters remain; one is the story of the historic presence of the energy crises, the other is that of America's thrilling exploits in space. Space exploration is a modern-day science, akin to the dawn of the electrical age in the 1880s.

PART TWENTY-TWO

REGULAR AND KING SIZE ENERGY CRISES

We have had our energy crises, local, national and international, in the past. From each painful experience, solutions were found, some ingeniously.

Energy Crisis of 1859

Depletion of whale oil was America's first historic energy crisis. Civil War whale oil shipments for the country's lamps had been disrupted and the price jumped from 25 cents to $1.45 per gallon. The solution: drill an oil well. Someone very brightly drilled the nation's first oil well in Pennsylvania in 1859. Lamps glowed again, this time burning kerosene.

Energy Shortage of 1900s

In Washington State, when pioneers completed the world's first underground hydro electric plant under the cliffs of Snoqualmie Falls in 1898, the owners predicted their hydro power would supply the state's electric needs for the next 50 years. To their chagrin, the dazzling demand brought a power shortage within 5 years. It was barely averted by a competitor building three more power plants — Post Street, Electron, and Georgetown.

SNOQUALMIE
(1898)

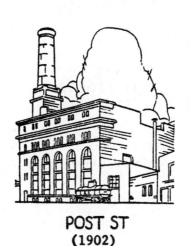

POST ST
(1902)

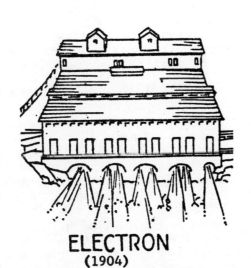

ELECTRON
(1904)

GEORGETOWN
(1906)

Droughts Bring Shortages

Areas like the Pacific Northwest long have depended upon hydro power; at times of low stream flows, the generation of electricity fell. A drought in 1928 forced the municipal plants of Tacoma and Seattle to curtail the use of electricity. Puget Power had built its Shuffleton steam plant and weathered the 1928 crisis. The solution was to build reserve plants, some oil-fired.

Again and again, regional shortages developed which were met by building larger generating stations, until by 1970, most rivers and lakes were fully harnessed. So for diversity in supply, utilities would eventually turn to coal and atomic energy for new power sources.

Petroleum Crises

Petroleum, too, has given this country many energy crises. For example, in 1917, as a boy, I was dismayed to learn that the supply of gasoline would be gone within the next 5 years. I read it in the papers. It shattered my dream of driving a spanking new Model T Ford. Then, oilmen drilled more wells. Oil and automobiles became the nation's biggest industries.

A gasoline shortage of another sort occurred in 1941, when, during World War II, rubber supplies were cut off and petroleum was diverted to make synthetic rubber. Now, Americans submitted to gasoline rationing and a speed limit of 35 miles an hour. With peace, industry drilled many new oil wells, mostly on foreign soil, and our economy grew tremendously — until the Arab oil boycott in 1973. Also in 1973, a drought hit the western states like the one of 1928, causing low water in reservoirs and some electric power curtailment.

Oil Embargo of 1973

It was an "oil shock" that came on the heels of the October 1973 war between Israel and its neighbors. Israel had bombed ships and shores and in so doing plugged the Suez Canal with sunken ships. This triggered an Arab oil embargo which lasted six months.

Shock waves from the embargo caused spiralling inflation throughout the world and also an economic recession that extended through the 1970s generally.

What amounted to the first test case of a potential Arab oil monopoly was effected in Beirut, Lebanon, on May 15, 1973, when four Arab countries — Libya, Iraq, Kuwait and Algeria — got together to announce a temporary halt (24 hours) of their westward oil flow, a symbolic protest against Western help to Israel.

They knew very well that the United States was importing about 3.6 million barrels of oil a day, though producing about 9.6 million barrels a day of its own oil. The cost was less than $3 a barrel, and total imports were $9 billion a year. Following the embargo, a cartel, the Organization of Oil Producing Countries (OPEC), was formed, which soon embraced thirteen countries. For the next ten years it was one of the most successful cartels in history.

Both the amount of oil imported by America and the price per barrel rose. Average daily oil imports rose from 3.6 million barrels a day in October 1973 to an all-time peak of 7.1 million barrels a day in July 1977. The price of imported oil rose from roughly $3 a barrel in 1973 to about $15 in 1978; $22 in 1979; and to between $37 and $38 in mid-1981.

A Homemade Shortage

The above facts tell us something. With hindsight we know that the oil crisis was in large measure a homemade shortage. The United States had met its own energy needs till 1969. In 1970 our domestic oil production peaked at 9.6 million barrels a day and we were running out of "easy oil." Either we would accept a steep rise in prices to pay costs of drilling, or import foreign oil.

Moreover, to nip the trend of inflation that had started in the roaring 1960s the Nixon administration in 1971 imposed a wage and price freeze. So we turned to foreign supplies for our oil. By 1973 we were importing 30% of our oil needs. Only after the embargo did we start drilling new oil wells at home. The myth of an oil shortage continued for an appalling ten years because liberal congressmen were able to extend oil price controls.

The high OPEC prices sent geologists searching for oil reserves all over the world. Norway and Britain developed wells under the North Sea. Mexico stepped up production dramatically. In America, the Alaskan oil fields were tapped with the trans-Alaska oil pipeline. By 1979, President Carter finally was convinced that price support was self-defeating, and planned to phase out controls in 1981. Ronald Reagan was elected as president in 1980, and after only a week in office lifted price controls on American oil. This scrapping of price controls ended the oil crisis of the 1970s.

During the summer of 1981, oil imports dropped below 4 million barrels a day. And we can say that America finally faced its energy problems and began to withdraw itself from the opiate of imported oil. Still, the 4 million barrels a day now cost more than $70 billion a year, a sum about equal to the 1981 federal deficit.

The high price of cartel oil had sparked a drilling surge throughout the world, so by March 1982 there was an oil glut, and caused prices to fall. Even OPEC could not stem the price collapse.

Much of the reduced United States demand for oil came from its people switching to a variety of sources, coal, natural gas, and to wood-burning stoves, as well as from other conservation practices. By 1985, use of oil was cut 21%.

It took America nearly ten years to learn that a price freeze only produces shortages, and that a free market through the operation of supply and demand is the soundest system.

A National Program for Action

The 1973 energy crunch was twenty years in coming. With abandon we had used coal, gas, hydro, and oil, and drifted towards a 38% dependence on foreign sources, without shaping a basic national policy. President Nixon had asked his chairman of the Atomic Energy Commission, Dr. Dixy Lee Ray, to undertake a national study on power sources and research. The study was completed in 1973. The voluminous report was optimistic.

After five months of labor by 16 panels of experts recruited from 36 federal departments and agencies, who were assisted by 282 consultants drawn from the private sector, the Commission covered more than 1,100 specific proposals for energy research and development. America, they said has the imagination, the know-how, and the physical means to achieve energy independence. Dr. Ray's team called for a five-year, 10-billion dollar program of federal and privately funded research. Five simultaneous goals were set:

1. Conserve the energy sources on which we now rely. Tremendous savings can be achieved merely by salvaging wasted heat, by insulation and by increasing the efficiency of machinery.
2. Increase domestic production of oil and natural gas, meaning "improved drilling methods for offshore sites, release of gas from tight formations and extracting oil from shale."
3. Substitute coal for oil and gas, "on a massive scale." America has the world's largest coal reserve.
4. Move ahead on crash programs for developing atomic energy, then solar power.
5. Still more distant, develop energy from wind currents, geothermal resources, and from ocean thermal gradients.

Changing Direction

In 1973, the nation measured its energy resources and started to do an about face. Its use of petroleum products was staggering: in refineries to produce gasoline, diesel fuel and lubricants for ships, airplanes, cars, tractors, locomotives and factory machinery; feedstocks for petrochemical and plastic resins industries; and oil for asphalt to pave highways and freeways. In 1973 the tally of energy used was: Oil 50%, natural gas 30%, coal 15%, hydro 4%, and nuclear 1%. The tally of fuels used to generate electricity alone, as reported by the U.S. Department of Energy, was:

1973: Oil 17%, gas 18%, coal 46%, nuclear 4%, hydro 15%.
1983: Oil 6%, gas 12%, coal 55%, nuclear 13%, hydro 14%.

As the energy crisis crackled and stirred across the country, new rules were imposed. The highway speed limits were reduced from 70 miles per hour to fifty-five miles per hour. People were sharing rides, buying compact cars reducing room temperatures in homes and offices, wearing sweaters and long johns, and also burning wood in fireplaces and installing wood-burning heaters. Self-dependence was the national goal. This was the pattern for the winter and spring of 1974, a quick-fix, yet, with attitudes changed, ten years later, most families adhered to this austere mode of living.

By 1985, what happened to the Nixon administration's 1974 Project Independence, that counted on nuclear power to provide 40% of the U.S. electricity by 1990, 50% by 2000? What about alternate energy sources, coal, oil from shale, solar, wind, geothermal? All alternates were researched. The greatest progress was in coal-fired electric generating plants. From 1973 to 1985, 93 were built in the United States, with compliance to strict antipollution rules.

Coal by Enlightened Methods

Though sitting on a storehouse of energy — coal — that exceeds even the oil wealth of the Arab nations, we were loath to use it. To environmentalists nothing was quite so ominous as the nation's colossal reserve of coal. Strip mining was the most economical recovery technique for coal, but it had ravaged Appalacia. David Freeman, director of the Ford Foundation Energy Policy Project, said, "We can't mine it and we can't burn it in a socially acceptable way."

Despite this, in the last ten years, strip mining, too, was made beautiful in such areas as Mine Lake, Illinois; Centralia, Washington; and Colstrip, Montana. At these and other places coal is removed, then the land reclaimed with lakes, grass, and trees.

With these new-era power plants there also was a push to build the cleanest coal-fired generating stations in the country. For example, at Colstrip where Units 1 and 2 cost $280 million, $50 million was used to install three scrubbers for each unit, which in operation met and exceeded air pollution standards.

Bloom and Wilt of Nuclear Power

The electric utilities entered the nuclear age with high hopes of leading in nuclear power and veering away from dependence on Arab oil. They were encouraged by 42 nuclear plants in operation in 1974, with performance costs that were competitive with coal and below oil. These were fission nuclear plants using uranium-235 as fuel. The utilities were to experience a boom and a bust.

Organized antinuclear forces bedeviled the industry. The lead time of "nukes" was stretched to an agonizing thirteen years, because of lengthy licensing and environmental reviews. (In the meantime, Japan and France were building new nuclear plants with an average lead time of six years.) The protestors were a dedicated and imaginative group with obstructive skills that harrassed and delayed construction to unconscionable lengths in an economy of double-digit inflation and interest rates.

Other woes descended on the U.S. nuclear industry. The most dramatic was the accident at Three Mile Island, on May 28, 1979. A stuck valve and personnel error caused the reactor to overheat. The core was not damaged and no one was hurt, but the publicity, avidly seized upon by the activists, put a blight upon the nation's nuclear growth.

New reviews on safety practices became an obsession, and for a number of years no licenses for nuclear plants were granted. Since 1979, 78 were cancelled, including 28 already under construction.

Even so, with rigorous licensing terms, there were 87 nuclear power plants in service in 28 American states by the first of 1985. Thirty-five plants were under construction and scheduled for completion by the early 1990s. Twenty percent of the U.S. demand was to be supplied by nuclear-generated electricity by 1990.

Elsewhere in the world, by 1985 there were 227 nuclear plants in operation. European nations, committed to nuclear energy, wonder about the slow pace in America. France now gets 60% of electricity form this source, Japan 21%. The U.S. stands at the bottom of the list with 14%.

Crisis of Energy Dependence

Concluding this review of regular and king-size energy crises, it is clear that our nation always was able to meet its energy crises domestically. The "king-size" crisis is one of dependence on foreign energy sources.

Since the 1973 Arab oil boycott, we have struggled forward with a goodly measure of energy independence — but not totally — in 1983, oil imports totaled over $50 billion.

Said Senator James McClure, chairman of the Senate Energy and Natural Resources Committee, "There is one area in which I am absolutely confident. There will be an interruption of oil supply that affects this country within the next two years ... it has happened to every decade in the last fifty years, and three times in the last decade ... reduce your vulnerability to the interruption of energy supplies from overseas."

Where should our electricity come from? Our energy sources are underfoot. According to a recent international survey, the U.S. has more than 400,000 tons of reasonably assured resources of uranium, and the world's largest reserve of coal deposits. So we must use both. The National Academy of Sciences and other experts have said that America must not become dependent on a single fuel, but must use alternatives, and all of them. Over-dependence on any one is risky and unreliable, as witness gas cutoffs, coal strikes, and warring nations.

Donald Hodel, Secretary of Energy, said, "We need a balanced mix of energy sources ... nuclear power is an imperative, not an option, for assuring reliable and adequate electricity supply in the United States and the rest of the world."

The U.S. Committee for Energy Awareness in a report said, "Between 1960 and 1982, United States industry dramatically improved its efficiency, reducing its total energy use 41% for each unit of output. But during the same time, industries used 10% more electricity for each unit of output." They pointed out that there is a second wave of electrification, because electricity is flexible, controllable and available.

In the decades ahead, we must do as our friends around the world are doing, assuredly build more nuclear and coal-fitted electric generating plants, with the future weighted heavily toward nuclear-powered energy.

PART TWENTY-THREE

SPACE EXPLORATION

In this book, vignettes on local and national history seem necessary to put into perspective influences that give direction to electric utilities. They, like other industrials, such as The Boeing Company, must adjust to the state of the art, or sink or swim with the ebb and flow of the national economy. Space exploration has relevancy.

In the span of one generation, we entered the space age. When World War II ended (1945) and our homesick men returned, the nation used a work force and a coterie of scientists to pursue peacetime research on the solar system. As space exploration unfolded we were thrilled and awed.

First, unmanned spaceships were designed and launched for flyby of planets. Then followed the spectacular exploit of placing men on the moon and returning them for a splash-down in the Pacific Ocean. Later, shuttle spaceships were put into orbit and returned with astronauts at the controls for airfield landings.

Spaceships were designed and launched for flyby of planets as follows: Mars in 1960, Venus in 1962 and 1967, Jupiter in 1973, Mercury in 1974, and Saturn in 1980 and 1981.

Remarkable information was yielded by each probe. For example, on December 3, 1973, the news of science-fiction-come-true was flashed by Earth pictures of Jupiter from the unmanned spaceship Pioneer 10. It had been launched in March of 1972, first to orbit the Sun, then to swing wider to photograph Mars. In 1973, it plunged through Jupiter's deadly radiation belts to swoop within 81,000 miles of Jupiter's orange-grey clouds. The pictures promised to unlock age-old mysteries. Scientists were elated.

Other spaceships were launched using new techniques for reaching distant planets such as the Boeing-built Mariner 10. It flew past the Moon calibrating its cameras, then swung past Venus, taking marvelous pictures. Next it was directed to the sun-seared planet Mercury, and once past Venus it was breaking new ground. On March 2, 1974, it came nearest to Mercury in the 22-day automated survey. Here it discovered a mysterious magnetic field. Flying within 120 miles of Mercury it mapped this field of the "Evening Star." Then with its altitude-control gas used up, it went into permanent orbit around the sun.

Two sister spaceships, Voyager I and II, in 1980 performed staggering complex missions to photograph Saturn, its rings, and its moons. They needed to play planetary billiards on the way, and swing past large planets to pick up

MOON BUGGY, designed and built by The Boeing Company, appears a bit like a 1909 Ford (page 22), otherwise it is a marvel of sophisticated ideas of physics, chemistry, metallurgy and electronics. Collapsed for transit and unfolded for use, the 462-pound vehicle functioned safely in space. Electrically driven, through research spin-off it just might be a forerunner of an electric car. Price of 1909 Ford f.o.b. Dearborn, $900. Price of the Moon Buggy f.o.b. the earth, $8 million. (Photo courtesy of Boeing).

gravitational boosts. All went well. Voyager I swept past Saturn and its moons and Voyager II took a look at Saturn's rings and swirling clouds on August 29, 1981, to race on to a 1986 meeting with the planet Uranus.

The launching of a manned craft, Eagle, and placing men on the moon took place in 1969. It astonished the world. Pictures were relayed to earth for the world to see. The return was a safe splashdown on the Pacific Ocean. On a 1971 flight, Apollo 15, astronauts walked in spacesuits and unlimbered the Boeing-built moon buggy to explore 17 miles of moon terrain and collect rock samples.

In 1980, another stride in science was taken when a manned spacecraft, the Columbia, was launched from Cape Canaveral. It was designed with heat tiles to protect itself from re-entry heat of the earth's atmosphere. Projected into an orbit of about 100 miles above the earth, the Columbia spent a six-day spectacular flight in space, then with astronauts in the cockpit landed on a desert lakebed, triumphantly touched the gravel, raced along the runway, and braked to a halt. On Earth the Columbia was transported "piggy back" on a Boeing 747.

The Columbia made six flights proving the economy of space experiments. It was succeeded by shuttle Challenger which also made six flights. Then a third shuttle spaceship, the Discovery, was launched; in 1985, a fourth shuttle craft, the Atlantis, was launched and more were to come later. Now there was a fleet of shuttleships, to make scheduled on-time launches.

The Discovery, in its maiden flight of August 1984, routinely spent six days in space with a crew of five men and one woman, and glided to a picture-perfect dawn landing on the desert lakebed — with an empty cargo bay — solid proof of its success in launching three communications satellites on a single flight. In mid-November an epoch in space occurred when sky-walking astronauts wrestled two wayward satellites into the cargo bay of the Discovery to return them to Earth for repairs.

Significantly, any space trash can be collected from orbit and thus space travel can be made safer. These fascinating exploits by the National Aeronautics and Space Administration (NASA) have opened breathtaking new horizons, all of interest and value to the nation's electric utilities.

Appendix

Puget's Presidents

Jacob Furth
Alton W. Leonard
Frank McLaughlin
James H. Clawson
Ralph M. Davis
John W. Ellis

JACOB FURTH

Jacob Furth, a long-time prominent figure in banking circles of the Northwest, at the age of sixty became the president of the newly organized Seattle Electric Company in 1900, and was the dynamic, masterful, commanding force in molding it by 1912 into a larger utility company, the Puget Sound Traction, Light and Power Company. In 1919 its name became Puget Sound Power & Light Company.

In 1899, when Stone & Webster had decided to come to Seattle and put together the various electric trolley and power firms into one system, they first asked a local electrical equipment dealer, William J. Grambs, to buy as their agent, controlling interest in the Union Electric Company. This was done. Then Charles A. Stone himself came and ran into difficulties. Grambs admitted that he knew one man who could be of inestimable help.

JACOB FURTH

"Who, then, is this one man you say can reconcile all the conflicting elements and enable us to get control of all the lines?" asked Stone.

"Jacob Furth," replied Grambs. "He knows the situation better than any other man, has the confidence of everybody and is the one man in Seattle who can serve your interests best." So an interview was arranged.

Mr. Furth showed such extraordinary grasp, not only of the local situation, but of the task before any corporation that would attempt to reduce Seattle's chaotic street railway system to one smooth-running whole, that arrangements were made forthwith for him to join his interests with those of Stone & Webster.

Under Furth's leadership, by 1914, Seattle had one of the finest street railway systems in the world.

Said Clarence Bagley, in his *History of Seattle:*

Mr. Furth had no special advantages beyond those which others enjoy, but he worked perhaps a little harder, a little more persistently, studied business situations and questions more thoroughly, and thus was able to make more judicious investments and to direct his labors more intelligently, with the result that he won a place among the most prosperous citizens of the Northwest, ranking too with those who while promoting individual prosperity, advanced the general welfare. Indeed, it was his public service and his kindliness that gained him the affection of those with whom he was brought into contact.

Came As An Immigrant

Jacob Furth came to the United States as an immigrant at the age of sixteen. He was born at Schwibau, Bohemia, on November 15, 1840. He arrived at San Francisco, stayed one week and spent his last ten dollars to go to Nevada City. Here he immediately found a job in a clothing store, working mornings and evenings and attending public school in the daytime to acquaint himself with the English language.

After six months, he began working full time at forty dollars a month; within three years, he had advanced rapidly and was earning three hundred dollars a month. In this start he reveals his astonishing energy.

In 1862, he opened a clothing and dry-goods store, believing that most progress is made by individuals acting freely. After eight years, he moved to Colusa, California, and started a general mercantile store which he operated twelve years. Then he headed for Puget Sound country.

In Seattle, just a village in 1882, Furth recognized opportunities for himself. He resolved to start a bank. With San Francisco friends he organized the Puget Sound National Bank and took charge. He was its cashier, receiving and paying clerk, teller, and bookkeeper; in fact, the only employee as well as the officer. This wasn't for long, as business and earnings grew. In 1893, he was elected to the bank's presidency, and so continued until consolidation with the Seattle National Bank, after which he was chairman of the board.

By now, Furth was recognized as one of the foremost factors in banking circles in the Northwest. He organized other banks and businesses.

To assist farmers in eastern Washington he organized the California Land & Stock Company in 1884, himself owning a farm of nearly 14,000 acres in Lincoln County. This was one of the largest farms in the state, mostly devoted to wheat growing. He organized the First National Bank of Snohomish in 1896. He also was president of the Vulcan Iron Works and held investments in Seattle real estate and in splendid timber lands throughout the Northwest. In 1900 he assisted in organizing the Seattle Electric Company, of which he became president, and aided in organizing the Puget Sound Electric Railway in 1902, of which he also was president.

Greatest Moment of a Busy Life

As his affairs grew in importance, the name and reputation of the man grew with him. In 1906, Jacob Furth was marked for a great honor. He was chosen to distribute a large sum of money to the stricken city of San Francisco following an earthquake and fire, April 18, 1906. Throughout the world, hearts were touched and purses were opened. The state of Massachusetts raised a million dollars by public subscription. It was decided to employ some agent whose honesty and judgment would best serve the purpose of the subscribers. Jacob Furth, a banker thousands of miles away, was the man chosen.

He was handed a million dollars with the simple direction that he spend it for the interest of the people of San Francisco. He accepted the trust and handled it with calm dispatch.

Some months later, he journeyed to Boston to give an account of the funds. They honored him at a dinner attended by the governor of the state, the mayor of the city, and many notables. Furth's shrewd appraisal of the values placed this incident where it belongs, among the greatest moments of his busy life.

A Man of Admirable Balance

Following the death of Jacob Furth, which took place quietly at his home, June 2, 1914, much prominence was given in the papers to his character. *The Seattle Post Intelligencer* said in part:

> More than half a century ago, a Bohemian boy left the confectioner's shop in Buda-Pesth to seek his fortune in the golden West of America. The boy brought with him a heritage of virtues — sobriety, thrift, industry and honesty ... His rugged face spelled power and self-mastery, and the eyes were a fascinating reflection of the mind of a man, at times kindly and smiling, at times commanding, often sympathetic. Always this intelligent gaze was leveled on whomever Mr. Furth addressed, a direct fearless glance which judged rapidly and accurately.

Said one who knew him intimately:

> Mr. Furth could put himself in place of a boy of ten who had broken his skates as readily as he could understand the feelings of a man or woman in their greatest misfortune.

Judge Burke wrote:

> Jacob Furth was an unusual man. He never lost his head no matter how great the agitation around him. No one could hold fifteen minutes conversation with him without feeling that he was talking with a man of great reserve power.

ALTON W. LEONARD

Alton W. Leonard, born and educated in the East, became president of the Puget Sound Traction, Light & Power Company in 1914, in an aura of well-being and success. After the stock market crash in 1929, the nation did a political and financial about-face, and in the trauma of the times, Leonard was forced to retire in 1931.

In the 1910s, Americans believed that their country was the greatest in the world and that anyone, with hard work, could achieve his goal. Leonard had come up the ranks and was considered an alert, resourceful, and enterprising rising young businessman.

He was typical of his age and had studied every phase of the business. In an interview with several of the Seattle dailies in 1924, he said: "We vision the ultimate completion of a gigantic super power system, with high-power transmission lines connecting the water power plants of Washington, Montana, British Columbia and Oregon — and ultimately California." It was prophetic.

ALTON W. LEONARD

Leonard was a quiet man, finding his greatest pleasure in the companionship of his family. He greatly enjoyed outdoor sports, fishing, hunting, boating and golf. His fellow employees viewed his vitality with pleasure. He, in turn, was keenly aware of the willingness and energy of his employees and relied upon them repeatedly to defeat initiative measures aimed at weakening private power companies.

A Rising Young Man

Alton Leonard was born on April 8, 1873, at Monmouth, Maine, and received his public school education at Brockton, Massachusetts, following which he found a job as a bookkeeper which he held for five years.

He was subsequently employed as assistant treasurer of the Edison Electric Illuminating Company of Brockton and advanced to superintendent and manager. This company was managed by Stone & Webster, who saw executive ability in Leonard.

In 1901, Leonard went to Houghton, Michigan, as superintendent of the Houghton County Electric Company. Shortly he became its manager and was also given the post of manager of the street railway.

In 1905, he was appointed manager of the Minneapolis General Electric Company. He next became vice president of this firm. All these jobs indicated a young man on the rise. Within a year Stone & Webster named him district manager of their interests in the Middle West of the United States.

In 1912, Leonard came to Seattle as vice president and manager of the Puget Sound Traction, Light & Power Company, which had just been consolidated under the leadership of Jacob Furth, its president. Upon the death of Furth in 1914, Alton Leonard succeeded him as president at the age of 41.

As a man highly trained in business management, he knew how to put a handle on a complicated package. There were rapidly developing times. The electric business was undergoing deep changes. It was moving away from trolley service towards electric service for the home, the farm, industry and commerce. These changes he saw more clearly than most of his contemporaries.

Moreover, almost immediately, his greatest challenge was in how to manage his company in the face of growing political incitements, labor unrest, wartime inflation, and competition from the City of Seattle. He did mitigate or resolve most of his political problems as they arose and his company grew vigorously.

Seattle's trolleys became an explosive political issue. And across the nation, big business was singled out as a whipping boy, especially railroads and trolley lines. Leonard's company was fair game. The City of Seattle wanted to run the trolleys. The cry was, "Buy out the private trolley lines!"

As in Seattle's past, raised voices became brash, loud, bold and rough. An impasse was reached. Accompanied by much recrimination in the newspapers, in 1919, the company sold its trolley lines to the City. The public power advocates termed it a victory. But Leonard, too, had scored. He had divested himself of a declining business and no longer had a bear by the tail.

Imaginative Moves

Now Leonard could turn his energies to a bigger plan. In the decade of the 1920s, with its boom-bust economy, he distinguished his career by deftly consolidating isolated, ailing, and inadequate electric companies serving some 350 communities scattered across 19 counties in western and central Washington and also in parts of Oregon. These were integrated into Puget Power's rapidly expanding network of lines and power plants. It was a herculean achievement.

He had a sincere purpose. He knew he could provide significantly better electric service to thousands of farmers and residential customers, and by diversity in use, he would be able to reduce rates. Customers welcomed the change.

A Battle of Initiatives

Although Leonard had remarkable success in enlarging his company, he was faced with the polarization of opinion on the public power issue and his adversaries mounted campaign after campaign. In Seattle, the public power faction was led by J. D. Ross, the "father of City Light," and in Tacoma the leader was Homer T. Bone, a former mail clerk, and a self-taught lawyer, who was elected a state legislator in 1922 as a farm-labor repesentative. Bone was a fiery orator, intense and intelligent, who projected considerable charm. His single theme was, "Water power is a God-given resource that belongs to the people."

In the ensuing years, Seattle and Tacoma tried repeatedly through the state legislature to win rights to serve outside their city limits, and also, through other initiatives to promote public power operation statewide. Leonard had always taken a strong stand against these measures, which were repeatedly defeated by the voters.

Career Ends Abruptly

Alton W. Leonard had been able to cope with the social, political and corporate attacks on his company for many years during times of deep-seated social stirrings, war, erratic economy, and beyond the devastating crash of the stock market of October 29, 1929. The crash marked a turning point. New voices were heard and others took charge. Old careers were broken. Two harsh blows were dealt him.

In the election of 1930, in a mood of mystical idealism fired up by Leonard's old adversary, Homer T. Bone, the public voted to establish Public Utility Districts throughout the state of Washington.

Futhermore, in 1931, upon returning from a fishing trip, Leonard discovered Stone & Webster had sent a new man, Frank McLaughlin, to Seattle to replace him. It struck him like a thunderbolt. He was disposed of because of a fight within Stone & Webster, one between a management faction and a finance faction. The management group thought Leonard was the best man; the finance group thought otherwise.

He went into retirement in Seattle. Leonard passed away at the age of 85, on March 11, 1959.

FRANK McLAUGHLIN

Frank McLaughlin was president of Puget Power from 1931 until his retirement in 1960. Most of those 29 years he presided over a company held under siege by public power adversaries.

Frank McLaughlin was born January 24, 1895, at the village of Hingham, Massachusetts, in the shadow of Plymouth Rock. He had graduated from high school with honors, and later, pieced in with busy days, completed selected courses at Brown University. In 1917, he joined the U.S. Air Force, and served in Britain where he advanced to the rank of Captain. On his return, he was married to Jean Gilchrist of El Paso, Texas, an understanding helpmate.

He had began his career in the electric industry in 1912 at the age of 17. As a high school graduate, he worked as an office boy for the Boston firm of Stone & Webster. When he arrived in Seattle in 1931, he was 36, a seasoned executive, having risen rapidly in management positions with utility companies in the East, South, and Mid-West. At the time of his coming to Seattle he had been the operation executive, (one step below the president), of Stone & Webster, in charge of their nationwide multimillion dollar complex of utilities. His mentors had stated: "McLaughlin undoubtedly has broader experience than any other of our executives."

FRANK McLAUGHLIN

In all his efforts McLaughlin had a way of getting the ear of the public and gaining goodwill and approval where before there had been ill will and mistrust. When he was sent to Seattle, it was a last-ditch effort to salvage Stone & Webster's investment in Puget Power. McLaughlin wryly observed that it also was on April Fool's Day.

Confronted with aggressive socialism and political agitation aimed at nothing less than the destruction of private ownership of electric power companies, he made his strategic decision, to go to the people. In his first 20 years he racked up at least 3,000 talks to groups, large and small, and countless conversations with individuals. He sought out people of all kinds in all walks of life.

Meets an Editor

On one of his "missionary tours" after only a few weeks on the job, late one moist evening he arrived at the plant of the *Northwest Farm News,* in Bellingham, and entered the office of the editor and publisher, Harry L. Allyn. Allyn wrote as follows:

I was working late and looked up surprised when the door opened and a total stranger stepped inside. His was a tall impressive figure, refined in clothes and manner, and with an air of quiet dignity and importance, firm and resolute in movement. He had a bearing and presence that inspired respect.

I took the man's measure instantly, and thought I saw more stature and character than had gladdened my senses in many a day. I glanced at the card he handed me "President of Puget Sound Power & Light Company." He asked if I could tell him something about the farmers, and about the electric service they were receiving.

True he appeared much younger than would be expected in a man assuming such a high post. There was something about him — I do not know how to express it precisely, other than that his inner qualities and outward demeanor seemed to be one and the same.

He spoke without hesitation about the Company, the whole situation and the difficulties he faced. He hoped to save the Company and get on a basis worthy of everybody's trust. His first concern was the preferred stockholders, many of them western Washington people who had put in their savings.

McLaughlin told me, "I am going to save them from losing their money if I can." Finally as he left he assured me, "We are turning over a new leaf, If the slate isn't clean it's my job to clean it!"

As I listened, I thought of the tremendous faith and trust placed by ownership 3,000 miles away in that young man. When he got up to leave that night, I felt as if I had known him all my life.

A Promise Kept

There were no illusions in McLaughlin's mind about the difficult times ahead. The Great Depression of the 1930s had settled with deep gloom across the nation. Earnings sank in 1931, 1932 and 1933, taxes rose and employment and production in the state soon hit bottom. One banker advised that Puget Power was a more dangerous speculation than a bet on a horse race.

McLaughlin met his problems by belt-tightening and when the Rock Island hydro plant was on line with abundant cheap electric power, management sought to lift itself up by its bootstraps with a vigorous sales campaign on all fronts. By 1936, dividend payments were resumed.

The year 1943 was a milestone in the history of Puget Power's progress. It refinanced its debt, recapitalized its stocks and met a federal order by divorcing itself from its holding company, the Engineers Public Service Company. The promise — of saving local stockholders from losing their money — had been kept. But financial woes had not been the only problem.

The Big Fight

In 1931, when McLaughlin took over the top job of Puget Power, the people had voted into state law the enabling act for public utility districts under county leadership. It was McLaughlin's job to persuade the people that under fair treatment their interests would be best served by private power. The big fight began in 1933 when socialist leaders in the state legislature singled out Puget Power as the largest plum.

From that time on, McLaughlin was confronted with innumerable campaigns to bring about the demise of his company. The siege continued for more than 20 years. Even when our nation was at war, in World War II and then in the Korean War, there was no letup in the efforts to tire, harass, hamstring, and take over by condemnation suits.

Countered with His Own Campaigns

McLaughlin countered each threat firmly, often by court action, and by going directly to the people through sales, newspaper advertisements, radio shows, and electric rate reductions. He believed in the innate fairness of the American citizen; he also knew that deeds speak louder than words.

Closeknit Team

Without doubt the tensions and challenges thrust upon his company brought about a very closeknit management team. Of this team McLaughlin later said reflectively and with a great deal of warmth, "God sent me good men!"

House in Order

He steered a steady but difficult course of survival during the 1930s. In the 1940s, the whole of Puget Power's magnificant system was threatened by condemnation and confiscation — federal, PUD, and municipal. Now, to buy time, and also to keep his head above water financially, fragments of Puget Power were sold. To the adversary, this was a taste of blood. In 1951, 1952, and 1953, Puget Power was pursued intensely with lawsuits, and the battle swirled from courtroom to boardroom and across the front pages of the press of the nation. The company's brightest claim was its financial position; it stood like a jewel. Its long-term debt was only 35% of its total worth, and even this was covered by a cash reserve of almost a like amount. Its financial house was in order, amazingly so.

It was a "Lively Corpse,"as managing editor Edward T. Stone of the *Seattle Post-Intelligencer*, wrote in 1953, saying in effect that the people wanted and needed Puget Power. Also, Dwight D. Eisenhower had been elected president of the nation. He believed in a partnership with private enterprise. The New Deal and the drive for public power collapsed. So, in the end, by public consensus, condemnation efforts were abandoned. For Frank McLaughlin, at long last the sun came over the mountain. Un-fettered from political harassments, McLaughlin's exuberance was understandable.

In 1955, he spoke jubilantly "Life Begins at 70!" He was speaking of Puget Power, because in 1885 its earliest predecessor was organized. He himself was 60.

An Aging Man

Just as surely as men try to shape events, so also events will shape men. His top officers of 1931 were no longer alive and with the younger ones, McLaughlin now was withdrawn. All being responsible leaders, the younger officers frequently spoke for management, when in former days their boss was the spokesman. This nettled the old warrior. In a bright move, he hired the nationally known consulting firm, Boos, Allen & Hamilton, to review Puget Power's plant and operations.

On their advice, well-located new division headquarter buildings were constructed and company-wide operation methods were revised. The company's plants were put in tip-top shape. At the time of McLaughlin's retirement in 1960, this was a heritage he left.

Friends Spoke Feelingly

The many years of "cliff-hanging" had brought to McLaughlin an insight and a serenity which caught the attention of leaders throughout the nation. When he retired in May 1960, plaudits came from a wide range of people. They were editors, political leaders, clergymen, educators, businessmen and financial associates. They characterized him as a battler for business, and a thoroughly alive, virile, dynamic, and human person.

After his intense career in Seattle, although retired, he maintained an office for years as a consultant to gradually unwind. Frank McLaughlin died on May 28, 1972, at the age of 77.

JAMES H. CLAWSON

James (Jack) H. Clawson, was elected president of Puget Power on September 18, 1959, at the age of 60, following the unusual experience of working successively and intimately with two of the firm's former presidents, Alton W. Leonard and Frank McLaughlin.

In successive steps — auditor, comptroller, assistant treasurer, treasurer, vice president-treasurer, executive vice president-treasurer — Clawson helped his predecessors guide Puget Power through turbulent and hectic years. By 1959, the company again faced a bright future and Clawson found himself at the helm of an alert, modern corporation, managed by vigorous and imaginative men.

Jack Clawson was born on April 18, 1899, in Providence, Utah. There he attended local schools and in 1920 graduated from the Utah State University in the top 10% of his class. He received a master's degree in business administration in 1922 from the Harvard Graduate School. He married Leona Gibbs, whom he had met in college, on September 23, 1925. It was in the same year that Clawson began his long and impressive utility career.

JACK CLAWSON

He joined Stone & Webster as a traveling auditor, and soon worked full-time with Puget Power as an auditor under the leadership of Alton Leonard. He had part of the action of the giant steps taken to integrate into one unified electric system nearly 100 small properties located in western and central Washington and part of Oregon.

Clawson had witnessed expansive growth, and was seasoned by the shock of the 1929 stock market crash and the ensuing deep Depression. Barely emerging from the harsh trials of the Depression, he was tested by the perils and pressures of a political siege by public power zealots. This only subsided after 20 years.

In those 20 years, Clawson was working closely with his new boss, Frank McLaughlin, and had a hand in the fiscal operations and the heavy burdens of the management team. He advanced to treasurer. Decisions were crucial and even brilliant. In one instance, to secure funds for the firm, Clawson visited mid-Western bankers, impressed them with the booming Northwest, and secured short-term loans for Puget Power totaling $30,000,000.

The honesty and integrity of his Mormon background always shone through, as well as his innate poise and enthusiasm. When faced with belligerence, he could speak his mind with friendliness and candor. In his philosophy of management he strongly advocated delegating authority to others, believing that the soundest decisions come from those closest to a problem, who also are likely to possess the best information.

When Clawson took over the top position of Puget Power in 1959, he could speak with pride of his company and felt a like pride in the state of Washington and the area his firm served. One of his first actions was to reorganize Puget Power as an independent Washington corporation. It had been a Massachusetts company since 1912. This change was one of the major marks of his career. He also guided Puget Power as it moved its headquarters from Seattle to Bellevue, and entered its stock for trade on the New York Stock Exchange.

In 1962, Clawson was elected chairman of the board and chief executive officer. He retired in 1965, and continued on the board of directors until 1970. He remained a personable man, truly concerned about the people who worked for his company and its community responsibilities. Said one employee: "He was the kind of a man where if you had something to say, you could march right up to his office and tell him. And, he'd sit there and listen. After you were finished, he would thank you for taking the time to let him know how you felt."

Jack Clawson died on May 28, 1984, at his home. He had given more than 48 years of service to Puget Power.

RALPH M. DAVIS

Ralph M. Davis was president of Puget Power from 1962 to 1976 and continued as chairman of the board till his retirement on September 1, 1979. He served as a modern-day executive of an ongoing electric utility company. Energetic and versed in present-day technology, he presided over his firm in a period of accelerated expansion. Moreover, he came to Puget Power after training in state government, and brought a citizen's viewpoint to his job.

Davis was born on August 4, 1919, at Doutchet, Oklahoma and came west to Oregon with his parents as a youngster. Then, at the outbreak of World War II, and in his third year at Linfield College, he joined the U.S. Air Force, staying six years as a pilot and administrative officer. Returning to civilian life, he enrolled at the University of Washington for a bachelor's degree in science in 1946 and a law degree in 1948. He was married during his Air Force days, to Evelyn Steahly, and became the father of three sons.

RALPH DAVIS

Ralph Davis was admitted to the bar and entered private law practice in Bellingham. A year later, he was tapped to serve as a law reporter for the state Supreme Court. Now, situated at the state capitol in Olympia, he was named assistant attorney general and legislative counsel to the governor in 1952; from 1955 to 1957, Davis was chairman of the Washignton State Public Service Commission, which regulates rates and operations of private utilties.

In 1957, Davis left state government to become the secretary of Puget Power. In 1961, he was also given the post of vice president, and in 1962 that of president, at the age of 43. Jack Clawson then moved up to executive officer and chairman of the board. When Clawson retired in 1965, Davis became both president and chief executive officer of Puget Power.

In his work in state government, Davis had been an observer of business; now as a key man in private industry, quietly but surely, he set Puget Power on a new long-range course, from the historic hydro power supply, to coal and nuclear for new energy sources. This meant changes in technology. Also he judged accurately new environmental demands, gauged political trends, sensed impending energy crises, and deftly made adjustments.

Now discernible too was a trend to bring specialists onto the management team, men with expertise and intimate knowledge of separate areas of operation. For example, early in the 1960s, the nation's mood was to preserve the environment, so a special staff took on beautification projects, such as the Snoqualmie Falls tourist park where a smartly designed viewing structure was erected and the grounds tastefully landscaped; at Baker Lake, a similar tourist park was provided; and employee camps at Lake Tapps and at American Lake were fitted with new cottages and trailer stations. These additions were in keeping with a sensitivity to current thinking.

As a lawyer, Davis had a keen interest in pursuing an American-Canadian pact to build storage dams on that part of the Columbia River located in Canada for downstream benefits of hydro dams in Washington. Davis selected an outstanding fellow attorney, John Ellis, and a gifted engineer, David Knight, to represent Puget Power on a negotiating committee. In 1964 the treaty was ratified by both countries, and by 1973, three dams had been built.

In the somber area of politics, Davis's experience enabled him to shape changes in the punitive Public Utility Law of 1931. At long last in 1969, the legislature was responsive to amending this law: now the voters' approval is required before a PUD can begin condemnation proceedings against privately owned companies.

Davis had a sharp intellect and the gift of giving a caller his complete attention. Seated at his clean desk, he would listen; then, without notes pick up the points of the presentation and answer with lucid thoughts.

Though he practiced the team approach — in which the chief executive is everybody's assistant — in crucial times, Davis went right to where the action was. For example, when voters were concerned about utility issues, he joined his employees out on the streets doorbelling. When the devastating Columbus Day storm of 1962 struck with fury, felling trees and power lines, he stood at the load dispatchers' center to expedite crucial calls for help.

He was willing to take risks. In 1964 Puget Power embraced the concept of total underground wiring to beautify residential developments. The idea had been thoroughly engineered, researched, and tested. To bury the wires was costly and critics told Davis, "You will lose your shirt!" Approval was given, and poles began coming down. The concept was sound. By 1973, about 90% of new installations were totally underground.

Past leaders of Puget Power had grappled with the problems of the times; each faced problems alone. Now, in Davis's time, partnerships eased the risks and responsibilities. In consort with others, huge new power plants were built. Regional planning was an exciting new field. In the 1970s, five major coal-fired projects were undertaken by Puget Power in partnership with other utilities.

Shared risk and shared responsibility with other leaders eases the load on the separate utility heads. With joint construction of huge developments, there is sharing of wisdom and experience; the projects are soundly conceived; there is a clear economy for each partner; and problems of siting, licensing, and ecology become more manageable.

Davis was much encouraged by this trend.

In time, Ralph Davis attained a high profile in the community and among business leaders. He served on the boards of the Seattle University, Doctors Hospital, the Seattle Chamber of Commerce, the United Way of King County, the International Trade Fair, and the Edison Electric Institute. He was chairman of the Economic Development Council of Puget Sound and of the Helium Breeder Association, an international organization for research and development of gas-cooled fast breeder reactor technology.

Upon his retirement in 1979, after 22 years with Puget Power, Ralph Davis cheerfully commented: "I have enjoyed an extremely exciting and pleasant career with Puget Power." Now he could be more relaxed and enjoy continued work in community activities, and also devote more time to his family.

JOHN W. ELLIS

John W. Ellis, president of Puget Power since 1976, has become a role model of a present-day corporate leader — one who is expected to effect a balance between profit and social conscience. In this, Ellis must take pains to explain that balance, to the firm's various publics — employees, the customers, the investors, the retired, the poor, and the needy. For all are users of electricity and are rate-payers.

He has managed this role very well and also the role he was picked for, that of managing his business. Articulate, personable, kindly, and sensitive, he is a keen judge of people and warmly interested in them. He had been tested by events that were not to his liking and to which he responded with a fresh viewpoint, and in several instances, with new programs that were innovative and won national recognition.

JOHN W. ELLIS

Ellis first caught the eye of Puget Power management as a company attorney, when he was a member of a team to consummate a landmark pact for building dams for storing Columbia River water in a steep stretch in a wilderness area in Canada. It took tireless effort. The treaty was ratified in 1964, by Canada and the United States. In 1970 Ellis joined Puget Power as vice president of utility management.

He was born in Seattle, September 14, 1928, and graduated from the University of Washington in 1952 with a bachelor of science degree and with a law degree in 1953. He joined the law firm of Perkins, Coie, Stone, Olsen & Williams and also was married to Doris Stearns. He now settled into home life and the practice of law. The tour of duty with Puget Power opened vast areas for a test of his many talents.

Ellis unquestionably became one of the movers and shakers of Washington business. Financial pressures on the state's tenth largest corporation and threats to the earnings of its 95,000 stockholders devoured his time.

For, from 1976 to 1980, the area experienced a business boom in a time of inflationary money costs. In these five years, 132,212 new customers were added to Puget Power's system, mandating construction of new energy sources that cost in excess of $800,000,000. Power projects included hydro, new coal-fired plants, gas-fired peaking units, and nuclear projects.

The venture into nuclear was aborted by antinuclear activists, who for more than six years bedeviled the siting and licensing of the projects.

In contrast, Ellis was warmly applauded for a variety of programs in the area of social concern. Each was deftly designed to help others and also to be beneficial to his company. He was one of the first to plan an energy conservation program for all classes of users, providing energy audits and consultants, as well as loans, believing that to give the customer more for his money is also good business for the company. There were other strategies to meet change.

A program of customer advisory councils was begun in 1980, as rates rose steeply and rate-payers started to get angry. Even the loudest critics were invited to take part. Friends said, "Don't do it, you will only give dissidents a platform!" Ellis believed in fairness, and the results were proof. The panels took their work seriously and the company was listening. Hundreds of vital ideas were submitted and almost all were implemented. This innovative program of enlisting customers' ideas won a national award.

One of the consumer panel recommendations challenged the company to be creative in developing new ways to help senior citizens. In 1985 this program was chosen as a finalist of the Edison Award. The citation read:

> The program reached far beyond those normally offered by electric utilities and included the formation of partnerships of corporations and state agencies, initiation of an aggressive referral program to put elderly customers in touch with appropriate social agencies, and organization of voluntary activities of caring employees, all of which have alleviated the distress and needs of elderly customers, reduced complaints, and positively influenced regulatory climate in the area.

In his community leadership roles, we again sense Ellis's interest in social concern. He had served as president of the Bellevue Boys Club, as board member of the Seattle-King County Boys Club, the Overlake Hospital, the Evergreen Safety Council, The Washington Round Table, the Seattle Sailing Foundation and has headed the United Way's annual fund drive. He also brought his casual and engaging leadership to many business organizations, including several banks, the Edison Electric Institute, and the Pacific Northwest Utilities Coordinating Committee. In 1984, this Puget Power president was honored with the Seattle Municipal League's Outstanding Citizen Award.

Ellis's stongest defenders can be found among his staff. He is a highly accessible and loyalty-inspiring boss. Said one veteran employee, "John is always poking his head in the door wondering what you are doing."

In the years 1980 to 1984, when a depression hit the state and the utility reduced staff by 140 positions, he made a point of hitting the road to talk with employees. Ellis did the explaining at a large staff meeting. Moreover, with a deep and sympathetic understanding, he challenged all employees to meet the lean, and tough years with "working smarter" efforts; and monetary prizes were given for cost-effective ideas from employees.

His personal feelings are expressed in his own words, taken from the 1985 annual report to stock holders:

> To our 2,374 employees, many of whom are also shareholders, I want to say thank you for the dedication and commitment you have demonstrated during the past year. You've not only "made do" but you've done with less. I recognize that senior managment has placed high expectations on all of your work areas. I am proud of the way you have performed and I know our customers and shareholders are too.

BIBLIOGRAPHY

Ackley, Daisy, *Wagon Wheels a 'Rollin'*, 1960
Aldwell, Thomas T., *Conquering the Last Frontier*, 1950
Bagley, Clarence B., *History of Seattle, Vol. 1, 2 and 3*, 1916
Blanchard, Leslie, *The Street Railway Era in Seattle*, 1968
Boy Scouts of America, *Boys' Life*, March and August, 1971
Carhart, Edith Beebe, *History of Bellingham*, 1926
Dwelley, Art, *Tenino the First Hundred Years*, 1971
Ford Motor Company, *Story of the Race*, 1909
Gellatly, John A., *History of Wenatchee*, 1957
Journal of American Society of Civil Engineers, "Handling Facilities Baker River Project," November 1961
Lucia, Ellis, *Head Rig*
McGraw-Hill Publishing Co., *Electrical World*, June 1912, March 1924
McGraw-Hill Publishing Co., *Electrical West*, March 1944
McGraw-Hill Publishing Co., *Electrical West, 75th Anniversary*, 1887-1962
Mansfield, Harold, *Vision*, 1966
Newall, Gordon and Don Sherwood, *Totem Tales of Old Seattle*, 1956
Phillips, James W., *Washington State Place Names*, 1971
Pierce County Auditor, Deed Archives
Puget Sound Traction, Light & Power Company, *Electric Journal*. January 1913, April 1915, August 1922, October 1922, January 1923, April 1923, June 1923, January 1924, October 1924, March 1925, January 1926, February 1926, February 1930, March 1930, October 1930, January 1931, May 1931.
Puget Sound Power & Light Company, Reports to Stockholders, 1928 to 1985.
Rathbun, J.C., *History of Thurston County*, 1895
Reasons, George and Sam Patrick, *They Had A Dream, Vol. 1*, 1969
Saturday Evening Post, December 1975
       "Nuclear Energy, What Kind of a Bargain?," by Dr. Edward Teller
Strong, Anna Louise, *I Change Worlds*, 1937
State of Washington, Original documents on file at Olympia
State of Washington, Initiatives and Referendum Measures, 1966
State of Washington, District Power Bill Chapter I Laws of Washington 1931
Technical Publishing Company, *Journal of Electricity*, June 1, 1912
Tacoma City Light, Report and Information, 1919
Thurston County Auditor, Volume I of Deeds
Volcan Iron Works, *Alaska-Yukon-Pacific Exposition*, 1909
Washington Water Power Company, *Story of Washington Water Power Company*, 1930
Washington Water Power Company, *The Illuminator*, February 1961
Welsh, William D., *A Brief Historical Sketch of Port Townsend*, 1943

INDEX